PRISONERS
OF
MEN'S DREAMS

BOOKS BY SUZANNE GORDON

Black Mesa:
The Angel of Death

Lonely in America

Off Balance:
The Real World of Ballet

Economic Conversion:
Revitalizing America's Economy
(coedited with David McFadden)

Prisoners of Men's Dreams:
Striking Out for a New Feminine Future

PRISONERS
OF
MEN'S DREAMS

Striking Out for a
New
Feminine Future

SUZANNE GORDON

LITTLE, BROWN AND COMPANY
BOSTON　　　TORONTO　　　LONDON

Many of the names in this book
and identifying details have been changed
for reasons of privacy.

Library of Congress Cataloging-in-Publication Data

Gordon, Suzanne, 1945–
    Prisoners of men's dreams: striking out for a new feminine future
    Suzanne Gordon. — 1st ed.
        p.   cm.
    ISBN 0-316-32106-0
    1. Feminism — United States.   2. Women — United States — Social
conditions.   I. Title.
HQ1426.G657   1991
305.42'0973 — dc20   90-13309

10   9   8   7   6   5   4   3   2   1

HC

Published simultaneously in Canada by Little, Brown & Company
(Canada) Limited

PRINTED IN THE UNITED STATES OF AMERICA

For
Steve

The subjugated, whose acts and integrity are granted no recognition, may, even in the very act of emancipation, remain in love with the ideal of power that has been denied to them. Though they may reject the master's right to dominion over them, they nevertheless do not reject his personification of power. They simply reverse the terms and claim his rights as theirs.

— JESSICA BENJAMIN,
The Bonds of Love

The Republic can survive its problems. The question is, Can it survive its politics?

— JACK BEATTY

CONTENTS

ACKNOWLEDGMENTS

Every book is, to some extent, a revelation to its own author. If the analogy to childbirth and rearing is apt, it is because what we create seems both wholly our own and wholly other. To me this book has not only been an essay on a theme — that of care, collaboration, and interdependence — it has also been a constant revelation of the power of such human interaction.

Although this book has my name on it, it is, in the most profound sense, a collaboration that belongs to the many people whose ideas have helped me shape my own and whose conversations helped me clarify my subject and goals.

I would first like to thank Jean Potter and Joan Fernandes for helping me understand the realities and imperatives of care as they are lived in complex human lives. And I want to thank Gerry Stechler for illuminating the dilemmas of both caring theories and the many conflicts involved in fulfilling our duties to ourselves and others. Although they are far too young to appreciate their mother's gratitude, I want to thank my daughters, Alexandra and Jessica, for giving me the opportunity to understand the problems I am writing about. As a mother, I have lived what I write about, and it is because I am a mother that I feel so acutely our need to value our caregiving work and make care an equal part of our world.

My agents, Anne and Georges Borchardt, have once again not only shepherded this work through the market but nurtured its author. My editor, Fredrica Friedman, has helped me find the book within the book that sometimes eluded me and persisted in encouraging me to find the voice that would convey my commitment to its subject.

Katrina Lewers gave me much needed advice and support. And Kirk Scharfenberg was there, almost minute by minute, when confidence faltered, words escaped me, and energy lapsed. I cannot thank him enough. I want to thank Nick King, Ande Zellman, and Louisa Williams for their encouragement.

My twenty-year conversation with Isabel Marcus continued throughout my work on this book and enlivened its analysis. Gar Alperovitz's insights were a much needed source of inspiration as well as of concrete suggestions for change. Diane Margolis's own work as well as her subtle and shrewd advice were invaluable guides. Patricia Benner and Bernice Buresh were sources of true moral support. And Joan Lynaugh, Claire Fagin, and Chris Allen helped me sharpen my ideas and examples.

I want to thank my mother for all the confidence she has had in me over the years. But finally, I want to thank my husband, Steve Early. He was indefatigable throughout every stage of this book. He edited and typed copy, prodded me when I procrastinated, and, most importantly, took care of our children so I could find time to do and finish my work. His shifts not only doubled but sometimes trebled, and he never hesitated to help, sustain, and nurture.

If this book succeeds in rekindling a societal discussion about the importance of care and women's role in transforming and taming the market, it is only because it is an embodiment of so many people's capacity for empathy and community. This book is a gift to them all.

PRISONERS
OF
MEN'S DREAMS

Introduction

WOMEN AT RISK

WOMEN and their vision of a more humane world are at risk.

Only a few short years ago, women's liberation promised to change our world. Our emphasis on the value of relationships, interdependence, and collaboration sought to balance work with love, hierarchy with healing, individualism with community. Through our profound commitment to caring, we hoped finally to teach American society that care was neither a reward for hard work nor an indulgence meted out to the infirm and vulnerable, but rather a fundamental human need. Many women who participated in our movement demanded that equality make a difference — not only for our sisters and ourselves, but for men and for generations to come.

Now, two decades after the great social upheavals of the 1960s, women are in danger of becoming prisoners of men's dreams.

It has required centuries of excruciating struggle, but we have finally arrived on the shores of the masculine world. And yet, as we have moved inland, slowly, almost imperceptibly, too many of us seem to have been wooed away from our original animating goal of changing this landscape.

We have not attained as much power and influence as we'd hoped. Although millions of us live in poverty that has been increasingly feminized, we have nonetheless been assimilated into the American marketplace. Millions of us now participate in an economic, social, and political system that is highly competitive, aggressive, and individualistic; a system that values workplace success and the accumulation of wealth, power, and privilege above all else.

Many of us are now doctors and lawyers, bankers and stockbrokers, scientists and engineers, legislators and congressional representatives, mayors and even governors. We are telephone workers and underground miners, carpenters and house painters, auto mechanics, mailpersons, and cab drivers. A few of us sit on the boards of the nation's major corporations. We have started our own magazines and secured positions of influence in the media — editing newspapers, producing network news shows, writing and directing for television, running major motion picture studios and determining the content of at least some of the films they make.

Some of us supervise not only other women but men. We boss secretaries, give orders to nurses, hire nannies, and are served by flight attendants as we fly the nation's skies. Not all of us, but some of us, participate in making the decisions that govern other women's lives.

We are lobbyists, political consultants, and politicians. We advise women — and sometimes men — how to run campaigns and shepherd bills through state legislatures and Congress. We may not have all the votes, and we certainly do not have the final veto — but to our constituents we interpret reality, define the possible, and help create the probable.

We have entered the male kingdom — and yet, we have been forced to play by the king's rules.

That is not what an important segment of the feminist movement promised.

Feminism was, and remains, one of the most powerful social movements of the twentieth century. When women marched and protested and united to recast the contours of our world, many of us carried a very different transformative vision in our hearts and minds. Twenty years ago, a significant group of feminists believed in women, in the potential of femininity and the transformative

power of feminism. It was clear, these transformative feminists*
argued, that our masculine socialization — our ingrained insecurity about our competence and talents outside of the domestic
sphere — was a wound. But our feminine socialization, so many
sensed, was a source of strength to be mobilized not only for the
private but for the public good.

Socialized in the home, the community, and the helping professions, women devoted themselves to nurturing, empowering, and
caring for others. In a society little dedicated to sustaining relationships, encouraging cooperation and community, recognizing
the value of collaboration, or rewarding altruism rather than
greed, women have historically defined, defended, and sustained
a set of insights, values, and activities which, if never dominant,
at least provided a counterweight and an alternative ideal to the
anomie, disconnectedness, fragmentation, and commercialization
of our culture.

Many of us saw women's experiences and concerns as the source
of a sorely needed transformative vision. And our dream of liberation was fueled by the hope that we could carry this vision with
us into the marketplace and encourage a new ethic of caring even
as we demonstrated our own competence. Our vision of a more
humane society was based on a profound commitment to caring —
to the emotional and physical activities, attitudes, and ethical com-
portment that help people grow and develop, that nurture and
empower them, affirming their strengths and helping them cope
with their weaknesses, vulnerabilities, and life crises.

Thus we hoped to create a less hierarchial workplace, one in
which people could help others grow and develop; in which knowledge, experience, power, and wealth could be shared more equi-
tably. We wanted both the private and public sector to allow and

*There are many different ways to refer to the feminisms and feminists that I
am describing. In her work, Nancy Cott distinguishes between those who focused
on equal rights and those who were concerned with using the insights of feminine
socialization to show that women could make a difference in the world. Some
feminists refer to "liberal" and "radical" feminists. Nel Noddings distinguishes
between first, second, and third generations of feminists and Jane Mansbridge
talks about "nurturant" feminism. For the purposes of this book, I will refer to
"transformative" and "adaptive," or "equal-opportunity," feminism.

even help us fulfill our caring responsibilities by implementing the kinds of social policies that are essential to any real integration of work and personal relationships. And we wanted to infuse our society with a greater respect for the caring work that women have so long performed and refined both inside and outside the home. Most importantly, we wanted men to value and share that caring with us in the home and the workplace.

American society has made it enormously difficult for women — or men — to hold to such an alternative ideal. Many men have sabotaged women's struggle for equality and difference from its inception, and they continue to resist our every effort to improve our lives. When America's masculine-dominated, marketplace culture has not openly thwarted women's hopes and dreams, it has often tried to co-opt women's liberation. Thus while many women have remained faithful to this transformative vision and still struggle valiantly to make it a reality, it has been difficult for millions of others to resist a barrage of messages from corporate America and the media that define mastery and liberation in competitive, marketplace terms. Corporate America and the media have declared that feminism triumphs when women gain the opportunity to compete in what Abraham Lincoln once called the great "race of life." Following a classic pattern in which the victims of aggression identify with their aggressors, many prominent advocates of women's liberation within the highly competitive capitalist marketplace have themselves embraced this masculinized corruption of feminist ideals.

Placing competition above caring, work above love, power above empowerment, and personal wealth above human worth, corporate America has created a late-twentieth-century hybrid — a refashioned feminism that takes traditional American ideas about success and repackages them for the new female contestants in the masculine marketplace. This hybrid is equal-opportunity feminism — an ideology that abandons transformation to adaptation, promoting male-female equality without questioning the values that define the very identity it seeks.

Betty Friedan, whose important work launched the liberal branch of the feminist movement, was one of the first to give voice to this ideology, in 1963 in *The Feminine Mystique.* For her, feminism and competition seemed to be synonymous. "When women take their education and abilities seriously and put them to use, ultimately they have to compete with men," she wrote. "It is better for a woman to compete impersonally in society, as men do, than to compete for dominance in her own home with her husband, compete with her neighbors for empty status, and so smother her son that he cannot compete at all."[1]

From the equal-opportunity feminism first envisaged in *The Feminine Mystique* to that promoted today by *Working Woman* and *Savvy* magazines, and the dozens of primers that promote the dress-for-success philosophy that often pretends to speak for all of feminism, progress and liberation have been defined in male, market terms. While some equal-opportunity feminists pay lip service to the work of their more care-oriented sisters, claiming that they would support a broad agenda that addresses our caring needs, the overarching mission of many is to help women adapt to the realities of the masculine marketplace. This brand of feminism often appeals to women's understandable fears that to discuss human beings' mutual need to care for one another is to argue that only women — not men — shoulder the duty to care. Rather than reaffirming our caring commitments so that we can all — male and female alike — share them, equal-opportunity feminism often seems to define caring as a masculine attempt to imprison women in the home and caring professions.

In this environment, the goal of liberation is to be treated as a man's equal *in a man's world*, competing for oneself against a very particular kind of man — the artists, scientists, politicians, and professionals that Friedan speaks of throughout her book. Or, as a recent *New York Times* series about the progress of women and feminism stated, "The basic goal of the women's movement was to eliminate the barriers that kept women from achieving as much as men and which did not allow them to *compete* with men on an equal basis"[2] (my italics).

For equal-opportunity feminism, then, the ultimate goal is traditional American success — making money; relentlessly accumulating possessions; capturing and hoarding power, knowledge, access, and information; grasping and clinging to fame, status, and privilege; proving that you are good enough, smart enough, driven enough to get to the top, and tough enough to stay there. In America — particularly the America of the Reagan and post-Reagan years — this is, after all, the meaning of "having it all."

In a world where allegiance to family, community, and politics has eroded, the American marketplace, with its glittering prize of success, has co-opted many of us, undermining our hopes and expectations. Others among us had a different vision. We had hoped that by going into the marketplace and taking our posts there as individuals, we would somehow subvert it. Many believed that our femininity would protect us, that the force of our feminism would make us invulnerable to the seductive logic of either patriarchy or capitalism.

In fact, we were remarkably naive about this foreign land into which we had journeyed. Yes, we were quick to admit that American society is too ruthless, too violent, too aggressive and uncaring. But many of us believed that the market's ills were a direct result of the sex of those who ruled and served it — men. As Betty Friedan, among so many others, has said over and over again, "Society was created by and for men."[3]

It seemed logical, therefore, to argue that the aggressive, elitist, hierarchial attitudes, values, and behaviors that kept women oppressed served the needs of and benefited all men, and that the natural solution was simply to change the sex of the players. It seemed natural to believe that putting women in power — without radically changing the system of power — would improve things for *all*. After all, like so many oppressed groups who believe oppression is a shield against the temptations of tyranny, women, who had been oppressed and subordinate for so long themselves, would never turn around and oppress and dominate others.

What we had not counted on was the strength of the marketplace, its ability to seduce and beguile the best and brightest, and its capacity to entrap us in its rules and entangle us in its imperatives. A few women have won great wealth and privilege. But, not unlike men in similar positions, many of them are unwilling to jeopardize what they've acquired in order to work for change. Some are so caught up in their own personal sagas of success that they have forgotten the women who have been left behind.

It is, of course, true that a great many professional women are

deeply concerned about the fate of personal, political, and social
life in modern America. They express great disenchantment but
nonetheless seem caught in gilded cages — unhappy with their lot
but too fearful of losing what they've gained for the promise of a
richer life or the fulfillment of a common morality.

Just as generations of men have succumbed to the lure of the
American dream, so too have millions of women scrambled after
an illusion.

Just as transformative feminism insisted that following this fantasy did not make men winners but rather victims, so too it has
made us victims of a different oppressor — the market. Instead of
attaining mastery and liberation on our own terms, we have become clones of what economist Adam Smith called "economic
man." Now standing beside him, we have economic woman — a
group of women who have grown so competitive and individualistic that they can think of little but themselves and advancing in
their careers. Committed to the bottom line of short-term profit,
these women have become oblivious to the needs and ambitions
of those who work with them or under them; some actually try to
thwart other women's efforts to improve their own lives.

To these women, self-esteem is not the expression and realization of women's different voice and behavior; it has become completely dependent on their accomplishment in the work world. So
obsessed are they with work that many now consider it to be a
panacea for the human condition. Just as Friedan believed that
work would make women less personally controlling, less apt to
compete for empty status, less eager to smother their children with
their love, so too many women today believe that work — pref-
erably in the highest-paying, highest-powered, most traditionally
male job possible — will be their salvation. "If only she had gone
to work, she wouldn't be like this," we say of our mothers, aunts,
or grandmothers, as if work engenders civility, eradicates prejudice, and guarantees rational appraisal and action in all of life's
dilemmas.

But all too soon we learn that work in the competitive marketplace is not necessarily a substitute for love and caring or a cure
for neurosis. Quite the contrary. While many women today have
"made it" in material terms, it has been at great cost. Thousands

have forfeited intimate relationships with lovers, family, and friends as we have devoted our lives, like men, to clawing our way to the top. But unlike men — who are generally able to find a woman to tend their personal lives, raise their children, and construct for them a haven in a heartless world — many of these women are unable to create even the facades of relationships with mates, families, and friends. Married to their jobs, they are divorced from a relational world.

These economic superwomen are not, however, the main victims of this new "masculine" mystique. It is the rest of us — women who never aspired to stardom, who never wanted to be the head of a major motion picture studio or of a state, who didn't care about making millions and taking over as CEO of a Fortune 500 company — who are its chief victims. Most of us hoped for more truly enriching rewards. We wanted careers in which we could expand our knowledge and skills, jobs in which we could master new challenges and make contributions to society.

We also hoped to maintain lives outside of work that included intellectual and spiritual pursuits, friends, love relationships, family, and community. But in today's world, where the fast track has become the only valued track, where nothing less than a 100 percent commitment to one's firm or field will do — and where many people must work two or three jobs even to survive — many women are finding that reconciling working and caring is impossible. Rather than being gratified by our many successes, too many of us are haunted by our compromises. Trying in vain to juggle private and professional lives, we are not allowed to find peace and happiness in either one. Our lives are run by the clock and so severely regimented that we have no time for friends, family, children, or community.

Too many of us wake up one morning to discover that we no longer know who we are, or what we really want, and we wonder how we became entangled in this web of expectation and disappointment. And then we look for someone to blame. It is men, we say; the fault is all in their failings. None of them have changed enough, none of them share enough, none of them do enough. Or it is feminism itself that is to blame, and with it every woman who ever dreamed a different dream or hoped for a better world. And we ask bitterly, "What has feminism done for *me*, why has it failed me?"

What we do not ask is, "Do we want to pursue these market-place goals?" "Is the fast track the best track?" "What can I do for feminism, and for other women?"

With such intense pressure from the masculine marketplace as well as the guidance of equal-opportunity feminism, many women have had to become so obsessed with their own individual strug-gles and strategies for survival that they no longer even remember how to reach out to each other in the workplace and community. Rather than recognizing the potential power of our numbers and our ideals, we feel alone, bereft. We can no longer even imagine the possibility of change. "It feels like attacking a mountain with a piece of sandpaper," one young investment counselor said, de-scribing why she felt she had to leave her former company rather than stay and fight to change it. "We used to feel so much a part of something. Like we were doing something for our world, and now, I wake up and feel alone."

To this young woman and so many others who are unwilling to sacrifice caring to competing in the workplace, the only solution seems to be flight rather than fight. Thus, a great many women are now leaving large corporate institutions to raise families, work part-time, or open their own businesses. This exodus from the competitive marketplace represents a mass protest movement of major proportions. But it is a sadly ineffective one. Once again it leaves men — and their female clones — in charge.

If the marketplace has compelled us to silence our own inner voices, robbed us of our sense of achievement, and made change seem a utopian fantasy, it has had an even more insidious impact on human caring. Feminism promised to demonstrate to American society that it is caring, not competition, that fosters human con-nection; that it is caring activities that enable human beings not only to survive but to thrive. We hoped to persuade men to share the duty to care both in the home and workplace, so that women would no longer be the sole caregivers in our society.

Today, many women have also joined men in denigrating the caregiving activities that they used to protect, preserve, and de-fend. It has become all too common for professional women to look down on those who have continued to do caring work in traditional women's professions like nursing, social work, teaching, and mothering. Nurses and others are constantly asked, "Why didn't someone as intelligent as you become a doctor?" or "Why didn't you become a psychologist rather than a social worker?" Teachers who leave the profession to become entrepreneurs are promoted as examples of "career courage," as if maintaining one's commitment to educating the young were an act of cowardice.[4]

Even our child-rearing practices have been affected. Today more and more mothers — particularly those among high-powered two-career couples — are told that good parenting equals pushing their young children to learn competitive, cognitive skills that will supposedly pave the way for future career advancement. In the process, they are producing families in which both parents now subscribe to the kind of performance-oriented, competitive child rearing so often associated with masculine parenting styles. And we, as a culture, risk dissolving the positive bonds of love and nurturing and losing the irretrievable freedom of childhood.

The fact that women are now encouraged to devalue caring work has exacerbated a widespread societal crisis in caring that has deep political and social roots. As a society we cannot seem to muster the will or political courage to care for the most precious things we produce — other human beings.

By devaluing care we have, for example, abandoned our moral responsibility to the children who represent our future. The United States has risen to twenty-first in its infant mortality rate. Twenty percent of America's children are destitute, and American poverty is increasingly feminized. Over thirty-seven million people have no employer-paid health insurance coverage, and twenty to thirty million more are under-insured. Even those who can produce an insurance card when they arrive at the hospital may receive inadequate care. Moreover, older Americans are denied even catastrophic health care coverage and must pauperize themselves before they are eligible for government assistance with long-term nursing home care.

America's public education system — once the cornerstone of our democracy — is in a shambles. Millions of Americans today are homeless. Childcare is unobtainable for many, substandard for most, and frequently unaffordable for women who work in the home and also need support and respite. The only kind of parental and medical leaves that Congress seems willing to legislate are unpaid ones that will never be utilized by the majority of Americans because they cannot afford the loss of income involved. And presidential vetoes are threatened even for those.

Our need is greater than ever for more people to care for our children and teach them the cognitive, moral, and social skills they will need to grow and develop; to tend the sick; to nurture the emotionally vulnerable and physically handicapped; and to help an aging population deal with infirmity, chronic illness, and death. And yet our society's widespread devaluation of care is discouraging potential recruits — whether male or female — from entering the caring professions and making it more difficult to induce those already in those professions to remain. These negative attitudes toward care pose a severe threat to existing political programs and policies that support and sustain caring activities. And if women retreat from caring, how can we possibly expect men to enter the caregiving professions or to be more caring in their personal and professional relationships?

The crisis in caring that women — and society — face today is more serious than many of us could have imagined. Yet, too many acknowledge the problem by essentially denying it. Like male CEO's rationalizing their failures to promote more women to positions of corporate power, they insist that the enemy is not their own values and beliefs, but rather time. It takes years, men often say, to produce women who have the skills and knowledge required to follow the commands, execute the orders, and play the game to win. Change, they insist, is forthcoming — dozens of women are in the pipeline; just wait and you will see them.

Some contemporary defenders of feminism echo these same rationalizations. Understandably concerned about providing antifeminist ammunition for the right, they insist that the problem is time, not values; quantity, not quality. Women have not been liberated long enough, there are not yet enough of us in positions of power. If the ratio of women to men were just greater — then things would definitely change for the better.

Of course, all this is true. But it is only a partial explanation. A

cold, clear look at reality reveals that these, if not amplified, are
but empty assurances. Yes, we do need more time. Of course, it
takes years, perhaps even decades, to change human behavior. But
change is a *process,* not an *event.* If the women waiting in the
wings for their moment on stage have been trained in the male
method, if they behave like men, abide by the rules of the male
marketplace, and merely join men in administering the status quo
rather than taking risks to change it, then only the names and
shapes of the players will have altered. The substance of our lives
will stay the same. Indeed, things may be even worse. If women
abandon caring for competition, rather than working to encourage
all of us to share in the real work of the human community, then
who will care? What kind of liberation will we have purchased?

Many of the books written by and about women today are sagas
of personal betrayal. Their authors lament the fact that feminists
and feminism have fed women misinformation and disinformation,
or that individual women have betrayed friends and colleagues,
lovers and children. This book is not a story of personal betrayal.
I have never felt that in a society as divided, cunning, and complex
as ours, feminism owed me a good outcome. Throughout my adult
life I have been a feminist, committed to a transformative vision
of women's liberation. The commitment and enthusiasm I felt
when I entered my first consciousness-raising group over twenty
years ago, the conviction that this experience and those ideals
would change my life, have never flagged. That is why I am writing
this book today.

It is not just a record of women's confusion and a critique of
the masculine marketplace and equal-opportunity feminism.
Along with many other works by other feminists, it is also a record
of women's hopes, a call to action, and, I hope, a challenge.

The stories that more than one hundred women have shared
with me are not only accounts of disillusionment. The tales of these
lawyers and doctors, scientists and social workers, nurses and secretaries, telephone workers and politicians, teachers and investment bankers are also cause for celebration and action. Some of
these women are committed feminists. Most are what I call
"Yes . . . but" feminists — women who sympathize with women's

struggles for equal rights, but who have been reluctant to fight for a broader agenda for social change. But nearly all of these women have one thing in common: the frustration they feel as they try in vain to juggle professional responsibilities and personal priorities. And this discontent positions them on the borders of dissent. Their very crises present an enormous, perhaps even unprecedented, possibility.

The women I interviewed are not unusual. They reflect the experiences and problems many others share. For the past decade, too many of us have lived out the fantasy that we could, individually and collectively, find happiness and completion in the marketplace, often as clones of economic man. Many believed that if an elite group of women benefited from the many victories of feminism, then millions of others would slowly follow in their footsteps. Well, now we have seen reality: women do not change the world by becoming more like men; many women who do not want to be like men feel they have no alternative but to leave the marketplace; even more women who are trying only to stay in place find that the bottom is falling out from under them and that the victories of their more fortunate sisters may be of little help.

Transformative feminists have been struggling to fulfill their vision of feminism in spite of the tyranny of the market. As more women realize that the dream of success in the male marketplace imprisons us as tightly as it has always imprisoned men, more of us can join in that struggle for real change. We can once again begin to dream our own dreams, to ask new questions and revise our goals. The question can no longer be, can we compete and succeed in traditional terms?

The question needs to be, what do we want to do, be, and become? The issue can no longer be only body counting — calculating how many women have attained positions of power and where — it must be quality counting. What kind of women are we putting in power? What do we want them to *really* stand for? What do they believe? Do they practice what they preach? To whom are they accountable? Will we make them accountable to the majority of women, not just an elite?

The task is no longer to find role models, it's to determine which kind of role models we want to promote. Are women who have

succeeded in male terms and in male-dominated arenas the only
women we want to emulate? Or are many of us looking for our
role models only in the corporate headquarters of Exxon and
American Express, rather than also in the caring professions,
where some of the most interesting experiments in transformative
feminism are taking place? Are we looking so intently at the model
that we no longer ask what role that model actually performs in
the world — what actions she takes, whom she serves?

The goal is no longer to work only for ourselves, but to regroup
so that we can determine how best to work for others.

Many women have been working together for years to achieve
equality with a difference. I believe those the market has disempowered can also relearn how to work with one another for real
change. Indeed, we cannot afford not to. Individual inaction poses
a far greater risk for most of us than does collective action. We
must all become creators of and participants in a mass transformative feminist renewal. If we do not, then we risk losing whatever
we have gained. If men and women do not work together to tame
the market — and to forge a new definition of freedom and self-
worth — then it will defeat us all in the end.

Recent debates about women and men, women and work,
women and family, women and relationships have concentrated
on the wisdom or folly of creating new tracks for women in the
workplace. But the real issue is not what track women are on, or
who will arrive first at the glittering station of individual success.
What should concern us instead is the context in which we find
ourselves today — a competitive, goal-oriented consumer culture
that bears little resemblance to the balanced, more compassionate
society envisaged by so many of us thirty years ago. I believe our
most daunting problems represent, in fact, a great and exciting
challenge: we must demystify the mistaken models of liberation
that have been constructed for us of late and, using the vision of
a more transformative feminism, together craft new alternatives
based neither on a nineteenth-century sentimentalization of wom-
en's caring roles nor on a celebration of late-twentieth-century
economic man.

Chapter One

THE MASCULINE MYSTIQUE

IN 1900, approximately one in five women worked outside of the home.[1] In 1950, 28.3 percent of all women were in the work force. And in 1970, that figure had increased to 43.3 percent.[2] In 1970, 5.4 percent of all law degrees and 8.4 percent of all medical degrees were awarded to women candidates. By 1979, those figures jumped to 28.5 percent and 23 percent respectively.[3] In 1970, 38.6 percent of all professional and technical employees, 15.9 percent of all managers and administrators, and 30.9 percent of all operatives were women.[4] By 1982, those percentages had increased to 43.2 percent, 29.2 percent, and 29.7 percent respectively.[5] By the mid-1980s, then, more women than ever before had entered or were preparing to enter the American labor market, many in positions that had traditionally been held by men.

This era was one of both extraordinary gains, in which women felt they were participating in an exciting new gender revolution, and also one which presented us with wrenching personal dilemmas. Most of us were, quite simply, ill-equipped to cope with these dilemmas.

Institutional discrimination was, and still is, one of the most prevalent problems women face in the marketplace. Men who have been nourished on sexism and marketplace ideology for centuries have been unwilling to redistribute or share power with the women who have been deprived of full rights, respect, and citizenship throughout history. Men's resistance to accepting — and advancing — women's liberation has also been exacerbated by our market society's emphasis on the struggle to compete in a zero-sum contest in which one is either a winner or a loser. In such an environment, both men with power and those with none have been unable to imagine a world in which men and women can all share in the benefits and progress of an advanced technological society. The model of winner-take-all success that drives our society decrees that men at the top cling desperately to power, wealth, and privilege, and that men at the bottom — who often feel worthless and powerless — hang on to the "privilege" of having someone less worthy and powerful than themselves to dominate and feel superior to.

While feminists were fighting institutional discrimination through the courts and Congress, the social and cultural obstacles the marketplace had long constructed proved just as hard to tackle.

On the most basic level, what women had not considered was just how much their traditional caring values and empathic interpersonal skills seemed to inhibit rather than enhance their efforts to succeed in the workplace.

To prove themselves to their male colleagues and bosses, who were hardly delighted by their arrival, women — particularly those entering business and the professions — soon realized they would have to do more than master the subject matter and technical details of their jobs. Success in the marketplace would entail far more than the ability to get the job done; it would mean conforming to the stereotype of how a successful person thinks, acts, and looks.

As numerous "feminist" success counselors have since pointed out, little boys learn the requisite blend of competitiveness, individual self-reliance, and aggressiveness at their fathers' knees and on their coaches' Little League teams. Little girls, on the other hand, know neither the written plays nor the unwritten psychological and moral rules that make one a "player" on a very specific kind of team. Women, who had been sidelined for centuries, now had to learn rule number one as they finally entered the game: the goal is to win. To get on and stay on the team, they would have to achieve the requisite blend of detachment and jocular camaraderie that would allow them both to be "team players" and to "look out for number one," while also dealing with those in power and those who had none.

For some eager 1970s neophytes, these lessons presented an entirely welcome challenge. All they wanted, it seemed, was to master the skills required to get ahead, do well, and be noticed. A great many other women, however, approached this "challenge" with trepidation. The competitive demands of the marketplace were, after all, antithetical to the values and activities many women truly cared about.

Many of the women who entered the work force in the mid- to late seventies came of age during the radical antiwar and civil rights movements of the sixties. Some wanted to revolutionize capitalist society, not administer it, and thus they had little that was positive to say about corporate America. The prospect of entering mainstream institutions meant not only abandoning any hope of change, but acquiescing to the values of an "establishment" they abhorred.

Other women were less concerned about becoming female *capitalists* than about becoming female "company men." For years, more radical women had been criticizing the male model of career advancement and the success ethic it engendered. Women exchanged apocryphal tales of men — in many cases their own fathers and husbands — who had sold their souls to the corporation and who had lost all ability to function as normal, sentient beings. Business thus seemed a no-win game. Men had blocked most paths to the top, and women had to struggle relentlessly even to gain entrance into their world. Furthermore, the occasional women who *could* squeeze through the cracks and achieve business success would have to pay for it with a kind of emotional death.

Women, moreover, were soon to find that the positive aspects of their feminine socialization — their caring insights and their positive views of human relationships — hampered their ability to internalize male rules of power. The very nurturing, empathic, empowering qualities that helped women do their work at home

inhibited them in the workplace. Women with no profound ideological commitment to either feminism or radical politics found it
difficult to boss subordinates, to ruthlessly shut out the other guy
(or gal), and to maintain the appropriate detachment about the
human consequences of business decisions — to believe, in short,
that at work the bottom line is the only one that counts.

During this transitional period, when women were first entering
male-dominated institutions, many feminists tried to confront
these issues and to consider their impact on women's lives and
feminism as a whole. *Ms.* magazine and other feminist journals,
for example, carried numerous articles on feminism and power,
and consciousness-raising groups grappled with these issues in
weekly sessions all over the country. Many tried to distinguish
between power, celebrity, and self-aggrandizement and assert a
definition of power as empowerment. But as the seventies moved
into the eighties, the consciousness-raising groups, which had been
most women's link to feminist ideals and to a larger community
of women, were disbanding — in part because women's struggles
in the marketplace were so time consuming — and this kind of
transformative feminist voice was relegated to the margins. Another "feminist" voice was becoming increasingly audible. It urged
the women who were moving into American institutions to pursue
careers rather than crusades, to compete rather than to care, to
embrace rather than challenge the male side of traditional American values.

Throughout our history, mainstream society has been indifferent,
if not hostile, to any alternative to the kind of aggressive, competitive, radically individualistic, profit-oriented values and activities that have always represented "the American way." Since its
founding, the United States has striven to be a market society
without peer. Where other industrialized nations have tempered
the impersonality and ruthlessness of the marketplace with institutions that provide caring services to all citizens, American sociey
has remained relatively impervious to less acquisitive definitions
of human nature and individual success. As a nation we are still
skeptical of the notion that the purpose of government might in-

clude providing for human caring, community, and collective action to achieve broad public good.

"Man has almost constant occasion for the help of his brethren, and it is in vain for him to expect it from their benevolence only," Adam Smith wrote in *The Wealth of Nations* in 1776. "It is not from the benevolence of the butcher, the brewer or the baker that we expect our dinner, but from their regard to their own interest. We address ourselves, not to their humanity but to their self love, and never talk to them of our own necessities but of their advantages. *Nobody but a beggar chuses* [*sic*] to depend chiefly upon the benevolence of his fellow citizens"[6] (my italics).

Although some argue that Adam Smith applied the theory of narrow self-interest only to the *economic* marketplace, in contemporary America the ideology of individualism and self-interest informs our entire culture and has made America more than a market *economy* but a market *society* in which bottom-line, marketplace concerns dominate all areas of our lives. In it human beings — Smith's "economic," or "inquisitive," man — are considered self-sufficient, independent units who get nothing and give nothing outside the pursuit of individual self-interest. They live in a world governed by the principle of scarcity rather than sufficiency, a world in which people learn that their ability to purchase a limited number of goods and services is dependent upon the outcome of a zero-sum contest for achievement and accumulation.

In the world women entered, competition is the essence of the market. It doesn't merely describe the dynamic of the struggle over the distribution of scarce resources, it is the process that fuels every positive aspect of a market society. Without it, we believe that there can be no productivity, creativity, or initiative. And in this society productivity, creativity, and initiative are channeled toward very specific aims: the accumulation of wealth, status, and, ultimately, power.

To get and keep wealth and power we are supposed to be "separate" and independent not only in the workplace, but in personal relationships as well. Our most prominent theories of psychological and moral development — from Freud to Erikson, from Piaget to Kohlberg and Levinson — propose a model of development in which the healthy human being (always a man) is "separated," "individuated," "autonomous." His emotional development is, as feminist scholars Jean Baker Miller, Carol Gilligan, and Jessica Benjamin, as well as many communitarian critics of liberalism, explain, a journey of disconnection.[7] He does not consider himself to be deeply embedded in a network of personal and communal relationships that define and enrich his life. Rather, he is taught to view other people either as adversaries to compete against and overcome, or as objects to be manipulated in the service of his self-interest.

The repudiation of relationship and community, altruism and benevolence, in favor of America's radical self-help, self-reliant ethic breeds contempt for caring — for the idea that we all need support, affirmation, affection, guidance, education, sensitivity, knowledge, and mutual self-revelation. American society has reluctantly conceded that some of its citizens will require care — the very young and very old, the very sick and very handicapped, for example. But the idea that caring is a human imperative, essential to everyone no matter how weak or how strong — and that caring activities are not acts of charity but rather affirmations of what is human about human beings — this is utterly foreign to our dominant culture. Instead, the very need for care is considered proof of some underlying physical or emotional flaw. "Nobody but a beggar," Smith insisted, "chuses to depend chiefly on the benevolence of his fellow citizens." Or, as Michael Douglas tells Charlie Sheen in *Wall Street*, "If you need a friend, get a dog."

Since any definition of politics that stresses the public rather than the private good violates this individualistic, instrumental ethic, our political process also reflects these notions about human nature and community. "In America," wrote Richard Hofstadter in his classic *The American Political Tradition*, "the business of politics . . . is to protect this competitive world, to foster it on occasion, to patch up its incidental abuses, but not to cripple it with a plan for common collective action." The result, according to Hofstadter, is a "democracy in cupidity," rather than a "democracy of fraternity."[8]

Hofstadter quotes Abraham Lincoln as stating in 1861 that the purpose of government is not to forge with the people and implement through the state a plan for common collective action but rather to "lift artificial weights from all shoulders; to clear the paths of laudable pursuits for all; to afford all an unfettered start and a fair chance in the race of life."[9]

Women have long taken issue with both the patriarchy and the advanced industrial capitalism of American society, as well as with the "economic," "acquisitive" men who ruled it. When women came together in the late sixties, their links to other radical movements of that era helped many early feminists develop a transformative vision that fought for both equality and difference.

Many women hoped to revolutionize the market. "With both members of the husband and wife team working sensible hours, neither of them need suffer the syndrome of being trapped in an economic rat race," Roslyn S. Willett argued in an essay on work in a classic 1971 collection of feminist articles, *Woman in Sexist Society*. "Both could enjoy the freedom of thinking, reading, aesthetic experiences, continuing education and regular exercise. . . . With equal partnership arrangements in families, another blow could be dealt to the rigid hierarchies that pass for organizational structure in most working places."[10] Women's liberation would not only allow the freedom to enter traditionally male-dominated jobs, it would liberate women *and* men from the constraints of work in a competitive, advanced industrial marketplace.

Compassion and competition were not considered antithetical; on the contrary, at least some feminists wanted to gain greater respect and remuneration for the caring work they had so long performed in the so-called helping professions — teaching, social work, nursing, childcare. Once women were in positions of authority, they hoped, women would mobilize their newfound power to fight for better pay, greater opportunity for advancement, and increased respect for their "sisters" who still chose to work in the traditional female sphere. "Women in this country do not want to be free for ruthless competition," Vivian Gornick and Barbara K. Moran wrote in the introduction to *Woman in Sexist Society*. "They want to be freed from private curatorship of the happiness of individuals — too often victims themselves — to joint trusteeship of the common good. They want a place in public life for the values they have been forced to cherish in private for too long."[11]

Or as Robin Morgan put it, in her 1970 anthology *Sisterhood Is Powerful*, "We know that we want something more, much more, than the same gray, meaningless, alienating jobs that men are forced to sacrifice their lives to."[12]

Conducting a close accounting of the price men paid for their dominance, many feminists condemned, or sometimes even pitied, men because they had been forced to sacrifice their personal lives to their professional ones. Transformative feminism's promise was a world in which men and women could balance love, friendship, work, and community; a world that would encourage cooperation between men and women and a sense of social responsibility in citizens, who would recognize their interconnectedness and who would affirm rather than deny their need for relationship. And so, many women set about transforming male-female relationships and child rearing to encourage this emerging sense of shared responsibility and balance.

"The personal is political" and "Sisterhood is powerful" were also calls to arms, urging women into the political arena, with the objective of creating a more cooperative commonwealth that would finally include all women in a true majoritarian culture, replacing that democracy of cupidity that Hofstadter wrote about not with a democracy of fraternity but of humanity.

"As the largest alienated element in our society, and because of their numbers, passion, and length of oppression, its largest revolutionary base, women might come to play a leadership part in social revolution, quite unknown before in history," Kate Millett prophesied in 1970 in *Sexual Politics*. "The changes in fundamental values such a coalition of expropriated groups — blacks, youth, women, the poor — would seek are especially pertinent to realizing not only sexual revolution but a gathering impetus toward freedom from rank or prescriptive role, sexual or otherwise. For to actually change the quality of life is to transform personality, and this cannot be done without freeing humanity from the tyranny of sexual-social category and conformity to sexual stereotype — as well as abolishing racial caste and economic class."[13]

Today many women — particularly younger ones — do not even remember this powerful feminist vision of social transformation. That's because the feminism that dominates the news and

public debates is a brand of adaptive feminism that teaches us to
adopt and adapt to male marketplace values, activities, and beliefs. That's what equal-opportunity feminism is all about.

Look through the parenting magazines or those targeting
professional women that clutter the newsstands; leaf through the
success primers that have replaced the feminist classics of the early
seventies in the nation's bookstores, or pick up a copy of the latest
how-to best-seller telling women whom and what to avoid in personal relationships; tune in to the new television serials or made-
for-TV movies or the Hollywood films that feature "new women."
Equal-opportunity feminism has become the dominant mainstream voice of the era. All the major discussions about women's
roles today — about work, love, and family life; about mommy
tracks and daddy tracks, parental leave and childcare; even about
abortion and reproductive rights — attempt to resolve the differences of feminist philosophies by suppressing or sentimentalizing
the caring insights that have historically made women different from men, and celebrating competition, success, and equality
of opportunity as the male American marketplace has always defined it.

"In America, success has always meant making money and
transforming it into status, or becoming famous," observes Richard M. Huber. "Success was not earned by being a loyal friend or
good husband. It was a reward for performance on the job. It is
not the same thing as happiness — which is how you feel. Success
was brutally objective and impersonal. It recorded a change in
rank, the upgrading of a person in relation to others by the unequal distribution of money and power, prestige and fame."[14]

For all its rhetoric about providing equality to ordinary people,
American ideology has never been truly interested in equality of
result. "Americans believe in equality of opportunity rather than
equality of result. Equality of result argues that people are, in
some substantive way, equal in the kinds of lives they lead," says
Harvard professor Sidney Verba.

Equality of opportunity, on the other hand, means we believe
that all should have an equal chance to use their talents and resources to get just as far ahead as they can. "Built into the notion
of equality of opportunity is the notion that ordinary people can

do extraordinary things," adds Verba. "So our heroes are not people of humble origins who lead ordinary lives, they are humble people who accomplish great things or even ordinary people who have extraordinary good — or bad — luck, like those who win the lottery."

In American culture, the concept of equality of opportunity is the path that leads individuals to the ultimate state of disconnection. While equality and egalitarianism connote similarity and interconnectedness, equality of opportunity connotes upward mobility — a move away from where one came from, what one used to do, how one used to be.

The feminist voice that mainstream society finds most congenial takes these traditional notions about success, equality, and disconnection and skillfully applies them to women. In the process it has produced a peculiar hybrid — economic, or acquisitive, woman — a faithful replica of the kind of economic, acquisitive man who has historically denigrated the very skills, values, and activities that have been the substance of women's claim to difference.

Equal-opportunity feminism has had a tremendous impact on American women over the past two decades. Supplementing the dominant voice of corporate America, its message reaches millions of women. It tells professional women how to get richer and spend more and it tells middle-, working-class, and poor women that they can pull themselves up by their own bootstraps and that they're the ones to blame if they fail. Its original leaders were a burgeoning group of women who, in the midseventies, began writing books and magazine articles, conducting seminars on business success and assertiveness training, promoting new magazines, and founding professional women's networks and organizations. Madison Avenue also soon joined them, zeroing in on a promising new market of working women. Here was a brand new group of individual consumers who were suddenly considering work to be a permanent part of their lives. With their own checking accounts and credit cards, they could now spend their newly disposable incomes on a vast array of products and services geared especially to them.

The result of this collaboration between American business, the advertising industry, and equal-opportunity feminists was a new "masculine mystique." This masculine mystique is founded on the assumption that women can find happiness, self-esteem, and self-fulfillment by emulating and ultimately internalizing the ideology of marketplace society; in other words, by becoming the female equivalent of economic, acquisitive man. In different forms, it made its first appearance in the midseventies and early eighties. I remember, for example, leafing through the pages of the *New York Times* in 1979 and discovering a five-column, full-length fashion ad promoting Macy's spring collection. Macy's wasn't offering only apparel and accessories. To go along with the clothes that would make the woman, it was sponsoring a seminar entitled "Women Mean Business." At the seminar, female corporate executives who had known "what it's like to be low man on the totem pole" in the business world would give pointers to other women who hoped to climb to the top in their new Macy's wardrobes.

And then, of course, there was the ad campaign for Virginia Slims. Remember the first appearance of the glamorous, svelte model kicking up her heels and dangling her cigarette to the tune of "You've Come a Long Way, Baby"? There is no better example of Madison Avenue's contribution to the masculine mystique: success, maturity, and achievement were all rolled up in one pert little cigarette that fused women's traditional image — the chic, trim sex symbol — with the independent, macho image of the Marlboro Man.

If we now needed our own cigarette, we would surely need our own professional magazines in which to advertise it — along with all the other baggage essential for our new journey. In 1976, *Working Woman* hit the newsstands. And in 1980, *Savvy*, for "the successful woman," joined what would soon be a literal cascade of publications aimed at the "new" woman. Instead of concentrating exclusively on such traditional topics as food, fashion, fitness, and sex, these magazines featured pragmatic, hard-nosed advice on how to succeed on the job, manage investments, and handle subordinates, colleagues, and superiors. This new-and-improved women's magazine recipe would soon, in fact, be copied by old-fashioned standbys like *Mademoiselle* and *Glamour* and by many others whose pages began to fill with advice for the business and professional woman.

By the early eighties, this new feminist voice had reached book-stores as well. Instead of cover images featuring clenched fists and other feminist symbols, women's books now sported photographs of smartly dressed women standing in front of imposing desks in elegant offices; inside they contained the "game plans" that would teach women how to get ahead. The new feminist heroine was a tailored Charlie's Angel who carried an attaché case rather than a .38 and who could "role-model" for a new breed of "sisters" who wanted to "network" — that is, to cut deals, make killings, and get to the top of the corporate heap. Titles included *Games Mother Never Taught You, In the Spotlight, The Managerial Woman,* and *Targeting the Top.*

It comes as no surprise that these books and the magazines, films, and seminars of the late seventies and eighties followed on the heels of the era's self-improvement movement; after all, in-dependence, intense subjectivism, and self-actualization have al-ways been at the heart of America's success ethic. In that tradition, equal-opportunity feminism defined success and self-esteem in re-lation to on-the-job performance and the attainment of wealth or fame. The women hailed as role models were leaders, not follow-ers; high-fliers, not ordinary women leading their ordinary lives. When equal-opportunity feminism did focus on ordinary women, they were women who had moved up and away from their ordi-nary jobs, friends, or families and on to better jobs, more money, and friendships that reflected status. "Success," Ben Hecht ob-served, "requires us to change our friends, as does failure."[15]

But, of course, moving up and away created anxiety for many women. The first feminist success counselors tried to calm wom-en's fears that they would be selling out, forfeiting their caring agendas to those of the ruthless male marketplace. They reassured women that they would not simply be trading the prison of do-mesticity for that of masculine professionalism; in fact, they prom-ised women that they could be equally committed to their sisters and to themselves; to their careers and to their femininity; to com-petition and caring. The would-be female professional was per-suaded that there was a place for her in the male marketplace; that it was a place she would want to occupy; and that in taking it, she would transform that marketplace rather than be transformed by it. In other words, she could have both versions of feminism — the transformative and adaptive.

Relax, women advised one another. The business world can't be as bad as we've been taught to believe. Certainly managers control other people; certainly there's competition out there; certainly it takes time to construct a career — time that might otherwise be devoted to family and friends. Nonetheless, social reformers and those with other human concerns will find the corporation a congenial environment. Participation in business, Margaret Fenn wrote in her 1980 book *In the Spotlight: Women Executives in a Changing Environment,* "holds the key to release untold amounts of human creativity and energy which can be tapped for the good of the organization."[16]

Don't be misled by all those rumors of ruthless competition and jungle fighting, Margaret V. Higginson and Thomas L. Quick advised in 1980 in *The Ambitious Woman's Guide to a Successful Career.* In the world of business my success doesn't equal your failure, my success equals your success: "People who really climb far up the ladder tend to discover that the way to achieve is by developing their own talents, not by reducing the stature of those around them." Indeed, what the winners create is a "growth" climate for those around them.[17]

According to many of these accounts, women's very entrance into the corporation would eliminate the conditions that they feared would compromise either their feminism or their femininity. "Having women as managers will be therapeutic or corrective for men," Higginson and Quick prophesied.[18] "After men experience working with a woman as a peer for the first time, they often say that communication was freer and more open than when they worked only with men."[19]

Women would create not only a more open environment, but a more egalitarian one as well. "Today women are bringing a new dimension to the administrative process," says Margaret Fenn, describing the democratizing influence of women managers. "Women managers are helping to move business toward the adoption of an administrative philosophy that provides opportunity for all members to participate and contribute their skills and knowledge to the processes affecting them."[20]

All of this contained a distinct biologically determinist tone and harks back to the nineteenth century. Femininity was a kind of force that women carried with them wherever they might go, which would vanquish all forms of masculine evil. "Whatever else the entrance of women into responsible organizational positions may bring, this should be paramount: the realization that it is wrong to deal with people as groups and to treat all members of the group the same way," Higginson and Quick agreed.[21] The women's magazines echoed these rosy themes. In an editorial in the January 1980 inaugural issue of *Savvy*, editor Judith Daniels explained that professional women differ from others because of "the centrality of work in our lives." This did not mean, Daniels hastened to clarify, that "we aren't interested in husbands or friends or children or pleasant homes. . . . Nor does it mean we're all crazed, ersatz men trying to get man-sized ulcers and heart attacks.

"Despite our work orientation, we at *Savvy* don't think what's needed is another trade publication or an office manual. We want *Savvy* to reflect the many ways in which interest in work affects the rest of our lives. We want to show that women who are ambitious are not socially irresponsible. That women who are concerned about professional success and rewards can also make life choices of personal compassion and maturity. That self-development does not mean selfishness."[22]

This view echoed those of Friedan, who wrote that women would, naturally, fight *for one another* in the political sphere, and that individual career advancement and action on behalf of the majority were interconnected. "Every girl who manages to stick it out through law school or medical school, who finishes her M.A. or Ph.D. and goes on to use it helps others move on," she wrote. "When enough women make life plans geared to their real abilities and speak out for maternity leaves or even maternity sabbaticals and professionally run nurseries, other changes in the rules then may be necessary."[23]

Most of the role models this feminist voice promoted were, of course, head-starters — women from middle- and upper-middle-class backgrounds with good educations. By focusing on these women — the ones who could and would make it — purveyors of the feminist mystique followed a well-worn path. This formula, of course, is simply a female version of the all-American Horatio Alger story. Named after the popular nineteenth-century novelist Horatio Alger, this rags-to-riches myth holds that by dint of perseverance and hard work, any boy can pull himself up by his own bootstraps and run the race to win.

But, as we noted earlier, some women were reluctant to enter it at all. And so proponents of equal-opportunity feminism dealt with that hesitation by turning women's gaze from the system to the self, suggesting that those women who did not embrace success and who had trouble reconciling their values with those of the marketplace had only themselves to blame for refusing to move out of the "feminine ghetto."

This argument was put forth most forcefully by Colette Dowling in her 1981 best-seller, *The Cinderella Complex.* Dowling argued, "We have only one shot at 'liberation,' that is to emancipate ourselves from within. It is the thesis of this book that personal, psychological dependency, the deep wish to be taken care of by others — is the chief force holding women down today. I call this 'The Cinderella Complex' — a network of largely repressed attitudes and fears that keep women in a kind of half-light, retreating from the full use of their minds and creativity. Like Cinderella, women today are still waiting for something external to transform their lives."[24]

To "spring free," repair the "energy leak," and "wrench away from the dependency trap," Dowling advises women to seek a good psychotherapist and to keep a "running balance on the fear of success."

According to this thesis, then, women's fear that success would spell the loss of meaningful relationships, activities, and values was not based on an accurate reading of reality. Instead, their fears were unfounded or, worse, signs of serious emotional problems that should be remedied through individual self-help techniques or an extended course of psychotherapy.

Replacing the "fear of success" with the "will to win" was a crucial step in the transformation of the adaptive feminist vision.

Soon, however, the creators of the feminist mystique were compelled to admit that their liberated women would not, in fact, be much different from men. That's because the marketplace demands that both men and women play by *the* rules. And these rules have not changed and will not change just because women are on the field.

Take lesson one. About POWER. What you need to know about power, the new women success experts explained, is that it is the ultimate scarce resource for which you *must* compete. To get it, you must willingly, even exuberantly, engage in a zero-sum contest with anyone — male or female — who appears on the playing field. Once you've got power, moreover, don't think there's any virtue in sharing it. The idea is to keep it for yourself and then get more.

Just as male theoreticians of the marketplace have always considered their rules "natural" or God given, so, too, equal-opportunity feminists consider that exercising hierarchical power over others is part of the natural order of things. "An effective manager recognizes that power and influence are parts of everyday life." It's true that "organizational members are positioned in a hierarchy which implies unequal power and distribution." But such distribution emerges *naturally* [my italics] from ideas about social organization and behavior," Margaret Fenn argued.[25] "As a condition of employment, employees accept as legitimate the exercise of authority over areas related to performance and are indifferent to the fact that they have the ability to choose other alternatives. Subordinates in accepting the power of authority do not exercise their own evaluative functions in those areas of legitimate authority related to the task," Fenn elaborated.[26]

Betty Lehan Harragan boldly described the essential rules of the game in her still popular 1977 best-seller, *Games Mother Never Taught You: Corporate Gamesmanship for Women*. Depicting life in the battlefield and sports metaphors that have been traditionally reserved for male "games," Harragan outlines a female future filled with tactics and strategies, battles and wars, in which any woman can succeed if she simply masters the lessons that dads taught their sons but which moms, unfortunately, were unable to pass on to their daughters.

"The objective of the game is money and power." She insists "this time there's no reason for working women of any age to enter the action unprepared, ill-equipped or uncertain of their position or opponents. The facts can set you free to determine your own fate in the corporate plan."[27]

To attain power, women must be willing to accept the fact that they can't really be *that* different from men. Caring and competing in an American marketplace are indeed antithetical. If they want to get ahead, women must become as driven as their male colleagues. Thus in its September 1986 issue, *Savvy* discarded its inaugural dictates against women becoming as "crazed" as men. An article entitled "In Search of Stamina" featured profiles of super-achieving female professionals whose hectic schedules rivaled those of any male businessman. "It's not that we're not aggressive enough, or that we lack a drive for power, or that we're not motivated," the author commiserated. "It's just that we're so tired. But we don't have to be. Some of us, like caterer Martha Stewart and Wall Street investment banker C. Austin Fitts, have already figured out how to create and preserve stamina, that fund of usable energy that takes you through long meetings, endless business trips, deadline frenzy. The rest of us are just learning."[28]

Learning to value power and to manage one's time were only two components of success. An additional aspect of the game was learning to devalue the caring concerns of female socialization. Women would have to make sure that their friendships with other women did not interfere with their jobs. "Your relationships with former associates," Higginson and Quick warn, "must reflect position not emotion." "Women," they observe, "seem to have a special problem in this area. In the company cafeteria, for example, they will sit down with other women — even if these women are on a lower job level — rather than join men who are now their peers."[29]

Or, as Margaret Fenn puts it, "Associations and friendships reflect managerial values. These imply a degree of social distancing from subordinates."[30] An article on office politics warned, "The fact is, you were hired to get the job done, not to win friends, fulfill needs left from your childhood or work out unresolved conflicts from your past." Here again, any need for affiliation is turned into a neurotic symptom. "You don't have to be a cold fish or a cutthroat . . . but it's good politics to avoid becoming too people-oriented. You don't want personal relationships in the office to harm your work and career."[31]

In the service of success, one is also advised to eliminate any evidence that one has a personal life outside the office. "Be sure to acquire all furnishings, draperies, pictures and other accoutrements that go with your rank," Harragan suggests. "Check with the office manager or whoever handles such things when you're in doubt . . . Don't dilute the power symbolism of your office with home-decoration goodies. A professional army officer or football player doesn't encumber himself with personal mementoes, nor should an active business game player. . . . Family photographs are iffy — if your superiors set the tone, okay; if not, consider it in light of the signals you'll be sending. From women, the messages can be self-protective — 'I'm married with a family so keep your distance.' Or the message received may be — 'She's not a serious businesswoman, her husband and kids dominate her life. She doesn't care about getting ahead.' "[32]

The final step was eliminating any identification with the vast majority of other women to whom the aspiring career woman might feel responsible. In other words, equal-opportunity feminism teaches us that although sisterhood might be powerful, it is far less compelling than rank, wealth, and fame.

To solve your problems, a column in *Savvy*'s "Ideas and Strategies for Doing Better Business" advises, "You must deal with subordinates who challenge authority. Divide and conquer. The way your gang is acting, the time for group talk is over."[33]

Stick with your own kind, Jane Wilson recommends in a 1980 *Savvy* article entitled "The New Girl Network: A Power System for the Future." Here was the forum that would replace the nearly defunct consciousness-raising groups of the sixties and early seventies. "What is needed now," Wilson noted, "is a way to galvanize progress, and the 'new girls network' is proving itself an effective means of ending isolation and passivity among ambitious women. The 'old boys' have used this tool for getting things done since the first hunting parties set out from the caves and for them one of its chief benefits has always been access to information."[34]

Like the old-boy network, the new-girl version is also an exclusive club, and not all aspiring women can be admitted. Places are reserved for candidates who "reflect a high level of achievement," who are "successful individuals," and who share the same power goals. Describing a model network, Wilson explains that would-be members must determine "whether the principal goal is money, power, or fame. Apparently you can't go for all three at this state in the game and any other objective, such as contentment or intellectual stimulation, is presumed to be a by-product of the Big Three."[35]

Of course, many women were uncomfortable with these new feminist power rules. Some troubled professional aspirants questioned whether such "male" behavior was really necessary, and how the inequalities that resulted could be justified. The answer was typical of the American gospel of success. As Betty Lehan Harragan explains it at the end of *Games Mother Never Taught You*, "Those who win the money decide how to spend it, so if you want to change the things money is spent on, you first have to win it."[36]

Economic woman was told that the new values and attitudes she was to adopt, the new rules she would learn, were only costume — like the three-piece women's business suit — regrettable accouterments, but absolutely essential to her success, upward mobility, and acquisition of the power needed to change things from within.

By the late 1980s, however, it was clear that costume had become content. Liberation now meant becoming the twin of economic man, and equal-opportunity feminism had turned its back on any qualms or questions about the world it had reproduced.

Many of the role models given us today clearly illustrate this as they unambivalently choose competition over caring. They are women like Lorraine Mecca, the CEO of a fourteen-million-dollar business who explains the facts of life in *Inc.* magazine. "You have to give up something to be a success in business. There's not time for everything. Me . . . I have very little time for my spiritual life. I don't have a civic life. And I do very little with friendships — anything that doesn't have to do with business. I don't have time to cultivate relationships that aren't profitable."[37]

The success models who are married and have children tend to apply the same basic how-to's to mother-child relationships that they bring to employer-employee relations. Successful women, Asta Lubin comments in *Managing Success*, have learned a crucial skill — to compartmentalize. "They are able to focus on the present and tune out other areas of their lives. Their sustaining crowd says, 'she is all there,' with the subject at hand. They focus on the child when with the child, on work when at work, and so on, thus preventing one role from interfering with another. This is an invaluable ability."[38]

So is the refusal to complain about work-related, family-related, or social problems. "It appears that complaining is against the rules," Lubin writes.[39] The advice that Betty Harragan gave in 1977 still holds true over a decade later: "Don't talk back to the coach. The coach or captain is the ultimate authority and the motivator. He evaluates skills, assigns positions, decides who plays in the first line-up, who gets benched, who is substituted, and his authority is unquestioned."[40]

In the elaboration of this new feminism of the 1980s, it also becomes crystal clear that marketplace success and monetary success are seen as one and the same, that economic woman is also acquisitive woman. As Richard M. Huber wrote in *The American Idea of Success*, "Bettering oneself had to be socially recognized by translating money into status. . . . The process was the translation of an economic class position derived from making money to a social class position which was particularly established by the spending of it."[41]

On one level this emphasis on consumption is nothing new. Women have traditionally been the targets of manufacturers and their advertising associates. The traditional female homemaker was the one whose job it was to keep up with the Joneses by purchasing the requisite homes, fashions, household equipment, and furnishings. Indeed, one fear American industry may have had when women entered the marketplace was that they would be less available to spend their time consuming. Keeping up with the Joneses and with career demands as well might prove to be too daunting a challenge. But that was far from the case. According to the tenets of equal-opportunity feminism, after all, women should have it all. And that means jobs, money, *and* things. Thus consumption plays an important part in the contemporary feminist mystique. But now women are exhorted to buy not only clothes and household goods, but professional attire, office equipment and accessories, and a great variety of personal services as well.

The feminist mystique's well-heeled, well-attired heroines do not appear only in the pages of slick magazines and how-to-succeed-in-business books. They also swing into action every night on television and at the movies. For the past three years on "L.A. Law" Grace Van Owen has personified economic woman in Hollywood's rendition of life in the fast track. In one episode, Van Owen was appointed a judge. On her very first day on the bench, she sentenced a pregnant cocaine abuser to jail and a sixteen-year-old to life imprisonment for murder — thus earning an instant reputation as a "hanging judge." And when the secretaries at the L.A. law firm in the show went on strike to protest uncalled-for alterations in their lunch hour, the most bottom line–oriented female partner in the firm argued they should be unceremoniously fired.

If the heroines of the cinematic past were spectators at life's parade or victims of its cruelties, today's cinematic woman has gone far beyond assertiveness to outright violence. In the hit movie *Fatal Attraction*, Anne Archer out-machos her wimpy, adulterous husband, proving that in this new era, families that slay together stay together — any woman with guts can take aim and fire.

In their celebration of violence, such films follow the formulas established in male cop shows and buddy films — formulas that distance human beings from the consequences of even their most violent actions. *Fatal Attraction*, in fact, is a faithful variation on this male model. After "the other woman's" body is bagged and carried away, the film concludes with a shot of husband and wife linking arms and retreating into their comfortable suburban house. The camera pans away from them to a hall table littered with photos, where it alights on a picture of mom, dad, and only child — the happy family, serene and reunited at last.

Not surprisingly, the callous, tough, competitive offspring of equal-opportunity feminism have drawn criticism as well as kudos. In a number of recent attacks on contemporary feminism, women have lamented what has happened to their "sisters" in the

workplace and at home. In one of the first such pieces, entitled
"Women and the Spoils of Success" (*New York Times Magazine*,
August 6, 1981), Anne Taylor Flemming asked, "Have envy and
elbowing replaced the last decade's good feelings among career
women? Many of them now seem more threatened by one another's triumphs than they are by the successes of men." In the beginning, she recalled, there was the "exhilaration of our shared
promise, we were sisterly, custodial of each of one another's
dreams. It was a special moment, shared by many women all over
the country. It was also brief. After moving out into the marketplace and into the decade, women became competitive, first with
men, then — and it is this that lingers — with one another, a kind
of jousting among tokens. So that now . . . so many of the women
I know are driven people, more afraid of failure than of success,
more afraid of complacency than of competition, more afraid of one
another's successes than of the successes of the men in their lives."[42]

But forgetting the fact that the fond hopes women shared were
the product of an era when women were *outside* the marketplace
rather than within it, Flemming lays the blame on women themselves for their competitiveness and insensitivity.

Six years later, again in the *New York Times Magazine*, Mary
Anne Dolan echoed the same theme. "When Feminism Failed,"
the two-page headline trumpets. A disheartened-looking professional woman leans against a large wooden door in the accompanying illustration. Three daggers — their lethal points piercing a
chill sea of blue — seem to march toward her. Her head hangs
down in despair, despair she shares with the author, who considers
feminism's "lost promise."

A feminist, Dolan became editor of the *Miami Herald* and hired
a number of women in positions of power and authority. "This
was a moment when the promise of the women's movement could
be fulfilled," she writes. "We had permission at last. The joint
belonged to us! We would bring all those 'female' qualities we had
been boasting about on placards for years in through the front
door, into the open of the newsroom. We would be a family. Between male and female would be respect and generosity and
adaptability and warmth and comity and nurturing. Such an environment would make the most of our talents and, centrally, of

our work. We would have honest conflict and competition, but also compromise and consensus and, therefore, success. We would make mincemeat of the male business model."[43]

Instead, "the power grab began . . . In the unique laboratory of the *Herald*, women given large doses of power were transmogrified by it. Faced with the freedom to behave differently from the iconic male executive, the women chose the course of least change."[44]

The "monster," Dolan continues, "is within. Out of some ancient fear that the power is not truly ours, we set about destroying it. Like slaves who can't give up their masters, we cling either to male bosses or male models. We are responsible for keeping alive the 'he-Tarzan, me-Jane' ethic, rendering ourselves powerless all over again. But somehow comfortable."[45]

Analyses such as these abound in today's debate about the gender revolution. But I am convinced that they ignore basic realities about women's plight. Contrary to what Mary Anne Dolan seems to believe, women moving into mainstream American workplaces — whether they be the *Miami Herald*, Exxon, or even the academy — are not "faced with freedom." They do not "own the joint" any more than the majority of men ever "owned the joint." Thus, throwing women into positions of power — without educating them about how to use it for the good of the group rather than only for the individual, without fostering a community to whom women feel accountable, and without valuing caring — does not guarantee the warm, supportive environment in which so many of us hoped to work.

Adaptive, equal-opportunity feminism has failed to provide an analysis of American institutions that demystifies the notion that one can care and compete simultaneously. What's more, women entering the work force in the past two decades have also lacked a feminist community. The collective, transformative voice has been marginalized, and equal-opportunity feminism has filled the gap. And so, although we have entered mainstream American institutions in force, it is hardly surprising that more transformative hopes and dreams have not withstood the combined assault of corporate culture and the new masculine mystique.

What Richard M. Huber wrote of women and the success ethic in 1971 is true today: "The cultural definition of success was the

same for a woman as a man in American society if the woman
competed with the man in the world of work. 'Getting ahead' was
measured in the same terms as a man. They were both competing
for the rewards that success conveys."[46]

As transformative feminists long ago pointed out, the myth of
individual success, and the rigidly circumscribed personal qualities
and professional options that defined the successful economic man,
have never truly benefited the majority — even the majority of
men in male-dominated cultures. Why, then, should this myth
hold out any more promise for women?

How do women fare as economic "men"? What kind of lives do
they lead as professionals trying to inch their way to the top? How
does the new masculine mystique serve those women who continue
to try to fulfill society's caring needs as helping professionals,
friends, lovers, and mothers? What has happened to women who
work *for* other women — are they any better served than they
would be working for men? And finally, what happens to the project of human caring and the attempt to share the obligations of
caring with men and to value caring throughout our whole society?

Chapter Two

THE NEW JERUSALEM

THE SEMINAR is entitled "Standing Fast as a Female in a Male World." About forty women between the ages of thirty and fifty-five are gathered at Radcliffe College. Before the lecture begins, the speaker asks the audience a series of questions.

"Do you work outside the home?"

All hands go up.

"Do you feel you work too hard?"

This time a unanimous yes accompanies the flurry of hands.

"Do you have enough time to take care of your children?"

Heads shake sadly and about half the hands are raised.

"What about taking care of elderly parents, is that a problem?"

The rest of the women — some in their fifties — signal that this is also a major concern.

And the concluding question: "Do any of you have a particularly hot issue that brought you here?"

A petite, dark-haired woman at the edge of the room raises her hand. The speaker asks her to relate her concerns to the group and she begins breathlessly. Her name is Elizabeth Parker,* and

---

*Many of the names in this book and identifying details have been changed for reasons of privacy.

she's a psychiatrist at a local hospital. "I was in the class of 'sixty-eight, the first medical school class that was twenty-five percent female rather than seven percent. My husband is a businessman, and I have two young children. I feel like I work all the time. I work at work and at home. You get caught on a treadmill. You feel you have to be the high-powered professional who works full-time. Your husband also expects that of you. Then everybody tells you you're at the peak of your career. People are calling you, and it's flattering. So you keep saying yes — to more referrals and more work. And then, you find that one day your head is spinning."

In response, the speaker asks Parker what she would do if she could do anything she wanted — regardless of the expectations of her husband, employer, or colleagues.

She looks startled, as if she can't quite fathom the question. Then she smiles ruefully. "You know," she says, "I'm so confused, I don't know what I want, anymore."

The paradox of many women's predicament in the marketplace is reflected in Parker's baffled gaze and her ultimate reply. For millions of American women, as the gospel hymn–like theme song of the recent film *Working Girl* so aptly asserts, the marketplace has been billed as the New Jerusalem. But for women, the American workplace of the late twentieth century diminishes our lives as much as it enriches them.

We can't begin to understand the problems women confront today without looking closely at the context in which we pursue liberation — the economic marketplace of the 1980s and early 1990s. Without some understanding of this work world, no comprehensive discussion of women's dilemmas and prospects is possible.

There is, of course, much good news for women in the marketplace. In the last twenty-five years, record numbers of them have entered the labor market. In 1972, 38 percent of the labor force was made up of women, and 43.9 percent of all women were working outside the home. By 1988, that figure had increased to 56.6 percent, and 45 percent of all working people were women.[1]

According to all estimates, women are in the labor force to stay. By the year 2000, writes Ronald E. Kutscher in the *Monthly Labor*

Review, "Women are projected to account for 64 percent of the net increase in the labor force — slightly more than their share of the 1972–86 labor force growth. Consequently, by 2000, women are expected to make up more than 47 percent of the labor force."[2]

The bad news is that despite the vast influx of women in the workplace, the market in America remains relatively untamed. "The truth is," Woodrow Wilson said in 1912, "we are all caught in a great economic system which is heartless."[3] Unfortunately, there is no evidence that the system has grown any more compassionate since women have become part of it.

"The great attraction of the market is that it offers freedom, individualism, and self-confidence. And sometimes it delivers," says Alan Wolfe, author of a recent book on the marketplace and moral obligation entitled *Whose Keeper: Social Science and Moral Obligation.* "But there's always a Faustian bargain in market relations. You pay for what you get because the market is governed by iron laws. There's no room for sentiment, caring, loving, personal ties, or community. And because market rules increasingly have moved from the economic to the personal sphere, it has become ever more dominant in our lives."

We can see this dominance if we look at three major trends in the marketplace that have significantly influenced women's lives over the past two decades. The first is the increase in work time and the decline of leisure in America, the second is the resurgence of belief in competition and accumulation, and the third is the market's refusal to help its workers accommodate work and family responsibilities.

Perhaps the first thing women discover when they enter the marketplace is that they have, ironically, been liberated to work in a period in which, more than at any time in the last half century, Americans have become prisoners of work. The forty-hour workweek that Americans finally achieved in the late 1930s has become an anachronism. Whether they work for profit-driven businesses, for progressive organizations, or for human service agencies, American workers of all types are going back to a future of ten- and twelve-hour days and six- and seven-day weeks. And while much of the rest of the industrialized world relaxes at least once a year during legally guaranteed vacations of up to a month or more, most Americans make do with half that much paid time off, and many forgo even that amount of leisure.

The economic squeeze of the 1980s has been a major factor in creating the pervasive new work compulsion that is the rule rather than the exception in this country. But the workplace atmosphere is also to blame. In a society increasingly obsessed with productivity, competition, and consumption, working longer and harder than the next guy is seen as the key to profitability and success. Technological advances — fax machines, personal computers and modems, beepers and car phones — that could make work life easier have instead become instruments with which to speed it up, thus creating even more stress.

This prison of ideology and expectation has, in fact, become so tightly sealed that even admitting that one would like a weekend or evening furlough — that some respite, some outside life, is desirable — may invite the accusation that one lacks "commitment to the job."

Ellen Williams, for example, won't let me use her real name when she describes the time pressure imposed on her at work. This in spite of the fact that she no longer works at the company whose hourly demands were the most excessive. "I worked every day, ten or eleven hours a day," the thirty-seven-year-old marketing executive reports. "And I put in five hours on weekends. The expectation for everyone was that you work not one point zero jobs, but one and a half jobs. That was the corporate culture. I don't know if it was started by men or women, but by the time I got to that office, it was deeply ingrained and everyone shared those expectations — men and women."

Williams tells me that she sat on the management committee that honored workers for giving the greatest service to the company. "The four criteria used to judge for this award had nothing to do with the hours they put in on the job. But each time we discussed a candidate, the first and most important thing mentioned was always how long they were willing to work. Did they get to the office first and leave last? Were they willing to work on weekends?"

In today's work world, Williams adds, and many other women and men agree, you have to be *in* the office — on the court playing

with the guys — to prove your worth as a worker. Some consultants refer to time spent on the job proving one's commitment as
"face time."

That's why so many proponents of equal-opportunity feminism
preach about the virtues of working as long and hard — if not
longer and harder — as men. "Work longer and harder on tough
assignments," an article advising female corporate lawyers declares. "Don't shirk late hours or weekend projects. Don't go home
to cook dinner — or if you do, don't tell anyone. Get the work
done on time, and in the best possible manner."[4]

"Hard Work (alone) Gets You Nowhere," a 1989 advice column
in *Mademoiselle* proclaimed. What does get you somewhere, author Lorraine Dusky argues, is conforming to whatever rules your
boss sets forth. "For instance, is your boss at work early? Or does
he arrive late and stay later? Is he in the office on weekends?
Whatever he does, conform to his particular work habits as much
as you can, especially in the beginning."[5]

All the women I interviewed for this book obeyed this advice.
"When I was starting out in science," says Maureen Kennedy, a
research scientist in New York, "I really felt I had to prove myself.
In those days they were looking for women to put on study sections
[the prestigious panels that review grant proposals for various government foundations and institutes], and so I was put on study
sections when I was very young and because I was a woman. I felt
I had to be very smart and work very hard, which was why my
husband and I put off having children until I was in my late thirties."

Thirty-three-year-old investment banker Helena Walzer says
she thought nothing of working ten- to twelve-hour days when she
got out of business school. "The attempt to prove one could do as
well as men had turned into a kind of competitive machismo about
how hard you work. People begin to compete about how many
hours they worked last week, as if working long hours were a sign
of how important or successful you are." Overwork has become
such a common occurrence that when a forty-three-year-old
mother of two went out looking for a thirty-two-hour-a-week part-
time job, she couldn't even find a forty-hour-a-week full-time
one. "In my field, medical research, the only jobs available are

full-time jobs. That's full time at fifty plus hours a week. When I go to interviews and say I want to work thirty-two hours a week, interviewers seem to think I'm crazy. Why, they wonder, don't I want to work more? The concept of having a life outside of work is foreign to them."

Giving 100 percent (and remember, that's fifty to eighty hours a week in 1990s time currency) means that everything else — social life, personal relationships, even the occasional jog around the block — must be fitted into the cracks unfilled by job or career concerns. When a young female associate investment banker for New York's Salomon Brothers was assaulted in Central Park in the spring of 1989, the newspaper accounts of the tragedy revealed that she frequently ran alone after 10:00 P.M. Why? Because of the time constraints: her jam-packed workday offered no other opportunity for exercise or relaxation. And she was not unique. "She was a hard worker, but that goes without saying," a colleague remarked, explaining that the young woman's schedule — like those of her male colleagues — was the rule rather than the exception.[6]

It should come as no surprise that this widespread preoccupation with work and material success has been documented in studies and polls and has been the subject of numerous articles, TV reports, and dinner table conversations. Results of a 1988 Louis Harris poll reveal that this increase in work and the corresponding decline in leisure is "steady and unending."[7] It is perhaps even more revealing about a harried frame of mind that exists in most Americans as the 1990s unfold. Since 1973, Harris found, there has been a 15 percent increase in the work week and a 37 percent decrease in leisure time.

The median hours Americans spent at work were 40.6 in 1973, 43.1 in 1975, 46.9 in 1980, 47.3 in 1984, and 46.8 in 1988. (In these studies, "work" is defined as time spent on a job or occupation, including keeping house or going to school. "Leisure" is time available for relaxation, socializing, sports, hobbies, or entertainment.) By contrast, leisure time dropped from 26.2 hours a week in 1973 to 24.3 in 1975, 19.2 in 1980, 18.1 in 1984, and 16.6 in 1988. High-powered professionals, small-business owners, and working women were identified as the most hardworking, sometimes averaging sixty to eighty hours of labor a week. Indeed, in some professional fields the forty-hour week is now considered part-time work.[8]

One factor contributing to the leisure shortage that has been much overlooked in recent polling and media reports is the very American tradition of limited vacation time. Compared with citizens of almost every other industrialized nation, Americans get fewer vacation days and take far longer to earn them. Unlike most European countries, the United States has no federal law guaranteeing a minimum amount of vacation time. Vacation policy is either set through collective bargaining or, more commonly, left to the discretion of individual private and public sector employers. According to the Bureau of Labor Statistics, there have been no recent increases in vacation time in either sector. Workers in both receive, on average, a week of vacation after a year of service, two weeks after five years, three weeks after ten, and four after twenty.[9]

To earn the month or so of vacation that goes with twenty or thirty years of service, employees must, of course, remain with the same employer the entire time. If employees change jobs, their accumulated vacation time may vanish — a common occurrence in a country where job tenure averages less than seven years.

In contrast, workers in other industrialized countries enjoy — as a statutory right — longer vacations from the moment they enter the work force. In Canada, workers are legally entitled to two weeks off during their first year on the job, in both the private and public sectors. After two or three years of employment most get three weeks of vacation. After ten years, it's up to four, and after twenty years Canadian workers have five weeks off a year. In West Germany, statutes guarantee eighteen days minimum for everyone, but most workers get five or six weeks. The same is true in the Scandinavian countries and in France, where much of the country goes on holiday in the month of August.

In none of these countries do workers have to "earn" vacation time by putting in a certain number of years with one company. They are entitled to ample vacations immediately, no matter what their rank or position. In countries that are America's most successful competitors in the global marketplace, all working people — whether lawyers or teachers, CEO's or janitors — take the vacations to which they are entitled by law. "No one in West Germany," a West German embassy officer explains, "no matter how high up they are, would ever say they couldn't afford to take a vacation. Everyone takes their vacation. In fact, offices and factories often close down for three or four weeks because people are on vacation."

The one exception to this advanced industrial model is Japan.* Japanese workers get eighteen paid holidays a year, which most do take. However, they work five-and-a-half-day weeks, and they tend not to take their full allotment of vacations, which average twenty paid days. On average they take only ten vacation days.[10]

This increase in work time and decrease in leisure is all the more startling because it reverses gains which Americans fought for for over a century — and which culminated in the forty-hour work-week that became the national standard in the 1940s. Although the American work ethic has become famous throughout the world, Americans actually spent much of the nineteenth century trying to liberate themselves from work. As historian Benjamin Kline Hunnicutt recounts in *Work without End: Abandoning Shorter Hours for the Right to Work*, the forty-hour workweek was won after a century of struggle led by social reformers, labor, feminists, religious and community leaders, and progressive politicians — all of whom believed that freedom from work, as well as improvements in wages and benefits, was a paramount social goal.

"Some welcomed and promoted shorter hours, believing they were as natural and good a result of industrial advance as higher wages," Hunnicutt relates. "Others supported the process for work's sake, believing that by reducing the hours of labor and thence fatigue, work could be perfected and made a thoroughly joyous experience. . . . At the close of the shorter-hour era, a few intellectuals even promoted shorter hours as an alternative to work, as an avenue for human progress, leading the common man

---

*Although American employers laud Japan's dedication to work, the Japanese themselves are beginning to consider their national workaholism a serious social problem. Stress-related illnesses and even deaths have prompted the government to set up a commission that is trying to promote shorter hours and more leisure. But the commission is having a difficult time changing age-old patterns.

to exercise his higher faculties — body, mind and spirit — in a democratic culture."[11]

In 1840, in response to workers' initiatives, Martin Van Buren implemented gradual decreases in the workweek; by the 1920s it had been reduced to fifty hours, and by 1940 the forty-hour week became the nation's standard. During the 1940s, moreover, reformers hoped that the forty-hour week would serve as a new point of departure, as labor, key congressional leaders, and even officials within the Roosevelt administration fought for job-sharing and a thirty-hour week.

But the thirty-hour week was defeated. Through a series of complex political maneuvers, it was abandoned in favor of job creation, the touchstone of the Roosevelt administration. And, according to Hunnicutt's fascinating history, the idea that work should be the most important part of life — not simply *one* part of life — and that self-esteem and fulfillment should come almost exclusively from workplace accomplishment gained ascendancy and became a part of political orthodoxy. "Since the Depression," Hunnicutt concludes, "no major party has made shorter hours a political issue, no resolutions have been passed and no convention platform has been constructed with reference to this traditional reform. Indeed, the issue of shorter hours has ceased to be an important part of public discourse. The dreams of utopian writers and the hopes of those who believed that progress involved leisure as much as it involved economic growth have largely evaporated.

"The study of leisure, the word now appearing often in pejorative quotes, has been relegated to obscure scholars out of the mainstream of intellectual life by those busy with more important and serious matters, such as jobs and how to make more of them."[12]

In the 1990s Americans apply themselves to these "serious matters," settle for even longer days, and even boast about how long it's been since they took their last vacation. One reason for this, of course, is pure economic survival. Today, as anyone who wants to buy a house, raise a family, or educate children knows very well, it takes two incomes to provide the lifestyle that one income — generally the man's — paid for several decades ago. (Figures recently released by the Department of Labor reveal, for example, that the number of women working more than two jobs quadrupled between 1970 and 1989.)[13]

The 1988 median household income in the United States was $27,225. Of the 92,830,000 households in America, 18.6 percent of them earned between $15,000 and $24,999; 16.0 percent earned between $25,000 and $34,999; and only 20.8 percent of households earned over $50,000.[14] Over the past several decades, as economists Robert Kuttner and Stephen Rose have noted, there has been a growing income polarization in the United States and a concomitant "shrinking middle class."

The real wages and salaries of individuals declined at the end of the seventies, so that the average real earnings of a household dropped by 12 percent. During this time, gaps between rich and poor, middle and poor, and rich and middle widened. Those at the bottom of the income pyramid fared worse because of their great loss in what economists call transfer payments — money from welfare and other programs. "Lower real earnings caused the households in the third quintile to suffer a 9 percent real income decline," Rose says.[15]

The 1984 median income dropped for families of every size. But larger families suffered more. The median income of the two-person family fell by only 3 percent, while families with seven or more people saw an erosion of some 16 percent.[16] During this period, real earnings have declined, because prices of goods and services rose sharply. For example, between 1976 and 1984 the median price for existing housing rose from $38,000 to $72,000, and for new housing from about $40,000 to $80,000. To purchase increasingly costly homes, Americans acquired higher and higher debts. Before 1980 the cost of paying a mortgage rarely exceeded 15 percent of the owner's income. By the mid-1980s it averaged 33 percent of the owner's income — making the escalating price of home ownership the most important shift in economic reality.[17]

The cost of cars, health care, and education has also increased. In 1989, the average car cost $15,265, up 18 percent from $12,950 in 1986.[18] Americans also have to spend more of their income on health care costs. Almost thirty-seven million Americans have no health insurance, and those who do are increasingly being asked to pay more as employers shift health care costs from companies to their employees. An average family today might easily spend between $2,500 and $5,000 a year on health insurance alone. The price of higher education has also escalated in the past ten years. The average state university tuition costs between $6,000 and $8,000 per year, while tuition at private universities averages between $15,000 and $21,000. Moreover, financial aid was so drastically cut during the Reagan years that very few Americans are eligible for loans or financial assistance. Families who earn the median income are increasingly strapped for money if they want to buy a home, purchase a car to get to work in, pay for health care, and send their kids to college.

All of this has led to increasing personal debt. This is evident in increased defaults on mortgages and increased reliance on purchases with credit cards and defaults on installment payments.[19] To simply keep their heads above water — let alone provide the kind of standard of living that was considered the norm in the 1950s and 1960s — both partners in most couples *have* to work, and one of them may even be required to work two, or even three, jobs. Indeed, many upper-middle-class families today simply could not afford to buy a second car, own a gracious home, and send their kids to Harvard or Yale without two wage earners. And lower-income Americans are dependent on two incomes to maintain even the most modest standard of living.

Providing for the necessities of a decent standard of living, or sheer survival, isn't the only goal driving us to work harder and longer. Today, more and more Americans are consuming increasingly expensive inessentials — we take expensive vacations; purchase expensive cars, jewels, clothing, household equipment and furnishings; and indulge in a variety of services offered by burgeoning service industries. Americans have also incurred significant debts to pay for these products and services.

The gospel of consumption first preached in this country in the 1920s has, today, settled into a full-blown religion — a religion in which increased purchasing power is considered a sign of salvation. "The whole theological superstructure that had once supported work — ideas about vocation, being called by God to work, concepts about the purpose of work as meeting natural needs and progressing toward life that transcended material

necessity — these were replaced by secular goals, the most important of which was economic growth," says Hunnicutt. "Leisure
was seen to be valuable, not because it perfected work or led to
higher things, but because it was helpful in promoting consumption and more employment. Productivity was valued not because
it reduced the burden of working but because it allowed industry
to progress to new frontiers of goods and services."[20]

Although economic factors are critical in shaping workplace behavior, other factors also explain "our harried frame of mind."
One is an increase in the sheer number of professional and managerial jobs in the American labor force. "There is one important
kind of job in the economy involving mostly professional and managerial workers who have always been expected to set their own
pace and goals and internalize the values of the firm," says David
M. Gordon, professor of economics on the graduate faculty of the
New School for Social Research. "The demands of that kind of job
have always been to some degree unlimited."

Or, as Rosabeth Moss Kanter explained in her 1977 *Men and
Women of the Corporation*, "There has traditionally been no such
thing as a part-time manager." She explains, "Full time for a
manager is not confined to normal working hours; in some cases,
it literally means every waking hour. . . . In the midst of organizations supposedly designed around the specific and limited con-
tractual relationships of a bureaucracy, managers may face,
instead, the demand for personal attachment and a generalized,
diffuse, unlimited commitment."[21]

The demands for such diffuse, unlimited commitment to the
organization, David Gordon suggests, have not increased in the
years since Kanter published her book. What has increased is
the proportion of the labor force involved in those managerial
jobs. Moreover, Gordon adds, the number of people who are self-
employed has also risen. "Since the beginning of the nineteenth
century, the number of self-employed people in the economy has
declined, but recently that number has increased fairly dramatically. And in those jobs, the pressure never ends." With women
starting small businesses at twice the rate of men today, they are
feeling the weight of that pressure in dramatic numbers.

"Finally," Gordon says, "today, more and more couples consist of two individuals who work full-time as professionals or managers or are self-employed." In these cases, "the demands of the job are unsustainable, unless you don't care about a personal life or are so affluent you can hire someone to fulfill family responsibilities."

The pressures on professional workers are also a result of a resurgence of the traditional American attitudes toward individual success and materialism. The definition of success as performance on the job and accumulation of wealth, position, and privilege was briefly questioned in the 1960s. In those days activists of every stripe — from antiwar protesters to seekers after increased human potential — worried about the American work ethic and the behavior it spawned. In Studs Terkel's best-seller *Working*, working people from all walks of life complained of the lack of meaning and satisfaction in their jobs. The nineteenth report of a Special Task Force to the Secretary of Health, Education and Welfare, entitled *Work in America*, also drew attention to the fact that "significant numbers of American workers are dissatisfied with the quality of their working lives" and suggested that policy makers in business, labor, and government work toward improvement. Others, like André Gorz in his *Farewell to the Working Class*, promised that the coming decade would inaugurate the "leisure society." And finally, in 1974, the book *Type A Behavior and Your Heart*, by Meyer Friedman and Ray H. Rosenman, scientifically documented the detrimental health consequences of America's love affair with the macho work ethic and professional accomplishment.

Of course, as current statistics confirm, the dream of a leisure society did not materialize. Instead, "type A behavior" made a comeback in the early eighties and has been on a roll ever since. Today a frantic work life is just as much a status symbol as the car phone, beeper, home computer, modem, and personal fax machine that help make it all possible. Practitioners of this new corporate machismo are the new media icons.

For example, in a recent *Business Week* profile of high-flying futures speculator Paul Tudor Jones II, readers learned that "Jones lives and breathes the market. . . . Hardly a moment goes by when Jones isn't glued to a Reuters screen, telephone in hand. When he pries himself away from the two screens in his lower Manhattan office, a phone in his BMW keeps him in touch.

"Jones, who is single, also scans a Reuters screen every half hour at home in the evening. And his day doesn't really end at bedtime: He wakes up several times a night to keep checking. 'My subconscious knows when Hong Kong and London open . . .' Last summer he even installed a satellite dish at his rental house in swanky Southampton, so he could trade during his vacation."[22]

Jones's female counterpart, stockbroker Elaine Garzarelli, was profiled in the inaugural issue of *Ms.* magazine's 1988 make-over. Garzarelli's claim to fame is the fact that she predicted the crash of October 1987 and saved her clients from disaster. She is described as a woman whose "professional dedication goes beyond duty; it is her life. Small and intense, she is constantly alert, anticipating the unexpected at any moment, ready to seize any market opportunity that can give her a gain, any gain.

"She has eliminated unnecessary tasks and obligations from her life to maximize efficiency. Her social life collapsed with the Dow. Like a jealous lover, Wall Street keeps her in thrall. When she travels for speaking engagements, her hotel rooms must have two telephone lines. She paid $300 to have her constant companion, the FNN cable, run into her East Hampton weekend home. She can only fly when the stock exchange is closed. A virtual prisoner of the continental USA, she will not travel offshore."[23]

For millions who will never be profiled in *Business Week, Inc.,* or *People* magazine, these are the new success models that influence marketplace behavior. Many of us — both male and female — take our cues from such role models. Bill Wallace, who worked for a high-tech firm in the San Francisco Bay area when I first talked with him, is one of those who feels he must conform to the time expectations of the workplace. "No one tells you that you have to come in early in the morning and leave late at night," the thirty-six-year-old product manager explains. "They don't tell you that you have to work on weekends. It's just that the models of success in the company are people who do that. My boss is one of those models. In spite of the fact that he has young children, he works all the time. And if you don't work as hard as he does, you constantly feel you're shortchanging the organization."

"People in the company I used to work for used to voluntarily give up their vacations," says Ellen Williams. "You would accrue vacation time if you didn't take it and then lose it if you didn't take it by a certain deadline. People would almost brag that they were losing vacations because they hadn't taken any in two years. And they do the same thing here where I work now. They boast about the fact that they can't remember when they last took a vacation."

Ron Blake, an attorney át a high-powered Chicago law firm, concurs. "I tend to work pretty hard," Blake says, in deference to the demands that have become standard in his field. "I try to keep it from about nine to six-thirty. But then, usually one day a week, I'll be at work till about seven-thirty or eight. Then occasionally I have to stay longer. At the end of February, I had a stretch when something came in and had to be done on real short notice. So I had to stay about three nights till ten, and then when we closed [the deal], it started at about nine on Monday morning and ended about two A.M. on Wednesday, with five hours of interruption. There are a lot of people who come in for half a day on the weekend, but I don't unless I absolutely have to. I'd rather work later during the week, and occasionally I'll bring work home on the weekend." Blake told me he usually takes four weeks of vacation, but his wife reminded him that for the past two years, he's only taken two weeks.

The willingness to devote all one's waking hours to working also defines success in the architectural profession, says thirty-six-year-old Peter Quinn. "The minute I got out of school, I saw that most architects work far longer than the amount of hours supposedly required," he explains. "The understanding many of my peers have is that this is a rite of passage, and that things will normalize once they rise up the ladder. But that's just not what happens. When you agree to work that long, you're beginning a never-ending odyssey of working long hours for relatively little pay in a competitive buyer's market for design services."

Quinn believes that the euphemisms used in the design marketplace reflect its excessive time demands. "You're told that 'the work becomes a way of life,' you're supposed to sacrifice your social life, not so much to get ahead but to 'make a commitment

to the job.' And you fall right into doing just that because you've
dedicated four or five years to your training."

Unlimited time demands are prevalent not only in fast-track,
money-making professions like law and medicine, they're also the
rule in the human services and progressive organizations.

"My organization decided to begin conversations with other
women in the community around the issue of shorter work time.
We wanted to start a shorter-work-time campaign, and the most
ironic thing was, everybody said they wanted a shorter workweek,
but no one had time to come and talk about it," says Barbara
Neely, executive director of the Massachusetts-based Women for
Economic Justice. "I'm supposed to work a four-day week. I always thought I could do a fifty-hour work load in those four days.
But the work load is so heavy that I now try to stuff six days'
worth of work into four days. And it's absolutely insane. People
in the progressive community now judge themselves on the amount
of time we're putting in. We all labor under the assumption that
if we don't do the work, it won't get done."

Bill Fletcher, a thirty-year-old union organizer who represents
daycare workers, faces the same pressure. In Fletcher's union, for
example, organizers are actually called "unlimited-hour staff,"
people who are always on call. "This puts enormous pressure on
you," he explains. "Your hour limit is determined by whatever
deal you can make with whoever is responsible for you and upon
your own individual willingness to say no. When I talk about the
hours, some people say, 'Well, just say no.' But it's laughable. You
have the same problem when people say, 'Just say no to drugs.'
It's not simply a subjective statement of will. If you don't have the
kind of social supports to back you up, you either won't say no or
you'll increasingly be viewed as not a 'good team player.' "

Saying no to work is even more difficult today because of the
kind of speed-up that has occurred as a result of new technologies
that were supposed to make work easier and less time consuming.
Tom Peters, author of the best-selling *In Search of Excellence*,
said in a recent article, "The information-technology revolution,
leading to the creation of brave new organizational forms for the
first time in centuries, is creating new winners and losers." The
key to being a winner, Peters says, is to "liberate a work team by

using technology to assure constant customer contact." This in turn will produce a work force that works all the time, as "data are discussed during coffee breaks or bowling evenings."[24]

Clearly the barriers between work and leisure, home and workplace are breaking down, and the invasion of new technology into the home blurs the boundaries even further. In many companies, employees are now provided with free terminals and fax machines for their homes. The idea is that they will work more efficiently and leave earlier, knowing that they can tie up loose ends from home. In fact, almost all those who use such technologies say they do not leave work any earlier, but simply work more at home at night and on the weekends.

Bill Wallace saw his company's offer of a free home terminal as a mixed blessing. "For a long time I resisted getting one because I saw that the technology allowed so many of my colleagues to work all the time — even when they were home," he says. "When I finally agreed to take one from my employer, I really believed that this was going to help me establish a going-home time of five-thirty or six P.M. without the threat of all the work I hadn't finished — because I could always do it at home. But that's just not what happened. I still stayed late at the office. All the technology does is continue to exacerbate a problem that's there in the first place."

"You have no time for another life," Ellen Williams agrees. "There's nothing but work. Right before I quit, I brought a computer to do work at home. I thought it would be a terrific idea at first. But once I got it home, I realized it was eating up my personal life. I was working at home and at work."

Lawyer Ron Blake also attributes some of the pressures in his profession to new technologies. "The legal business is a lot more competitive these days," he says. "The days of the old provincial outpost are gone. We can do a deal with a client in Boston as easily as any law firm in that city. A lot of the deadlines are artificially imposed. There's no reason why a particular thing has to get done this quickly. So you get a lot of very unreasonable deadlines and you just have to meet them."

The technology that makes such cutthroat competition possible also eliminates "downtime" in the working day at many corporate offices. Blake says, "There used to be times when you had to wait for something to arrive, and that meant you could reflect on what you were doing or just get some breathing space. But with fax machines and overnight deliveries, you can get things done at a moment's notice. And so now you have to do things at a moment's notice."

In the professional world, time devoted to work has increased for another reason, too: today's model of professional success tends to be entirely one track — the fast track. The novice professional is expected to get out of school and immediately begin climbing the "ladder" in his or her profession. The aim is not to broaden and deepen one's knowledge of one's field so that one can develop oneself over the long term. The aim is to get to the top as quickly as possible. In corporate law offices, for example, young lawyers have about six years as associates before they are asked to become partners. Those who do not move up into partner slots are out. In academia, the assistant professor has a similar time period in which to prove that he or she deserves tenure. Again, those who don't move up are moved out. The same is true in the hard sciences and many other careers. The assumption is that once people have "made it" to the top, the pressure will be off. But by then total devotion to the job has become a habit — if not an addiction — and constant work has become a way of life.

Demographic changes have also helped make "workaholism" the rule rather than the exception. Today, greater numbers of men and women are waiting until their early to late thirties to have their first child. According to the National Center for Health Statistics, in 1986, four times as many women had their first babies between the ages of thirty-five and thirty-nine as in 1975, and a little over three times as many had first babies between the ages of thirty and thirty-four.[25] The U.S. Census Bureau reports that the number of childless couples in which both husband and wife were employed and the wife was of childbearing age increased from 3.0 million to 4.3 million between 1976 and 1987.[26]

These statistics may account for some increase in the acceptance of long hours and constant pressure as a way of life. In the past, family responsibilities have acted to temper compulsive commitments to work. Women who remained at home raising children, for example, often criticized their husbands for devoting too much time and energy to work and too little to their home life. And for women who worked, obligations to children and families limited their ability or willingness to commit everything to the job. But today, as more younger women work as long and as hard as their male colleagues and partners, and as they put off having children, they, too, become caught in the success trap, trading time and personal enrichment for recognition on the job. And, as we shall see in the next chapters, by the time these women do have children and realize they no longer can or want to put in ten- to twelve-hour days, they have already contributed to the very work-time standards and expectations which threaten their own desires to balance careers and families.

When a working person in America has a child or must attend to some other human attachments, he or she immediately discovers one of the most salient facts about life in the marketplace. "The marketplace turns people into commodities — like apples or oranges — or anything else that can be bought and sold," says sociologist Diane Margolis, author of *The Managers: Corporate Life in America.* "Of course, the human being is an odd kind of commodity — unlike apples and oranges, the human being is created out of social attachments and creates and lives through social attachments. But while there is some recognition that the worker is a biological organism that requires downtime in the form of vacation, that does sleep and eat, and that may get sick, about the only acknowledgment of his attachments is in the convention of a few personal days — where he is free to attend events like funerals.

"In order to deal with the peculiarities of the human commodity, the marketplace has to engage in a lot of mythmaking. For the men to whom the marketplace has geared its mythmaking, this has required the myth that their only contribution or obligation to the families most of them live in is making money. It follows then that the more devoted a man is to his work, the more devoted he is to his family. The good family, in turn, forces him to be a good commodity, to act as if he is unattached, so that he can go off to work each day and work as long and hard as required, free of worries and care. The family is supposed to stay off his back."

This male model, Margolis points out, has not been altered for women. "From the point of view of the employer, the good female worker is a carbon copy of the good male worker. And thus we have a situation in which her obligations to others are essentially invisible in the workplace."

Given this economic view of family ties, it is not surprising that, the gender revolution of the past two decades notwithstanding, most American employers continue to function as though their employees had no family commitments. They refuse to implement policies to help workers fulfill those commitments and they block passage of any national family legislation that could mandate such policies.

This has created a tremendous crisis in caring for millions of women and men. Today, approximately 70 percent of women with school-age children are in the out-of-home work force and about 60 percent of mothers of preschool children work outside the home. There are 27.8 million women with children under eighteen who are working and 11.8 million working women are single heads of families.[27] According to Department of Labor statistics, 80 percent of women working who are of childbearing age become pregnant at some time during their careers. Nor do these women stay home to take care of their children. Most will return to work.[28]

Moreover, 22.1 million men with children under eighteen are on the job, 96.5 percent of all men with children under six work full-time, and 2.8 million working fathers are single heads of households, making this the fastest-growing family group in America — an increase of 86 percent in the last eleven years in relative terms.[29] According to the U.S. Census Bureau, there were 13.4 million two-worker families with children in 1987, up from 8.3 million in 1976.[30]

"This whole issue of work and family is seen as a woman's issue," says Professor Bradley Googins of Boston University's School of Social Work. "This is not because it is a woman's issue, but because it is defined as such by the workplace. And that's not an accident. There are probably a lot of people who would like to keep it a woman's issue, for obvious reasons."

That's because American employers are not eager to call attention to the overwhelming numbers of working parents who are suffering today because our country has no coherent family policy system.

Federal policy requires that employers grant leaves to women unable to work because of pregnancy and childbirth on the same basis that they grant leaves for short-term disabilities of any kind. It does not mandate that employers establish new disability benefits or provide leave to parents to care for newborn infants. Most workplaces have no provisions for parents who adopt children, or who must care for sick children, even children who are desperately ill or dying.

We also lack any policies that help working people take time off their jobs to care for sick spouses, parents, or relatives. Today, as our nation's health care crisis worsens, the burden of care for spouses, parents, and relatives who have been discharged from the hospital — quicker and sicker — increasingly falls on their children or mates, who are asked to provide short-term care normally available in the hospital from experienced nurses. Although Medicare and some private insurance companies pay for the cost of visiting nurses and home health aides, they cover only a few hours a day. Thus, most people cannot afford to hire surrogate caregivers and must provide care themselves.

Furthermore, 80 percent of people sixty-five and over have one chronic illness; 23 percent are "functionally disabled" — that is, they need help with personal care or shopping and cooking; of these, only 9 percent receive care from a paid provider. The rest receive family care.[31]

As Americans live longer (and Americans over seventy-five are the fastest-growing segment of our population) more and more are being cared for at home. Women are their primary caretakers. And 33 percent of those providing short- or long-term home care for the frail elderly work. Whether female or male, these caregivers are often told they must choose between their families and their jobs or careers because nationally mandated policies that allow people to take off work to provide this kind of care — care which saves our health care system billions a year — are nonexistent. Or in order to tend to a sick child or parent, most employees must tell their employers that it is they, not their children or parents, who are sick and thus use up their own sick-leave allowance.

Compared with the rest of the world, this lack of family policy is remarkable, to say the very least. More than two-thirds of the nations of the world, including almost all industrialized nations, have enacted excellent parental and childcare leave policies. Such paid leaves vary from three months to a year. In France, a new mother is allowed four months of paid leave, at 90 percent of her salary, for her first two children and six months for each subsequent child. Her husband may take three days off per child. In the Scandinavian countries — which have the most extensive parenting benefits — either a father or mother may take up to a year off at 90 percent pay to take care of their newborns. Austrians receive twenty weeks at full salary; Canadians fifteen weeks at 60 percent of salary; West Germans fourteen to nineteen weeks with full pay; Japanese twelve weeks at 60 percent pay; and East Germans twenty-six weeks at full pay for the first child and one year of paid leave after the birth of the second or third child. Most countries also allow parents to take supplementary unpaid leave and grant some medical leaves to care for relatives.[32]

In this country there is no statutorily guaranteed paid or unpaid parental leave. For the past several years, congressional family policy advocates have tried to take a first step in addressing working parents' needs. Representative Patricia Schroeder (D-Colorado) and Senator Christopher Dodd (D-Connecticut) introduced the Family and Medical Leave Act, which, in its original House version, would have provided eighteen weeks of unpaid leave every two years for employees who have babies, adopt, or who need time off to take care of either a sick child or parent. (The bill also permitted employees to take a leave for a serious health problem of their own.) The bill would have covered every U.S. employer with fifteen or more workers and would have created a committee to study the feasibility of eventually introducing the kind of paid parental and medical leaves that workers have in other countries.

Although it had a great deal of congressional support, the bill's introduction triggered a major business offensive against it. Numerous bipartisan compromises were made to save the bill from defeat. In its revised form, the bill exempted companies with fewer than fifty employees for the first three years (thus excluding 90 percent of the nation's companies and half of its workers); employees would be entitled to only ten weeks of unpaid parental leave every two years; and the study of paid leave was eliminated. Yet, in 1990, even this watered-down version could not muster enough votes to override our "kinder and gentler" president's veto.

What is even more disturbing is the fact that some women in fast-track professions now seem to feel they must "give back" whatever maternity benefits their companies do provide. Because of the fear that they will lose their place in line if they aren't in the office working like everybody else, many women who have six weeks or even six months off after having a baby come back far before their allotted time is up. "It seems that among my friends in publishing there is an unspoken competition to see who returns to work the soonest after having a baby," an editor at a major publishing house recently told me. "I know an agent who was back on the job in two weeks — and proud of it — and editors who aren't even taking the full leaves granted by their companies. One admitted she was bored at home. Another told me, 'The dirty little secret is it's much easier to go to the office than to stay at home with a baby.' "

The editor felt that the main issue for her female colleagues was the escalating competitive demands that permeate corporate culture today. "People are afraid that if they're not at the office, things will be fine without them. Then their employers will feel that they just aren't needed. And then there's so much competition among editors for books that they feel they must be seen going to lunch, talking with agents and authors all the time, or they won't get ahead."

For men the situation is the same or worse. The New York–based research group Catalyst studied male utilization of parental leave, conducting a survey of 384 large companies to determine if they offered men parenting leave. If so, the group asked, did men take advantage of such leave policies? Of the companies questioned, only a third offered such leave. And only nine of those reported that men took it. Catalyst discovered that two-thirds of the companies studied "did not consider it reasonable for men to take any parental leave whatsoever." More importantly, of those with leave policies on the books, 41 percent didn't sanction men's using them. "If a man requested a leave for this purpose, his career would take a dive," a human resource manager at a large southern manufacturer reported.[33]

Jane Bermont, a consultant at Ibis Consulting Group in Cambridge, reports similar findings. "In our work on family issues," she says, "we've interviewed vice presidents of human resource departments at a number of progressive companies — companies that ostensibly have good work-family programs and policies in place — like parental leave and childcare resources. These vice presidents nonetheless report that men are reluctant to use parental leave benefits at the birth or adoption of a child. They do, in fact, take time off. But they tend to use vacation or sick time.

"I think there are two reasons for this," Bermont elaborates. "When parental leaves are unpaid, the reason may be economic. However, there's also a perception problem. Men may feel uncomfortable exposing the real reason they are taking time off. In our intensely competitive corporate culture, men may fear that their companies will view them as parents as well as workers. Their employers will, therefore, not consider them to be totally committed to their work, and they may be afraid that they'll be penalized for this over the long term."

Working parents must also cope with a seriously inadequate childcare system. Today, there are an estimated seventeen million school-age children whose mothers work. Eight point two million preschool children under the age of six have mothers in the workplace. And 52 percent of women whose children are under the age of one are working.[34] These children all presumably need part-time or full-time childcare. Moreover, an estimated seven to ten million children are what is known as latchkey children — they are school-age children whose parents work and who should have childcare. But they don't. They are thus left alone when they return home from school.[35]

By 1995, experts estimate, about three-quarters of all children will have working mothers. This means that about 14.6 million preschool and 37.4 million school-age children will need some kind of infant, preschool, and after-school care. To provide such care for children who need it through the age of twelve would cost an estimated $70 billion or more a year.[36]

Again, while many European countries have some form of subsidized childcare, nursery schools, and after-school programs available to all, regardless of income, very few subsidized programs exist in the United States, and subsidies are minimal. In 1970, the White House Conference on Children said that childcare was the most serious problem facing America's families. In order to deal with this problem, Congress passed the 1971 Comprehensive Child Development Act. But President Nixon vetoed the law and since then, according to Edward Zigler, head of Yale University's Bush Center for Child Development, "our nation has not come a single step closer toward providing a solution." This "serious problem" has grown so pervasive that it is now called America's "childcare crisis."

Today, of America's 6,000,000 employers, about 3,500 — or six one hundredths of 1 percent — support childcare services. And most of these only provide referrals to providers, who are often overburdened with requests they cannot accept. Only two hundred corporations and six hundred hospitals in the nation have on-site or near-site daycare centers.[37]

When women were excluded from participation in the work world, it was easy to believe that its main problem was men — the ones who dominated the workplace and determined its priorities. That men routinely sacrificed their nights and weekends, vacations, and, ultimately, their families to work was a fact with which most women were all too familiar. Like the optimistic immigrants whose hopes and dreams fueled the American success ethic for centuries, we believed we could dramatically change the masculine corporate culture we were about to enter by the sheer force of our numbers.

But this belief focused too narrowly on the sex of those in power and obscured all too relevant facts about the system which they served. The competition, individualism, and aggression that the contemporary marketplace now demands overpower the human capacity to care.

Chapter Three

TARGETING THE TOP —
GAIN AND PAIN

THE ENTRANCE to the Manhattan headquarters of National Financial Services — one of America's largest financial service corporations — is stark and imposing. An escalator in the middle of the glittering brass and marble foyer leads up to a mezzanine checkpoint, where security guards carefully scrutinize visitors before indicating the elevator bank that will carry them to the building's upper floors. It's lunchtime. Thousands of employees rush by, flashing identity cards as they return to work or move out to hail cabs or down to the basement complex where dozens of executive and clerical eateries are packed with workers on their lunch hour.

After writing down my name and the purpose of my visit, I'm escorted into the central atrium to meet Alice Hart, a middle-level manager at NFS. The thirty-four-year-old takes me to the comfortable company dining room. As we order, she begins to describe the preoccupations and problems she shares with countless other professional women.

Like many of the women I interviewed, Alice Hart says her choice of career was "an accident." After majoring in psychology in college, she went to work for a New York bank. A friend of hers was getting an MBA and so, "as a lark," Hart took a business course, liked it, did well, and decided to follow suit.

After nine years at NFS, she is well established — not in senior-level management (few women in the company are), but in a very respectable marketing career in which she earns over $60,000 a year. Her husband is a business executive at a smaller firm near their suburban Westchester home, and the couple has a two-year-old son.

Alice Hart says she likes her job and the challenges it presents. With obvious pride, she tells me she enjoys relating to people and helping them develop. She considers herself a talented and dedicated worker. But she becomes more somber when I ask her about the gender issues related to her work. She says quite candidly that she is disappointed and disheartened by the demeanor and attitudes she is asked to adopt, by the male behavior she is told to ignore or condone, and by the impact of the organization on her relationships with other female colleagues, on her family, and on her own definition of success and self-esteem.

"The biggest difference between women and men in this company is that men are able to deal with the side of business that is not particularly human," she explains, leaning across the table. "They don't really care if people's feelings are hurt. Their attitude is, 'you've got to grow up and be a big girl, that's just the way it is.' They don't fight the system much. They don't feel the inequities of the system the way I do or people in my peer group do. I, on the other hand, know how the system works and why it works, but that doesn't mean I don't think there are things that should be changed."

Hart's conversation is a compendium of anecdotes illustrating the intractability of male beliefs about power. "We will constantly have meetings in which my boss, two senior levels from me, comments on how people are doing their jobs. He will never tell the people who work for him, 'You've done a good job, but have you considered this?' It's always just 'Have you considered this?' There's no pat on the back or support. I don't care so much about this for myself, but I do care about it for people who work for me because they need it more than I do.

"I had a long discussion with my immediate boss about this," Hart continues, "and his attitude was, 'oh, Rand is just like that.'" She pauses, and with evident impatience, argues, "It's true that that's the way Rand is. But I still believe I have to fight for this, because I'm very concerned about how people are treated. My bottom line is that it's important to take the opportunity to motivate someone and make them feel good about what they do and how they do it. But this is not something that is measured or rewarded or valued in the organization. The company gives a lot of lip service to it, but there's a definite idea that you will do what the organization wants you to do, that employees shouldn't question, and that the people who are rewarded are those who follow the rules."

One of those unwritten rules governs the way men treat women: "Men at senior-level positions just get away with very outrageous forms of behavior." Her voice lowering as colleagues walk by, she says in a tone of disgust, "At sales meetings, you find these men in their late thirties and forties lusting after women in their twenties — not women from headquarters, but field-staff women who are much younger and on their way up and who feel flattered or obligated by their attention. I feel sorry for these women. On the books, the company takes all these issues of sexual harassment very seriously. It has all the requisite procedures in place. But in fact, the first step of talking about this kind of thing as a problem just never happens."

Our conversation inevitably turns to the family issues that trouble almost every working mother. Hart must commute an hour to and from work. She tries to get to work at nine and leave by five-thirty. Nevertheless, she constantly struggles with guilt because she spends so little time with her son. "I didn't have a son to have someone else take care of him," she says ruefully.

And yet, says Alice Hart, women like herself are trapped in a world that will not accommodate their needs and that eventually forces them out of the organizations in which they have invested so much. "Ten women in management here have had children and they have not come back. They are women in their thirties with good salaries. It used to be that women who stayed home with kids weren't like us, they were different. They didn't want to go to work and have a career. Now I have managers who worked under me, who were like me, and they are staying home. This sends a message to the organization that women with children don't come back, and I find that very scary."

Although Alice Hart recognizes that her corporation needs to change, her lack of awareness of the need for collective political action makes it hard for her to advocate for such change, either for herself or for others. I ask, for instance, if she considers herself a feminist. She thinks for a moment and answers with the qualified "Yes, but . . ." that characterizes so many professional women's relationship to feminism. She says she sympathizes with feminism as an idea. Women should be allowed to have greater choice and be equal to men. Then comes the "but." The idea that she herself could participate in a movement for broad social change is foreign to her. She is not a marcher, a protester, a fuss maker.

What's more troubling is that she has had little experience working with other women for such needed change, either inside or outside her workplace. Hart confesses frankly that she finds it difficult to talk about her problems with any but a few close colleagues. Moreover, her own fears and reluctance about really challenging her company limit her options. What, I asked her, would she do if she ever uncovered a serious case of sexual harassment? A look of alarm flickers across her face and she says, almost sadly, "I think I would be scared shitless." Several failed efforts to initiate collegial conversations or networks that could address women's problems in her organization have not increased mutual trust among women in the company. "I made a fuss once when I had a conversation with another woman on my level. I thought we were talking confidentially, but the woman told other people about my concerns. It was a very unpleasant experience."

As she talks, she seems to exude fatigue and defeat. A well-intentioned woman who is trying to preserve her personal integrity, she constantly encounters roadblock after roadblock. Wary of taking more detours, she is badly in need of guidance. When she looks for possible female mentors or role models, she finds that the women who have advanced into senior positions in her company over the past two decades are little help. Many of these women, she feels, are unhappy, or so obsessed with money, status, and power that she cannot identify with them. "As a woman in middle management, I feel the lack of women who have my values toward life and are still able to be successful. The women in management positions above me either have no children, or they have nannies and work till seven and eight at night. They are like men. They don't create a very good climate. I don't know if what I want is possible in a big organization. I would like to find women who are not so hung up on levels of organization that you can't talk to them without going through four layers of people to get to them. I would like to find people who are willing to listen to the opposite side of an argument without thinking the person is disloyal, or women who haven't forgotten their roots — who don't feel they've moved into another class just because they've moved up."

Surrounded by corporate soldiers both male and female, Alice Hart sighs and admits that she is in danger of becoming one herself. In a kind of corporate limbo, she does her job well and dreads the day when she will finally be pushed too far. Then, she says, she will choose not fight, but rather flight.

Alice Hart is one of the best and the brightest. Sensitive and thoughtful, she is ambitious in marketplace terms, but seems ultimately more committed to her own caring agenda than to fulfilling a competitive agenda that threatens to compromise it. The majority of doctors, lawyers, academics, scientists, and businesswomen I spoke with have much in common with Alice Hart. All were between the ages of twenty-five and fifty-five when we met. A few had been politically active when they were younger. Some of these women still considered themselves feminists, no "buts" attached, but only a handful are active in any women's or other political groups. However, no matter what their political orientation, all are torn between intense pressure to compete on men's terms and the deep need to be nurtured and nurture in a rich world of relationships. These women want to attain mastery and recognition in their fields. But because this means being treated as an equal to a man in a man's world, they are forced to sacrifice their commitment to their own caring goals — the desire to treat colleagues or subordinates well and nurture their development, empower others, maintain social relationships, and preserve a balance between work and love, and work and family life. They work to protect themselves as individuals, and sometimes they try to help other women. But as a rule, most fear any open public expression of their discontents and avoid collective action to resolve their problems. Even if they are feminists, their transformative efforts are often reduced to style, not substance — being warmer hierarchical employers, listening to personal problems, trying to empower others but too many times failing to do so.

There were some notable exceptions to this rule — a minority of women who seem to have uncritically adapted to the demands of the marketplace, avidly pursuing equal-opportunity feminism's competitive agenda to the exclusion of any personal or civic life. The personal histories of most, however, bear some resemblance to that of Alice Hart — tales of gradual and deepening disillusionment and resignation that begins during professional training, increases once they are on the job, and finally becomes a major preoccupation when they have children and find they cannot integrate work and family life. What most of these women report is that they love their *work* but have great distaste for the conditions under which they are forced to do it.

In her analysis of the rise of the middle class in America, social analyst Barbara Ehrenreich has argued that professionalization has been used as protection against the instability of "an increasingly uncertain world."[1] The development of a body of "scientific" objective professional expertise was the "capital" that professionals accumulated and sold in a market dominated by various professional organizations and concerns. By developing an ever more esoteric body of professional expertise, the rising middle class in America restricted entrance to professional and managerial positions and thus secured an ostensibly safe haven in the marketplace.

That marketplace has traditionally been inhabited by men whose families depended on their professional fortunes. Now, of course, men have been forced to share their status with an increasing number of women. And the latter are mastering what men have had to master before them — an education in professionalism. The education in professional expertise and skills does not only restrict entrance into the professions, it also restricts the behavior and actions of those who have been allowed into the inner sanctum.

Thus, soon after she enters her professional training, the female apprentice realizes that professional mastery and marketplace success will involve far more than learning a body of knowledge — how to diagnose an illness, write a legal brief, or make up a business plan. Women have to learn not only how to *do* medicine, law, science, or business; they have to learn to *be* professionals — doctors, lawyers, scientists, or businesswomen. In other words, they have to conform to the contemporary image of a professional in order to be taken seriously on the job.

This became evident to twenty-eight-year-old Lucia Santini as soon as she entered the MBA program at Boston University. Santini did her undergraduate work in French literature. Unable to find a job in that field, she went to work as a secretary for the asset management department of U.S. Trust in Boston. Inspired by the department's interest in socially responsible investing, Santini decided to go to business school at night. "I didn't want to go to business school in the first place, but I wanted to become a portfolio manager, and that was the only way to do it. What I found in business school is that the qualitative aspect, the human issues in business, and the ethics, are just not discussed."

More to the point, Santini found that her ideals of caring and empowerment were scorned as counterproductive in the business world. "When we learned bargaining strategies at school, they told us that in the long term, your best strategy was probably to take the cooperative tack and get the best solution for both parties. But in the short term, you were always going to do better by screwing the other guy and being aggressive. The class was game based and we were graded on this basis — on how you did against your partner as opposed to how others did."

She went to class and tried to play by her rules. "The whole thing really disturbed me. I had a hard time being nasty and screwing the other guy, and so I got a low grade. It didn't come naturally." But like a chameleon changing colors, over time, she had to adapt to her new environment. "I started to be able to look at these things and say, he's going to do this to me, and I can do it too. The point was, you have to screw the other guy to get a good grade," she says bluntly. "That's true whether you're a woman playing the game with another woman or a man playing it against another man. I have to admit, after a while, you begin to catch on."

In law and medicine, the same kinds of pressures cause conflict and confusion in thousands of new women entrants, says Dr. Emily Lowry, who discovered the "rules" of medicine during her own school days. "In medical school, we were constantly told we were supposed to be more 'aggressive.' That was the exact word they used. For example, the way you got the attending physician's attention was by volunteering to do minor procedures that you really didn't know how to do. Someone would ask, 'Who can do a lumbar puncture?' and a lot of guys would raise their hands, even though they in fact didn't know how to do the procedure.

"I could never do that. It was dishonest. I would have said, 'I don't know how to do it but I'm willing to learn.' They didn't say that; they said they knew how to do it. Yet they didn't interpret that as dishonesty; men thought of it as a mark of self-confidence.

"When I tried to do it my way, I was told I wasn't aggressive enough. After a while, I realized that the problem wasn't that I couldn't act that way; it was that I didn't want to act that way. I didn't want to engage in acts of medical bravado and become marginally honest. It was something I simply didn't approve of. And so I had to find other ways to define self-confidence to myself — like being more firm or more poised."

The core curriculum of female apprentices high in male-dominated professions almost always includes tutorials on how to hide all evidence of "femininity." Sometimes femininity is concealed to protect women against unwanted sexual advances from their male colleagues. "Because men have been taught to regard women as sex objects, not as coworkers, women going into corporate America quickly learn that men are uncomfortable with their femaleness," a management consultant and former high-level Carter administration official told me. "Men don't regard evidence of women's femininity as just another gender-related difference, they regard it as a sexual invitation. So women going into high-powered jobs in business discover that one of the best ways to avoid uncomfortable situations with male colleagues is to neutralize their femininity. This means never wearing clothes that could be considered suggestive or flirtatious."

Rather than addressing the problem head-on and insisting that men learn to deal with women's femaleness, most women feel they must deliberately neuter themselves. "A lot of the women you see nowadays," the consultant continues, "wear masculinized female uniforms — the classic grey flannel suit. It may work in business, but the result is that you see a lot of 'men' running around in women's bodies."

Some professional counselors advise women to conceal their femininity because any evidence of human vulnerability or gentleness makes men patronize rather than respect female colleagues. In a chapter on women lawyers in *Mapping the Moral Domain*, Dana and Rand Jack write that "in the *American Bar Association Journal*, 'female' characteristics are simultaneously designated and demeaned."[2] The Jacks quote from an article by N. Strachan entitled "A Map for Women on the Road to Success," which advises: "Dress and talk in a conservative professional style. Avoid wraparound skirts, casual shoes or hair-color changes. Dress like a lawyer, in a conservative suit. Don't chew gum. When called 'dear' or flirted with in business meetings or professional settings, respond only with entirely professional and business-like statements, so that all communications are placed on and remain on a highly professional plane."[3]

"Looking extremely feminine gives the message that you need to be taken care of," says Brenda York, president of the Academy of Fashion and Image Consultants in McLean, Virginia. In a *Wall Street Journal* article on success and fashion in the business world entitled "Businesswomen's Broader Latitude in Dress Codes Goes Just So Far," York and other consultants insist that even the slightest hint that caring needs can coexist with professionalism behind the businesswoman's carefully polished facade compromises the perception of "seriousness in the business world." Only conservative, that is, masculine, clothing is appropriate. "Indeed, the consensus seems to be that despite the relaxation of dress codes, it still isn't acceptable to look too feminine — or too sexy, or too cute — in corporate America," concludes reporter Kathleen A. Hughes. An accompanying chart correlates job performance with conservative dress, ostensibly documenting that "women in sales positions whose attire is described as conservative by their managers outperform their colleagues."[4]

Perhaps the most important lesson in women's professional training is that of collective disempowerment. Transformative feminism originally articulated an analysis of both patriarchy and capitalism that guided at least some women's attitudes and actions. We used to argue that the transformation of the American workplace would not occur only because an elite group of women advanced in high-powered careers: these women would also have to engage in collective action, both in their workplaces and in the political sphere. No individual, after all, is powerful enough to go up against corporate institutions alone. However, the curriculum of professional training, no matter where it is given — be it in a dress-for-success seminar, in medical, law, or business school, or through on-the-job advice from female or male mentors — has always ignored these elementary principles of social change (because, of course, adaptation, not change, is their message). Thus, such training channels women exclusively toward individual career goals. Acting collectively — whether inside or outside of the institution — women, like men before them, are constantly reminded, is out of bounds because it compromises rather than enhances individual career goals.

Helena Walzer offers a classic story. As a business school student, Walzer served as a summer intern at Bankers Trust in Manhattan. The bank's summer intern program recruited students from Ivy League business schools, screening potential candidates for future employment. Throughout the summer, the company wined and dined the students and provided weekly breakfasts with top bank officials. These were "test periods," during which students questioned officials about the bank to determine if they would be interested in permanent positions. The sessions also afforded management the opportunity to discern how "intelligent and aggressive" the recruits were.

At the first breakfast, the bank's president spoke about the company and then asked for questions from the floor. "I raised my hand," Walzer recalls, "and said I had been reading the annual report and noticed, both from this and just from looking around, how few women there were in senior management. As a woman in business this concerned me, I said, and then I asked him point-blank, 'Do I have a future at this bank?' He didn't seem to be at all affronted and he responded very nicely, explaining that yes, there were no women in top management, but that many were in the pipeline and would eventually make their way up.

"I learned later from another student that I had created quite a stir. Who was that woman, some had asked. It turned out that the female interns were very angry at me for asking the question. They said it was 'inappropriate and absolutely confrontational and adversarial.' And yet it was an entirely obvious and almost innocuous statement of fact."

Young women who are going into the legal profession, says second-year Harvard Law School student Caroline Lawson, have learned that success means adaptation to the professional status quo. "The women I know who are going into law firms fully expect to work between fifty and eighty hours a week for the ten years it will take them to become partners. They think they'll have children and work all the time. We don't question this, except in conversations with each other. At this point we accept that over-work is a systemic problem in the legal profession, and at this point we're acquiescing to it."

The idea that the demands of the profession could change and that female lawyers could help effect that change is, she says, outside the realm of legitimate discussion at Harvard Law School. "There are very few classroom discussions with either female or male professors in which issues of how the law is practiced are raised. The only reference that's ever made to the actual practice of the law is how you would make a particular argument when you stand up in front of the judge." In her experience, in the rare instances when feminist or professional issues are brought up, they tend to center around ethical problems, the discrimination women face, or discussions of abortion rights, battered women, or legal aid.

The profession has become so competitive and the women in it so concerned about their ability to compete that Lawson says she and her friends would be afraid to openly raise or participate in discussions of more care-related topics. "I think my friends and I would think that women who raised issues about overwork or family would be viewed as marginal, as not in the mainstream of Harvard Law School thinking. Even though we are privately very concerned about these issues, we wouldn't want to be considered outside the mainstream."

Some women are so wary of broaching such concerns that they refuse to wear wedding or engagement rings to interviews at law firms, even if the interviewers are other women. Similarly, they feel that if they ask about the family-related benefits their prospective firms may offer — like maternity leave, vacation time, and childcare — they will hurt their chances of employment or promotion. The idea that these subjects should be off-limits is conveyed to them not only by law school faculty but by female attorneys whom they meet in the process of interviewing for summer employment. "You meet dozens of women — associates, junior and senior partners — when you interview with law firms. Some of these women think open discussions about these issues (family-related policies and overwork) are threatening their opportunities to kill themselves and make partner and make two hundred fifty thousand a year. At least a half to a third of the women I met on interviews espoused the attitude that it's not a good idea to talk about these things."

A recent survey conducted by the *National Law Journal* confirms that this woman's experience may be the norm. Ninety percent of the female respondents (many of whom earned over $100,000 a year) to a survey about career pressures reported that they felt they would be penalized if they made use of benefits their employers offered. Ninety percent said they felt they would be unable to advance in their careers if they took advantage of part-time or flex-time work arrangements, and 43 percent reported that they were afraid to take advantage of normal maternity leaves offered.[5]

Many other corporate women I interviewed concurred. An established businesswoman said, "If you even ask about parental leave policies or childcare on your third interview with a company — right before you would ordinarily be hired — that's the kiss of death." When I interviewed a prominent feminist academic for a recent article I was writing and suggested using the term "feminist" to describe her, she practically leaped through the phone line. "Oh, please don't call me *that*," she begged. For a woman trying to advance in the mainstream, it appeared, the word "feminist" would compromise her efforts.

Today, women learn the lessons of professionalism not only in male-dominated institutions like Yale Law School or Harvard Business School, but also from equal-opportunity feminists who instruct those women who did not learn the proper skills and attitudes either at home or at school. The American Women's Economic Development Network is one of many that provide this help. Its executive director, Beatrice Fitzpatrick, a woman in her late fifties, works to fulfill the ten-year-old organization's mandate — helping women succeed in managing the businesses they start.

AWED offers a variety of programs on managing a business, including an eighteen-month training series for women who have been in business for a year or more; a two-year series of monthly roundtable programs for chief-executive women whose businesses gross more than one million dollars annually; counseling services; conferences and seminars; and peer support groups and networks.

In 1978, AWED's first year, only 4.6 percent of small businesses were owned by women; by 1988 that figure had risen to 28 percent, and it is expected to reach 50 percent by the year 2000. With so many women now starting their own businesses and with four out of five businesses failing within the first five years, Fitzpatrick says that good management and information are more valuable than ever.

"Women have been taught to be nurturing," Fitzpatrick explains. "They go into business and they still want to be nurturing. They love what they're doing so much that they want everyone to enjoy it. The fact that they love what they're doing means that they feel about their business the way they feel about their child. And they will no more let someone kill that business than they will let them kill their child. So, long past the time when most people would throw in the towel, they hang on until it takes off."

This kind of dedication is a quality that must be preserved, Fitzpatrick argues. What AWED tries to help women overcome is their fear of money and finance and of success. According to

Fitzpatrick, many women become frightened just when their small businesses are about to really take off. This fear of success, she explains, may be due to women's reluctance to have more money and power than their mates, and to their need to be caring and nice.

"It's hard for women to learn how to be boss, to tell people what to do, to expect things of them. It's not like being nice and kind and sweet. I would say that being a woman business owner puts you in the sharpest contrast with what's accepted behavior of any occupation there is. If you are a woman manager for a large company and you have to fire someone, you can say you're doing it for the company. If you're a woman business *owner*, you're doing it for your bottom line or profit structure. Well, women aren't supposed to do things for themselves. They're supposed to be nice, they're supposed to be taking care of everyone else. It's very hard for a woman to fire someone because she's supposed to fire them so she can make more money. That goes against everything women are taught."

But, Fitzpatrick seems to suggest, learning to sacrifice the caring to the competitive agenda is just what the successful entrepreneur must do. Eschewing what Carol Gilligan calls the morality of care and responsibility in favor of the morality of the marketplace, Fitzpatrick seems to believe that an employer's responsibility is to maximize her *own* self-interest and create a successful business. This fuels economic growth and thus helps others. The owner's obligation, she suggests, is to do what is best for her, which will, she insists, help her employees and colleagues who will benefit. She seems to want women, while pursuing success, to look like women and act like women, but she still appears to encourage them to be "hard-nosed, bottom-line, and tough." As she put it in a 1987 article in the *Nation's Business*, "We'll kill ourselves to help you learn to be competitive."

To do this, AWED offers seminars, lectures, and national conferences. The pamphlet advertising its eighth National Conference for Women in the Business of Fashion, Beauty, Fitness, Food and Home Fashion featured a picture of Joan Carpenter, president of Linens by Design, reclining on a proverbial bed of roses. "I used to lust after the success of others, until I cut it out," Carpenter says. Presumably, the conference participants will do the same. A course called "Learn to Mind Your Own Business" will show women that they *can* make a difference — that is, they can make money. "Yes," the brochure reads, " 'Mind Your Own Business' is the message . . . has always been the message that AWED has urged on women from its early days a decade ago! And those are fighting words; words AWED has given a whole new meaning to! No admonition to shrinking violets to apologize for their very existence, but a command to women to *learn* to mind their own business. To learn how to start it. How to run it. How to make it more successful. How to enlarge it, increase it. Raise money for it. Negotiate on its behalf. Take it to heights never dreamed of. From small beginnings to million dollar successes.

"Minding our own business? You bet we will. Right on, from the first penny of profit to the first million!"

As for fighting to make the corporate world better, well, that doesn't seem to be women's job. Women embarking on a career "should be aware that their role is not to fight constantly for more opportunity," writes Doris Shaw, cochairwoman of the AWED executive planning committee. "That will come with the evolution of a corporate society coming to grips with a new participant."

Although AWED cannot lobby for legislation in Washington, Fitzpatrick said the group does not support mandated unpaid parental leave — the Family and Medical Leave Act — because it would hurt small businesses. This stance, unfortunately, suggests that women small-business owners are no more enlightened or supportive of the majority of women than are their male counterparts. Following the lead of the U.S. Chamber of Commerce, small-business owners have been the most active opponents of the Family and Medical Leave Act and are responsible for the fact that, at this writing, the bill has languished in Congress. Thus, for this kind of equal-opportunity feminist, sisters may attain power and be powerful, but sister*hood* — the collective advancement of the majority — seems to be a distinct impediment to individual, professional women's climb to the top.

As Rosanna Hertz, author of the study of two-income couples entitled *More Equal Than Others*, points out, today women as well as men are "routinely advised that advancement is brought about by 'team' contributions to the organization, but most learn very quickly that a significant, if not more important, criterion for advancement is outstanding individual performance. The effect of such an emphasis is that individual performance is valued as the means to individual reward, and the virtues of collective effort are ignored or devalued. Given such an environment, collective action (even for goals shared by people in similar situations) is avoided in favor of individual action or individual solutions. Thus, even though people employed by the same organization may have similar situations or needs, they rarely consider collective claims against the organization as a viable alternative."[6]

A number of the women I interviewed had learned this lesson all too well. In their personal and professional lives, they seemed entirely committed to advancement and success as it has been traditionally defined. Despite their common dilemmas, they viewed other women as competitors rather than as possible cohorts. And, like immigrants who had "made it in the New World," they had little sympathy with the struggles of those who were unable to pull themselves up by their own bootstraps and "have it all." No wonder a 1987 *Business Week* cover described corporate women in the following terms. "The new crop, which entered the work force in the late 1960s and 1970s, is better educated, more determined to advance, and more apt to be 'Organization Women' keeping mum on gender-related inequities. These women are more likely to be managers, and they hold far more senior positions."[7]

At thirty-eight, Lisa Wu is one of those "organization women" who has taken all the requisite steps for a "fast-track" scientific career. Women's participation in the scientific arena has ebbed and flowed throughout the twentieth century. During the 1920s, women actually made significant strides in the physical and social sciences, holding 16 percent of the doctorates in the life sciences, 8 percent in the physical sciences, and 17 percent in the social sciences. These numbers declined during the Depression, rose again slightly during the Second World War, and fell off when men returned from battle. In the 1950s women earned less than 4 percent of the doctorates awarded in the physical sciences and 11 percent in the life and social sciences.[8]

With the advent of the women's movement, however, women

made significant advances.[9] Between 1960 and 1984 women earned 56,000 doctorates in science.[10] Lisa Wu was one of them. But she had to compete every inch of the way to get into the right graduate school, get a good postdoctoral fellowship, and finally become one of the 21 percent of the female scientists to be employed in a college or university.[11] Today she is a molecular biologist at a state university in California, where 20 percent of the academic staff are women.

Although Wu has worked very hard to get where she is, she will have to work even harder to stay there, thanks to the Reagan administration's drastic cuts in funds available for higher education and nonmilitary scientific research. As more and more scientists compete for dwindling fiscal resources, competition has become fiercer than ever. To get tenure, Wu must have a good publication record as well as a research grant. But today the national scientific institutes that finance research fund only a fraction of the grant proposals they receive.

In the competition for jobs and grants, women have not fared as well as men. Among the population with doctoral degrees, unemployment rates for women are two to five times higher than for men.[12]

"It's very high-pressure and competitive," the Taiwan-born assistant professor says as we talk in her drab office at the university, down the hall from her lab. "Ten years ago every good grant was funded by the NIH. Now they only fund fifteen percent of those that apply."

To make sure she gets all her work done, Wu goes to work at seven-thirty each morning. Although she leaves at five to pick up her seven-year-old son, she often must return to the lab at night to start, monitor, or complete an experiment. When she's teaching, she works at home preparing lectures and grading exams. And she generally puts in extra hours on the weekend. When I interviewed her, her husband, who is also a research scientist, was commuting to see her on weekends from another state. Because Wu cannot always take her son with her to the lab at night and on weekends, but has no one with whom to leave him, she has taught him how to use the phone in an emergency.

Extremely ambitious, Wu says she loves her research work.

However, she seems to resent the time she must spend teaching and relating to students. There is, she complains, a shortage of good graduate students in science and she feels shortchanged by having to deal with second-raters. "You have to spend a lot of time with them, but you don't get anything back. When you have good graduate students, you don't mind spending time with them because they produce good data for you. But if you just spend time with them, and they don't generate any data, then you have to do all the work yourself."

Wu believes her sex also puts her at a disadvantage: her female students expect her to be supportive and interested in their personal and professional problems, and this, she insists, represents a subtle form of discrimination. "I had two female students the first year, and they would have treated me differently if I were a man. They talked to me the way I wouldn't have talked to a professor." She says, still bristling, "For example, they'd ask me something without thinking it over first. They would interrupt me about a work-related problem when I was busy. Or they would tell me something I'm not interested in, because I'm not interested in their personal lives. I never talked to my professors about my personal problems. We talked about research."

In an attempt to enforce the proper professional distance, Wu seated one of her most "troublesome" female students as far as possible from her own lab chair. Finally, though, she got her transferred to another lab. "Now I have a male student and the relationship is much better," she says with palpable relief. "It's based on scientific things, nothing personal."

Although she struggles to juggle her career and family while coping with the competitive pressures of her work, Lisa Wu views her situation in isolation. It was her "choice" to become a scientist: since she made her bed, she must sleep in it — alone. The only person with whom she feels she can share her problems is her husband — when he's around. "It's very important to have a good husband in this profession," she observes.

For her, there is no question of getting together with other women to try to change the conditions that make their lives so harried. In fact, she does not even have time to form friendships with other women. Her life is equally divided between working and tending her family. "If you want to compete with men, you have to do whatever they do," she concludes. To prove her point, she tells me the story of a friend who worked for years toward a scientific career, then had a retarded son and was forced to quit. To her, this tale illustrates the fact that women must shoulder their personal problems by themselves. "If you have family problems, you have to give up."

In talking about her work life and her responsibilities to others, Lisa Wu seems cold, unsympathetic, almost heartless. In fact, I don't think she is a terrible or callous woman. Her inability to recognize the personal needs of her students and coworkers and her interpretation of their interpersonal demands is in part a result of her ethnic origins. Chinese immigrants tend to be very private, reserved, and family-centered. They do not believe it is appropriate to share personal experiences with those who are not close members of their families. Similarly, some of Wu's complaints about female graduate students stem from Chinese culture's respect for authority and traditions of deference.

Ultimately, however, Lisa Wu's lack of generosity seems to be a result of the competitive pressures of scientific life. She cannot overcome tradition because she does not have time to give to others. Young assistant professors trying to get tenure are encouraged to publish or perish. In considering promotions, universities do not give much credit to a candidate's teaching skills. It is research or "scholarship" alone that counts.

Add to this burden the demands of her job and her family, and the belief she shares with so many others that colleagues are competitors, not allies, and it is little wonder she cannot reach out to them and cannot respond when they reach out to her. As she sat in her bare office, groping for the right words, I felt somewhat shocked listening to her complaints, but finally, she seemed someone to sympathize with rather than condemn. Lisa Wu is trapped between two untenable options. Her experience as an immigrant has been multiplied two-fold. She must prove herself as a minority and as a woman, and in so doing she has been rewarded with as much loneliness as success.

While Lisa Wu seems torn by her experiences in the male work world, Meredith Jameson seems almost unconcerned about the paradoxes her experiences illuminate. Like many high-achieving professional women, she is an advocate of the philosophy that "the trouble with women is that they aren't enough like men."

The thirty-seven-year-old senior-level manager of a large San Francisco bank is seven months pregnant when she greets me in her twentieth-floor office with a spectacular view of the San Francisco Bay. Her office and her let's-get-down-to-business demeanor attest to the fact that, after sixteen years climbing the corporate ladder, she is a "success."

Her career trajectory, she tells me, was not without obstacles. In fact, she says she "fell" into the banking world when she discovered that a bachelor's degree in Spanish only prompted prospective employers to ask her the traditional $64,000 question: "Can you type, dear?" One potential avenue for a linguist was banking, and so she got an MBA. But, again, when she wanted to work in customer service in Latin American banking, many male bankers insisted that she had no chance: macho Latins would never consent to work with a woman. Her current employer was the one exception. The bank wasn't interested in her sex, the school she went to, or the fraternity she wasn't in, but only in her ability to get the job done.

After working on the international side, Jameson transferred to the domestic side, working with Fortune 500 companies and middle-market firms. Now she is working in domestic lending. She has supervised many men and women and knows that women have a number of justifiable complaints about the business world. On the other hand, she says her own experiences have convinced her that a woman who produces for an organization will be recognized despite her sex. If you act like one of the guys, she says, you'll be treated like one of them. This has been easy for Jameson because she was one of seven children, four of them boys, and her mother expected her to tough it out with her brothers. She knows that most women have not been as fortunate.

"Many of the women in our generation," she explains, glancing out on the gorgeous panorama below, "were raised without a lot of organized team sports, so women aren't used to reacting the way a man would, according to a team concept," she says, echoing the classic "male" interpretation of girls' noncompetitive, more cooperative style of play. "Women aren't used to behaving like part of a team because they played solo individual games. That's a real barrier to women getting ahead."

Jameson says that encounters with a number of "difficult" women have helped her understand why men often consider them "pushy broads." She describes, for example, a very bright young woman whom she supervised. "She wouldn't come to me with a problem like a male colleague would; she wouldn't come in and lay out the problem and essentially give me a recommendation. I had to force her to make a decision. But then, once I'd make a decision, with my full authority to do so, she wouldn't accept it if she didn't like it. She'd come back ten times [to question it]. She had no concept of what is best for the institution. And I've seen more than one woman like that. A man, on the other hand, would argue the case and then back off when he recognized that his goals weren't important for the organization."

Jameson's attitude toward feminine style also illustrates the tightrope many women in the business world now ask one another to walk. While she complains that most women aren't enough like men, she also says that many overcompensate and become too much like men — too tough, too unfeminine. Still, "you don't want to be too much like a floozy," she warns. "Women would do better by not worrying so much about women's issues and just relaxing." Like men, she doesn't want women to be either too aggressive or too passive. But just where are they supposed to find that elusive middle ground she advocates? Apparently, they're supposed to divine it by some process of osmosis, since she also believes women should avoid the women's groups that she considers "crybaby organizations, women just getting together to moan and groan about their terrible plight."

Jameson believes these kinds of conversations encourage competent women to concentrate only on the negative instead of getting them thinking about how they can contribute to an organization. She is optimistic that future generations of businesswomen will be better prepared for the realities of the business world, because today young girls are participating in Little League, soccer, and other organized team sports that will teach them the essentials of teamwork.

Jameson does acknowledge that women have special problems that need to be addressed in one area — child rearing. In her company, as in many other banking and financial institutions, there is no maternity leave policy (women must go on disability), no help with childcare or other family-related problems. "There are several women who did an excellent job before they had children and, therefore, when they came back to work, they were able to arrange flexi-time or part-time work. Other women, like a very senior one with children, can afford to have a nice apartment and live-in help."

Jameson has been able to work out a good maternity leave package for herself and can afford to hire a qualified baby-sitter. It does not seem to have occurred to her to work with any other women at her level to try to turn these ad hoc arrangements into policies that would be available to others. She realizes that for many of the 15,000 to 16,000 employees who work for her bank as tellers or clerks, motherhood may give rise to some difficult dilemmas. When I asked her if she or others could do something to alleviate their plight, she had nothing to offer except reasons why the banking community will be slow to change and will take years to consider the kinds of parental and childcare policies that will make their work lives easier.

Jameson's attitudes toward women and their problems is typical of a certain kind of corporate woman, and a number of the women in or near positions of power I talked to were similar. Raised predominantly with brothers, having benefited from rather than fought for the kinds of advances women's liberation's early struggles made possible, these women tend to see life in the corporation as a "great adventure" rather than an enormous battle. They acknowledge that women do have certain problems but do not believe they are a result of systemic discrimination or skewed marketplace values. In the tradition of the power of positive thinking, they tend to blame women for their own "failings" and argue that if women just tried harder they would succeed. Trying harder does not, however, include reaching out to other women and acting collectively.

Nor does it mean giving much consideration to the problems women have combining working and caring. Meredith Jameson, for example, does not seem to have reflected much about these issues until she became pregnant. Because her income is so high, she will easily be able to purchase surrogate care and will never fully appreciate the tragic situation of those who cannot. And of course, her job as a manager of other women and a superior in a large hierarchy is not only to serve customers but, as Ehrenreich puts it, "to keep workers in line."[13]

Personally Meredith Jameson does not exude much warmth. And her job does not encourage her to practice caring in the workplace. She is what some consider a classically "male-identified" woman, one who has internalized the rules of the market and its ideals of power and moral responsibility. Her responsibility is to herself and her team, not to the far more numerous players in the minor leagues.

Even though such women are, I believe, the minority, they wield power far greater than their numbers. As the "power models" women are asked to measure themselves against, they reaffirm the belief that achievement, self-esteem, and personal success must be measured in market terms and that women must adopt the male economic model in order to make it in their careers. Reinforced by the media and by the business world at large, this message causes confusion and sometimes despair in many women who suspect that their own goals and ideals are more complicated.

At thirty-two, Mary Moses has had a series of high-level jobs in state government in California and in Chicago. She speaks with a nervous intensity when we meet. She has recently been awarded a plum job in a major metropolitan city, working on new school construction for the Board of Education. Having worked in the Department of Transportation in a large California city, Moses came of professional age in a very male-dominated environment. But this, she says, was nothing compared to the Board of Ed. Here, she comments, "we're really talking *male.*" Moses is currently working within a male-dominated central administration with male-dominated construction unions and male contractors.

Often feeling that she is working in isolation and that she must constantly prove herself — because she is both a woman and an "outsider" who did not come through the ranks — creates a great deal of strain. "Sometimes I feel like, what if they ever found out? I have a feeling that I'm not quite real," she confides.

Moses finds it hard to adapt to the marketplace injunction that the "boss" must take credit for everything he or she and his or her team accomplish, denying the role of chance as well as the participation of others. "I find it hard to give myself credit for all I've done. I did some really good things at the MTA. I loved the job. I loved working in the public sector. I was lucky to get a job at the MTA when exciting things were happening. I was lucky to have a wonderful boss and other very smart, talented people around me. For me, I've always felt lucky, even though other people say, 'You're so amazing, you've made all these things happen.' I feel like they happen to me."

Like so many women who recognize that they alone are not responsible for their successes and that, even in the workplace, they are part of an interdependent community of coworkers, Moses feels uncomfortable with the masculine assumption that her advances are hers alone. She is, in fact, articulating something very important. Women are quite correctly uncomfortable with the kind of radical disconnection from others that masculine ideas of success have always extolled.

Men have been taught to capture credit for accomplishments which are not always theirs alone, but rather the product of contributions from many others with whom they work. They deny the fact of interdependence and conceal, far more than they reveal, the input of others who help make them who and what they are. Women, on the other hand, tend to recognize and respect collaboration. That recognition and respect are strengths they bring with them into the marketplace. But instead of honoring them as such, their employers and equal-opportunity feminist-success counselors tell them these are weaknesses and that women should mimic men — taking credit where it is not always due.

Today many would interpret Mary Moses' belief that "things happen to me" as a quintessential example of the "fear of success." On the contrary, it is very positive recognition of reality. But again, the market superimposes its categories on her feminine way of knowing and being. And so, rather than constructing a new set of relationships based on interdependence, in her new job she feels increasingly isolated and "relationless" and has no marketplace language or framework that can help her express or analyze her feelings and experiences.

Thus, she says that she finds it "hard to figure out how to act with people, how friendly, how emotional I can be." She is also worried about how she appears to people. On the one hand, she says she has to get things accomplished and must "step on some people's toes to do so." On the other hand, she feels that the isolation and adversarial atmosphere in her workplace cause her to "jump on people at work, and to jump to conclusions instead of listening to people."

She was never like that in her former job, she recalls, where she had support and worked on a real team. Perceived as a "success," Mary Moses is nevertheless looking for guidance and relationship on the job and finding neither. She concludes, "I love my job and hate my job."

The same love/hate relationship defines Helena Walzer's work life. A portfolio manager at a large bank when we first met, the thirty-four-year-old had begun to feel that the conflicts between her personal and her professional life were unbearable. For one thing, her sense of female integrity clashed constantly with the work-styles of the men around her. "Men bullshit a lot more than women," she observes. "Men will express themselves about things even when they don't know what they're talking about. It's important to men to be able to form an opinion, express it, and hold it, even without believing it or being bonded to it. Women feel they have to know things better before they express themselves. I feel I need perfect information to express or form an opinion."

More troubling, though, was the realization that her high-powered job left no room for a personal and family life. During the two years she worked for the bank, Walzer noted with growing concern that women who had children were unable to combine work and family, and thus most never returned from maternity leave. Even worse, the men who headed her department failed to recognize the reasons for their departure. "The male senior-level executives never realized the exodus was a result of their refusal to help women accommodate a career and family. In one meeting, the head of my department announced that women of a certain age were overcome by their hormones and couldn't resist the pull of staying home with their children. It never occurred to him that the problem wasn't hormonal, it was institutional."

Disturbed by the potential conflict between her company's business and her own personal priorities, Walzer tried to find allies — role models who could provide guidance. "I tried calling some of the businesswomen's networks in town, but they made it perfectly clear that they weren't interested in lower-level women like myself. They were interested in you only if you had some exchange value, if you could give them a tip about another high-level job for themselves. They're not interested in helping other women, just advancing in their own careers."

When I asked Walzer if she could imagine working with other women to change the corporate priorities that turn women's lives into such juggling acts, she shook her head. "It would be like attacking a mountain with a piece of sandpaper," she said regretfully.

The implicit suggestion that women must pay for their careers with their lives, their friendships, their families, their personal interests, and their "femininity" is as destructive as it is prevalent. Women who try to adapt to the expectations of the marketplace often find themselves unhappy and uncomfortable, disaffected with both the institutions in which they work and the brand of feminism that led them to believe they could "have it all." This widespread disaffection has been confirmed in a variety of media reports. In 1989, the *New York Times* published a three-part, front-page series on women's gains on the job. According to the *Times* poll of 1,497 adults, 83 percent of working mothers and 72 percent of working fathers reported conflicting demands of their jobs and their desires to see more of their families. Forty-eight percent of all women felt the costs of their professional lives were too high and that they were forced to sacrifice children and family life to their jobs.[14]

But what do women do to protect their families, their children, their personal ideals, and their integrity? When they discover the price of adapting, what action do they take? Does the fact that they have attained greater power in mainstream society encourage — as Friedan and others hoped it would — the exercise of voice, or do women, like so many other Americans before them, simply vote with their feet and leave?

Chapter Four

TARGETING THE TOP — FIGHT AND FLIGHT

WHAT OPTIONS do professional women feel they can exercise in a masculine marketplace? That is the question.

The well-known economist Albert Hirschman helps us answer it. In his well-known book *Exit, Voice and Loyalty* Hirschman argues that when human beings experience a decline in the products they purchase or the organizations to which they belong or in which they work, they have several options. One Hirschman calls "exit" and the other "voice." When people are discontented with the organizations and institutions that shape their lives, some respond by leaving — by "voting with their feet." Others respond with a protest or challenge — by raising their voices.

Hirschman explains that the exit option — the option that is often preferred in market economies — generally requires no more than a simple comparative choice between a product made by one firm and that produced by another. In some instances, mass exit does create an improvement in a firm or organization. But in most cases this very American strategy of escape, of flight rather than fight, leads to few improvements.

The exercise of voice, the ultimate description of collective political activity, is, on the other hand, much more complicated but potentially much more constructive. Unfortunately, however, "the

presence of the exit alternative can *tend to atrophy the development of the art of voice.*"[1]

Which is where loyalty comes in. Far from being "irrational,"
loyalty is crucial because it "can serve the socially useful purpose
of preventing deterioration from becoming cumulative, as it so
often does when there is no barrier to exit."[2] But in order for
loyalty to come into play at all, individuals must be loyal to some
ideal or institution.

Unfortunately, and perhaps not surprisingly, given the conditions in most workplaces, the response to job-related problems
seems to be some variation of flight rather than fight, exit rather
than voice. The majority of women I spoke with felt compelled to
choose exit rather than voice — with only a minority trying to
solve their problems through some sort of individual or collective
protest. This finding seems to be confirmed in research studies and
media reports.

Those who did try to stay and fight, for themselves or for others,
did so precisely because of a sense of loyalty to their own past
experiences of oppression and struggle combined with a feeling of
responsibility to a feminine/feminist ideal of corporate, societal,
and personal relationships.

For Janet Thomas, a forty-six-year-old neurobiologist and tenured professor at a major eastern university, fighting has become
a way of life. Now she is well established in her field, and we meet
while she is attending a prestigious conference in the mountains
of upstate New York. Thomas has been marked by the ordeal that
began in her student days. During her graduate training, her thesis
adviser and mentor began to make sexual advances toward her.
When she resisted, the harassment increased. Twenty years ago,
she says, this was commonplace. When she told other professors
about it and tried to get help, some said they were not at all
surprised at hearing the story. None, however, offered more than
the most minimal help.

After completing her thesis, Thomas moved to the East Coast
with a boyfriend. But things did not improve much. "I had a job
teaching medical students molecular biology. But they were mostly
guys who were only interested in setting up an office and getting

an accountant. They were very hostile and only respected men wearing white coats. And here I was, a woman."

When she was in the middle of setting up her own lab, the department chief who had acted as Thomas's mentor suddenly died. She grew more and more depressed and finally went to a psychiatrist. "I told him I didn't need to talk, I just needed anti-depressants and tranquilizers, and he gave them to me," Thomas recalls. "And I got hooked." Now she was not only depressed, she was addicted. Isolated from colleagues, far from family, she finally decided she wanted out. Twenty years ago, at Christmas, she took all the pills she could find and swallowed them. "They took me to a psychiatric hospital and locked me up. It was incredible," she recalls, crying silently at the memory. "Before, I had always thought that suicide was an out. When things were terrible, you just checked out. But here I was in this horrible place and I didn't have any choice but to fix my life."

While she was in the hospital, she says, she realized how adversely the competitive environment of academic science had influenced both herself and her colleagues. "Throughout all this there was a great deal of support for me from people in my department whom I barely knew. I thought everything that had happened was my fault. That I was the only one who was depressed about our work environment. But it turned out everyone was feeling that way, but no one felt they could talk about it; they all thought they had to walk around acting like everything was terrific."

Thomas and her colleagues all unwittingly obeyed a code of silence that tends to rule almost all institutions. If people are unhappy, they feel they have to keep their problems to themselves. Complainers — male or female — do not get ahead. Thomas's problems were so acute that she was forced to violate this code.

It was at this period of her life that Thomas learned lessons about the need for support in the workplace that she has never forgotten. She entered therapy and also began to attend a women's support group that has continued for many years. "It was incredible. There were administrative assistants and postdocs, students and professors."

Because she does not want other women to suffer as she did, Thomas says, she feels a keen sense of responsibility to her female students. "I have three female graduate students in my lab, and more than half the entering class is women. I know there are a lot of places in academia where you can't have emotions and discuss them and own them, but maybe in this lab I can promote an idea of being natural. It seems important, as I watch these women who come in, to give them an experience where they can succeed by being real, instead of having to go through what I went through."

She herself still grapples constantly with the complex issues of care and responsibility. Carol Gilligan, in her book *In a Different Voice*, describes this struggle as the "progression of relationships toward a maturity of interdependence."[3] As a woman reaches adulthood, Gilligan explains, "the moral dilemma changes from how to exercise one's rights without interfering in the rights of others to 'how to lead a moral life which includes obligations to myself and my family and people in general'."[4]

Certainly this has been true for Janet Thomas, who continues to seek the right balance between professionalism and compassion. "Because you're supportive of your students, and nurturing, you find yourself on the horns of a dilemma. You can't go overboard and rescue them too much. And then you also have to look at this as a challenge rather than a problem. There are times when I feel all of this is used to penalize me, because you get no points in academic science for worrying about how to treat other people. And then you feel resentful because you spend so much time sitting around feeling bad about these issues instead of doing science.

"I guess I think the real issue for women," she concludes, "is how do we take this caring thing we do and make it a positive force, something for which there is permission, while also protecting ourselves from burnout? I've always been so close to the burnout stage in caring for other people."

Her concerns also illustrate the difficulties of caring in an environment designed specifically to defeat caring. Many institutions define caring as a problem, a threat to the bottom line, not as a positive and valuable human activity. Thus finding the space to care involves scaling myriad barriers that limit us as caregivers. Before we are able to even make the space to care, we are exhausted. This, I believe, is the essence of the "burnout" that Thomas describes. Janet Thomas continued to try to care, but some women decide that caring itself is too difficult. Rather than attacking the institutions that make caring a mission impossible, they decide it's better not to care at all.

Many of the women I interviewed experienced the kind of care-related discrimination they thought they would never have to deal with after they had a child. Suddenly their bosses viewed them through an entirely different lens. Although they continued to work as diligently as before, the very fact that they now had other commitments in their lives — commitments they worked hard to honor — made them suspect. In the "if-you-need-a-friend-get-a-dog" world of the American marketplace, juggling work and babies is not a symbol of one's resourcefulness and stamina but rather the scarlet letter of failure, as Alice Hart's colleague, Jane Foley, a twenty-nine-year-old middle-level manager at National Financial Services, explains. "When I had been back at work for six months after having my daughter," she recounts, "my boss told me they were taking me off my job. He felt I had a major distraction at home; that my family issues prevented me from giving 100 percent to my job, and so he was going to move me to a less demanding one."

Foley, who grew up in a working-class home and attributes some of her feistiness to her father's strong trade-union allegiance, refused to accept her boss's suggestion. "My response was to tell him that he might as well fire me. I wasn't going to accept this. I was going to talk to whomever necessary." Foley did just that and was given another job, in which she no longer had to report directly to this particular male manager. Although she found at least a temporary solution, she realized that hundreds of other women in her organization had similar problems. "You can't come back and compete with people who are unattached. The choice shouldn't be to work here without any kids or not work at all."

The ideal option, she decided, was job-sharing at the managerial level. Foley floated the idea by Alice Hart and other women managers before approaching a sympathetic senior-level female executive, who gave her the go-ahead to put together a small pilot project. She then lined up six women who had already left the company because of family pressures and convinced them to come back and share three jobs. They agreed.

By the time the program was in place, however, all of her candidates had changed their minds. "Most of them had been out for six months to two years and said they'd already adjusted to being at home and they didn't want to go back to work yet." Forced to rethink her plan, Foley wrote an employee survey and distributed it to the four thousand members of her division to ascertain their needs. After this the company initiated a limited job-sharing experiment. "I want it for myself," she candidly admits. "I know that when they're looking for people to promote, I won't be on the list; people will say I'm not committed enough, but that's okay with me."

The women I described above are all "fighters." Their intra-institutional struggles involve battles over issues of discrimination with male supervisors or employers, and/or attempts to nurture a feminine/feminist alternative within the confines of their own workplaces: their offices, labs, or departments. In many important instances, their hard work has resulted in changes within larger institutions that are extremely resistant to any alteration in the way business is done and power is wielded. In some instances, however, the exercise of voice they describe has been limited by their own definitions of the parameters of acceptable protest.

Alice Hart, for example, tried to work collectively with other women by starting a network of women on her middle-management level. "We had a group of eight directors who used to get together," Hart explains. "We met four times over a period of six months. It was great. But one of the women got promoted to vice president and she wasn't invited anymore. She was the same person. But there was a degree of uncomfortableness about what you would say to someone who was not at your level and how it would be interpreted."

The group eventually disbanded, not least because it had no way to accommodate women who moved up. When I asked Alice Hart if she felt that excluding this senior woman had sent the wrong message, she agreed it had but could imagine no other outcome. "This is another example," Jane Foley, who was not a member of the group, commented, "of women's lack of comradely support. That woman should have been kept in the group as an inspiration. Instead she was penalized socially for her promotion. She was personally hurt."

Helena Walzer also recounted the same kind of female respect for career ladders that made it impossible for her to find a networking group that would accept a junior-level woman. In both of these instances, women's training in the rules of professional hierarchy made sisterhood a nostalgic ideal.

Our society's continued denigration of all alternatives to the marketplace model also makes it extremely difficult for these women to anchor their concerns, questions, and complaints in a feminine/feminist critique or vision of change. In fact, rather than trusting their own judgments and perceptions, even some of the most self-confident and combative women have been encouraged to view their strengths as weaknesses or deficiencies. Women like Alice Hart constantly berate themselves for not being "into power." Given the climates in which they work, these women find it hard to appreciate that their models of empowerment may be simply different, not inferior, to the dominant marketplace model to which they are expected to conform.

Moreover, because the male standard of professional conduct, rather than any feminist alternative, is the one these female professionals are told to measure themselves against, even the most feisty women often fail to challenge men when it would be relatively risk free to do so. Like Janet Thomas, Maureen Kennedy, another molecular biologist, says she feels that it is her duty to help her graduate students with their personal and professional problems and to create a warm and supportive environment in her lab. However, when she moves out of the confines of her own lab and onto male turf, she says, she feels obliged to "neuter herself" and act more like men.

When serving on study sections to review other scientists' grant proposals, for example, she says her first task is to gain "credibility." Because an applicant's livelihood and professional future are dependent on her ability to be an advocate for their work, Kennedy feels she must be strong and professional in her demeanor if she is to convince other panel members that her evaluation of a grant is correct. Kennedy feels that being "strong and professional" means suppressing all signs of emotion and making sure her colleagues don't consider that her femininity, her tendency to care about someone's future, will obscure her judgment.

Occasionally, she says, she has had to respond to the accusation that being a woman is an impediment to sound judgment — usually when a colleague suggests that she is "acting just like a woman." "You have to put that person down and make them realize what they're doing by denying that that's the case." With some surprise, I asked if she can imagine an alternative response and suggest something like, "Of course I'm acting like a woman; I *am* a woman. What's wrong with that? You're acting just like a man." After all, I said, men are always telling women it's no good to be feminine. Why not throw it back at men and suggest that strong silent masculinity may not be such a boon to society? She admits that such an alternative has never occurred to her. Indeed, she confesses more — that she is troubled by her tendency to care "too much." "You know what I hate about myself?" she asks. "I hate myself for having tears in my eyes when I'm arguing something. I feel I'm in an inferior position because the other guy wouldn't have tears in his eyes.

"Here's another thing I feel embarrassed about," she continues. "When someone calls me to be on a panel or study section, I tell them I have to talk to my husband because we have small kids and we can't both be out of the house at the same time. I say it softly, as if I'm embarrassed that I have to ask my husband's permission — which I do, just as he has to ask mine. Most people will say, 'Yeah, I know what you mean, I have a two-year-old too.' "

Mary Moses shares Kennedy's dilemma. "Sometimes in meetings," Moses says, "I get very emotional. I don't have a poker face. When I get angry and upset, I show it, and I'm conscious of men thinking it's not because Mary's just that way, it's because she's a woman. And I care that they think that. I think, a man would never do this. But then, I think, maybe it's because he just wouldn't care as much."

While women like Moses and Kennedy may express doubts about the lessons they have learned from market society when talking to an interviewer like me, when they're at work they tend, not surprisingly, to obey the final verdict of the marketplace: Caring is for sissies; tough girls don't care, question, or complain, or at least they don't show it or do it openly.

These women begin to feel that the market forces them to trade one form of subordination for another. In the home and family they had to submerge their so-called masculine side in favor of the feminine. Now, in the workplace, they are forced to conceal their feminine side and express only the most traditional, masculine competitive and aggressive behaviors. No matter where they are, then, the market will not let them be whole. And we are all suffering the consequences.

One of these consequences is that some women actually join men in arguing that women should not even try to speak in a different voice or act in a different way at work. To act differently than men, they believe, will jeopardize whatever advances we have made in the marketplace. Thus, when Jane Foley tried to institute job-sharing at NFS, she was surprised to discover that not all women were supportive. "One particularly high-powered friend who's very ambitious and has no children had a very negative response," she recalls. "She said a program like this just supports the idea that women can't handle it and need special treatment."

Unfortunately, many women — particularly younger ones — now put so much pressure on one another to conform to the male model that some are ashamed to admit how desperately they do need a different "deal" in the marketplace. In the spring of 1989, Felice Schwartz unveiled her controversial proposal for a special track for "career and family women" in an article in the *Harvard Business Review*.[5] Shortly thereafter, I and several other women addressed a crowd of 250 female professionals at Harvard University. During the question period, I called on a young woman who was eight months pregnant. She explained that she was a medical student at Harvard and that, after accidentally becoming pregnant, she had decided to have the child.

Her boyfriend left her, and she now faced the prospect of raising the child herself, while continuing to try to earn her medical degree in one of the most demanding and competitive schools in the country. Her school schedule precluded sharing an apartment and childcare duties with another single mother. Practically in tears,

the woman said she wanted to ask Harvard for a "different deal."
But would she be betraying feminism and other women if she
admitted how much she needed a "mommy track"? She turned to
the audience. What, she asked these women, should she do? Given
these parameters, what, indeed, could she do?

Even some women who actually do negotiate a different deal —
usually at considerable sacrifice to their incomes and careers —
find that other women often resent it. That's what Rachel James,
a magazine editor and divorced mother of a seven-year-old son,
discovered when she moved from the East to the West Coast to
take a job at a publication dealing with parent-child issues. "When
I was negotiating for the job, I made it clear that I could not work
fourteen- or sixteen-hour days in the office. I took a less senior
position and a large cut in pay in order to be able to leave the
office at five-thirty so I could pick up my son. I also made it clear
to my employers that I would do the necessary work at home to
get the job done. Those were the conditions under which I was
hired.

"The office was staffed with young women who had no families,
divorced men, and men with wives who stayed home to take care
of kids," James says. "And it soon became clear that everyone
resented the fact that I wasn't there till ten at night, even though
I was getting my work done at home. If you weren't in the office,
you were perceived as not working. To my female colleagues, it
was as if a chauffeur were picking me up at five-thirty every afternoon to take me out drinking and dancing, when in fact all I was
doing was going home to take care of my son and to do more work
after he was in bed. The incredible thing was, here we were publishing articles about these issues every day, and they simply
couldn't grasp the simple facts of a working mother's life."

Such morale problems are common, says Ellen Wallach, a career
consultant in Seattle, Washington, who works with women professionals in a variety of corporate settings. "Even if people never
discuss the rules that they work by in a particular office, they take
these unwritten rules as a given that everyone is supposed to live
by. And they feel that fair means equal. So if some people aren't
in the office when everyone else is there, even if they're working

at home and getting the work done, their colleagues may get angry. And if people's different arrangements aren't discussed with the group as a whole, but are worked out individually with an employer or supervisor, then people can get even angrier. People don't sympathize with someone who has special needs, or even with someone who has the same needs but has been able to satisfy them. They look upon that person resentfully and believe they're getting special treatment."

Unfortunately, many women confirmed this new phenomenon. In corporate law offices and brokerage houses, high-tech firms and large banks and insurance companies, everyone had a story to tell about younger women on their way up who resented and ultimately caused problems for older women who were trying to accommodate their family responsibilities to young children or aging parents. Many of these young women have become part of a large group of people in our society — what I call the No Cares Cohort. They don't have young children, so they're not worried about childcare. Their parents aren't old, so they have no elderly parents to nurse through an illness. They're not sick, so they're not concerned about health care. And if they're married or in a relationship, they may be coworkaholics with their mates (even if their mates are other women).

The main concern of many of these young women is to compete with both men and other women to get ahead. They perceive any special deal working mothers or fathers make with their employers to be an unfair advantage. And sometimes they speak out in anger to oppose the continuation of such "unfair arrangements." Because they are young and do not have to cope with the demands of reconciling work and family life, they are unsupportive of their colleagues who are grappling with these issues. And because corporate culture has become so competitive, generosity of spirit has been ruled out of order.

This self-centeredness is reinforced, rather than tempered, in the literature of equal-opportunity feminism. Most of the equal-opportunity "experts" who write for professional women's magazines like *Working Woman* and *Savvy* publish how-to primers and give seminars for the successful woman admit that "having it all" has costly side effects. But the message that now influences millions of women counsels only adaptation to or exit from the marketplace and its values.

The January 1988 issue of *Working Woman* — a magazine that now claims a circulation of 3,000,000 — considers one of the most notable side effects of the compulsion to adapt to the marketplace and "do it all" — the internalized prohibition against taking time off. "Are you a victim of vacation anxiety?" the author asks.[6]

In the same issue, a psychiatrist confesses that she cannot allow herself the "weakness" of getting sick. Like the most macho corporate executive, she refused to admit illness, and when she was finally felled by her own body, she resisted the efforts of physicians, family, and friends to care for her.[7] A March 1988 piece entitled "Fear of Tears: Crying at the Office" addressed the female manager's unfortunate inability to eradicate the last vestige of feminine vulnerability — the tendency to care and to cry. Like it or not, the woman manager must learn that "Upper-echelon executives realize that the bottom line is business and that their job is to function well enough to make a profit for the company. . . . You're expected to be able to put your feelings aside and get on with the task at hand. That's what being upper-level management means. Showing tears in the office is anathema."[8]

Job stress is also a recurring theme. *Working Woman* dedicated its April 1988 issue to "Managing Your Way Out of the Work Swamp," explaining, "High achievers are magnets for work. But when overload threatens to sink your career, it's time to take action."[9]

The prescriptions offered in these articles and many others never suggest that women's problems are the result of the fundamentally perverse and inflexible demands of the marketplace. Rather, they are personal problems — the result of ineffective "management skills" or symptoms of underlying psychological hang-ups. As Judith Briles puts it in her 1987 book *Woman to Woman: From Sabotage to Support*, women's work-related dilemmas, notably their inability to cooperate with other women, are "an unconscious reaction to and result of low self-esteem developed in childhood — low self-esteem that has caused us to feel inferior to men, anxious and doubtful about our abilities, fearful of female competition, and envious of female success and power."[10] She suggests that troubled women use standard self-help techniques to improve self-esteem and that individual psychotherapy may be useful. She also advises readers to find a powerful leader to follow, and to remember, as Betty Lehan Harragan said, "Never talk back to the coach."

Other dress-for-success feminists counsel withdrawal from relationships. In order to make time for a personal life, the professional woman is told how to "keep her eye on the goal and eliminate all inessentials." In this case, "inessentials" are noninstrumental relationships and non-work-related social encounters on the job. As one businesswoman says brusquely, "I never do lunches." Another confesses, "I used to spend a lot of time schmoozing with people — amazing how much time I spent." A corporate lawyer returning from maternity leave told me she had attended a seminar conducted by a local dress-for-success counselor. First-time mothers returning to work were warned never to talk about their babies or to display baby pictures on their desks. To do so would convince their male colleagues that they were not committed to their work. To suggest one has even bonded with another human being, some women who call themselves feminists or are otherwise committed to women's advancement now insist, is a no-no in the office.

Collective solutions to common problems are resolutely resisted. In his essay on the corporation as totalitarian state, Robert Jelinek counsels that the man to imitate is not the Lenin-like revolutionary or the Gorbachev-style reformer but the "corporate Kremlinologist." "There are basically three legal means available to an assiduous corporate Kremlinologist: *people* — setting up your own private network of them; *paper* — reading everything you can get your hands on about your company and your company's principal competitors; and *telltale signs* — keeping your eyes and ears open for them and learning how to interpret them."[11]

Total exit is the "final solution." Feeble as this may sound, it is advice that has been widely disseminated by equal-opportunity feminists. Judith Briles says "the wrong approach is to refuse directly when someone in power wants you to do something a certain way. . . . A person lower down in the business hierarchy

needs to respect the hierarchy and the relationships with colleagues which cross-cut it." If a woman is simply pushed too far,
or "if the whole company is unethical," Briles says, "it may be
time to leave."[12] Apparently, she can see no other alternative.

In a 1989 cover story entitled "The Rat Race," writers for *Time*
magazine proposed an even more drastic remedy for unbearable
job stress: if the work is too much with you, they say, perhaps it's
time to change profession or even move to a different city, state,
or region. Women who want to gain control of their lives should
open up small businesses or move to "habitable cities" such as
Fort Worth, Texas, Providence, Rhode Island, and Charlotte,
North Carolina; trade a high-powered job for a lower-level job
with more free time; or hire a professional time organizer.[13]

Given the difficulty they have integrating their caring and competitive agendas in the workplace and the lack of guidance from
within and outside mainstream institutions, it is not surprising
that, in my sample of professional women, exit was the primary
solution to workplace dilemmas. Indeed, "bailing out" seems
to be one of the most popular new trends among professional
women. For example, a recent *Business Week* cover story on corporate women contained a section entitled "Where Are They
Now? *Business Week's* Leading Corporate Women of 1976." Re-
visiting forty-six of the original one hundred, *Business Week* found
only twenty-seven still working, sixteen with the same companies.
Three women had changed employers but remained in the corporate world. "Seven left the corporate world to start their own
businesses or join professional firms. Only one left to start a family.
The other nineteen retired. In all, only five women are working in
the kinds of line jobs considered crucial for a shot at senior executive positions.

"What is more disturbing is that nearly one-third of the women
surveyed have left corporate jobs."[14]

Susan Shattuck is one of these corporate expatriates. An early
supporter of the women's movement, the forty-year-old mother of
two spent much of her twenties fighting to break down the career
obstacles facing women in the predominantly male world of television journalism. While she never considered herself addicted to

work, she willingly put in her share of twelve-hour days until she became one of the first assignment editors at WCBS, the CBS affiliate in New York. In a few more years, she expected, she would move into management or become an on-air reporter or a producer for network news.

When Shattuck was thirty-two, however, she became pregnant with her younger son, Aaron. "As soon as I became pregnant," she recalls, "things changed at work. The more you could see my belly, the worse things got. Network news is very macho, a very antipeople environment — even the men have trouble with it. But it's almost impossible for a woman, particularly a pregnant one. Instead of accommodating your needs, they punish you. When I was six months pregnant, for example, I was put on overnights. Finally I realized that, if I continued in that working environment, I would have nothing left to give my infant." So Shattuck quit. Like many professional women, and unlike most lower-income women, she was in a position to do so. Her husband, a tape editor for CBS's "Sunday Morning" show, earns a professional salary. Even so, the loss of her income entailed significant sacrifices.

A year and a half after our initial meeting, Helena Walzer had also left her job. She says she first tried to organize a group of women in her office. "When the senior staff went on periodic retreats to discuss the state of the economy, we decided to meet to talk about the state of women in the office. The issues we discussed concerned the company's failure to provide us with adequate information and help us grow and develop. We actually had two meetings with the men. The first was really unpleasant and uncomfortable. Either they got very upset or simply wouldn't engage. The second was somewhat better. But the whole effort just dribbled out.

"Nothing really ever changed. I think efforts like that die for lack of fertility. There's no fertile soil in the corporation. And then there was dissension among the women involved. Some just didn't want to rock the boat. There were others who didn't want to offend men whom they considered friends. It was a small office and there were a lot of personal relationships. And we would have had to be very confrontational."

In part, Walzer attributes the group's failure to her own

unwillingness to provide leadership. "For something like this to succeed," she says, "you need one person who's really willing to be labeled a screaming meemy. I would have been the obvious choice. But I didn't do it. I felt hopeless about the situation. I felt the men were really entrenched, and I didn't know how long I would be around. And then, most of the other women weren't real fighters, and I wasn't sure they'd back me up or follow through."

Finally, when Walzer accidentally got pregnant, she left and now works as a part-time consultant.

A marketing manager for a large high-tech company in San Jose, California, Susan Sullivan quit her job when she discovered that the exciting highs of making it as a frenetic dealmaker in the marketplace can be followed by ego-shattering lows. After leaving teaching and getting an MBA in her mid-thirties, she took a job marketing a new product for her prominent high-tech firm. "In the first year it was great," the forty-one-year-old explains. "I was cutting deals with third parties, getting grants, negotiating all the time. I loved it. The job was full of long, exciting, intense hours. I was excited by the product. I could believe in it."

As quickly as the roller coaster went up, however, it plummeted. The company discovered that the technology was more complex than first imagined. Nor was the line producing the expected profits. Suddenly, Sullivan was no longer the hot new "guy" on the block. "No one told us they were pulling the plug. The group just got ignored. We didn't get the resources and people just relocated within the company or left."

Sullivan stayed on to navigate her product's transition. After having been the ace entrepreneurial broker, she found herself working with old-line "tough cookies" who tried to undermine her authority. Her immediate boss's behavior became increasingly erratic. One day she heard, quite by accident, that he planned to move his office and *her* secretary to an entirely new location, without informing her about the move.

Her reaction to this was to blame herself. "I started wondering what I'd done wrong," she says. "I began to think perhaps I was like one of those cases I studied in business school — a woman who just wasn't politically savvy enough to know what was going on and act to change it."

When I asked her if she felt she could talk with coworkers about her problem, she explained that that is out of the question in corporate culture. "I obviously felt I couldn't talk to anyone on the male staff. But I also felt I couldn't reach out to other women," she adds. "The unwritten rule is that, within the organization, you just don't reveal negative things about what's going on. If you do, you'll be looked at as someone who 'can't handle it.' People will think it must be your fault. There's a basic lack of trust within the organization. And then people don't want to hear about what's awful and bad. It's as though it will rub off on them and they'll get tainted. Sometimes, if you talk to someone, they'll sympathize. But nobody wants to rock the boat. People want to protect their positions and get to a better position. And that extends to women as well as men and women's dealings with each other."

Given these taboos, Sullivan felt she had no option but to leave. The experience, she recounts, has had a lasting impact. "It made me a person who is not trusting," she observes candidly. "In the political corporate battlefield, I've seen people shrivel up when support systems were withdrawn. I'm glad I went through it," she concludes, "but I may not like what I've become."

Exit does not always involve leaving one's job. Distressed by their employer's values and priorities, some women stay in their jobs, while engaging in a kind of internal exile, in which they give up any hope of change. They may have experienced too many disappointments trying to address the corporate policies that make their lives so difficult. They may understandably feel that the time demands of contemporary professional work preclude political activity. But most have been so well schooled in a culture that teaches people only to seek individual "how-to" solutions that the idea of collective action to advance the *individual* as well as the *common* good is entirely foreign.

Alice Hart is a case in point. A year after our initial interview, she had moved out of her company's headquarters in lower Manhattan to another office farther uptown. With a great deal of bitterness she explained why. "I came in to work about nine months ago, after having had excellent reviews, and my boss told me that his perception was that I would rather stay at home and be a mother than be at work. I was pregnant at the time, although he didn't know it, and I was an emotional wreck when I heard that. I tried to talk with him about it, but he's one of those conflict-avoidance types, and he finally just said he was tired of hearing about it. I had had excellent performance reviews and I did my work. I worked from about nine until five-thirty and did about an hour and a half of work at night at home. But I suppose the fact that I wasn't in the office doing it, and the fact that I used to talk about my son — I'm just so proud of him — made them feel this way.

"I knew that saying that kind of thing was discriminatory and against the law, but I just felt there was no one in personnel that I could talk to. I didn't feel comfortable enough that there was an open door to complain without it coming back to hurt me in the long run."

After this experience, Hart feels that any hope she may have had for improving the quality of life at NFS was naive. "If you don't give a hundred and ten percent to the specific job, they don't value you. I don't want to be a senior vice president in three years, I just want to do my job and enjoy it and have a family. But if you're not on that fast track, they think you're not interested in your work and not competent to do it. You're just not recognized if you don't have that dog-eat-dog kind of drive."

The fact that the head of personnel at NFS is a woman and that a female senior vice president enjoys a reputation for fighting to improve women's lot in the corporation has not helped, Hart says. "The fact is, I don't think I could talk to either of those women. The head of personnel is a woman, but she's single, and I don't think the word of a working mother means anything. I'd be scared she'd just say that these are the rules at this company and I've been wearing rose-colored glasses."

When I mentioned the job-sharing experiments her company has initiated which have attracted significant attention, she simply laughs. "It's all P.R. They implement the most minimal experiment in job-sharing, all at lower levels, and they get a lot of mileage out of it."

At this point, Hart says sadly, she never mentions her son at work and plans to stay on only until she has another child. Although she is aware that thousands of women at her company share her problems, she does not reach out to any of them because she does not believe that change is possible — not for her generation. "Those are the rules," she says stoically.

Some women have managed to negotiate individual deals that change those rules. But these women are often afraid or unwilling to put themselves on the line to help other less fortunate women — even women who are professional peers. "Women seem loath to use collective strategies within their companies," says Ibis consulting firm's Jane Bermont. "In my work with professional women, what I see instead is that they try to become invaluable to their companies and thus get a 'good deal' as an individual. For example, I recently attended a meeting where a woman attorney spoke about her own personal situation. She said she had been able to negotiate a part-time schedule because she was perceived as an exceptional contributor to her firm. She recognized the problems other women faced reconciling work and family life. Ideally, she said, she would have liked to help women find solutions to these problems within her firm."

But, Bermont said, the woman insisted she would not speak out to help other women because she was unwilling to put her own individual deal at risk. "She felt she had been done a favor," Bermont explains. "She did not want to appear ungrateful. She said the only way she would work for change was within her professional organization." Bermont added that even working within this professional organization, the woman appeared unwilling to allow her name to be used. There was no place, it seemed, where she would go on the record with either her sympathies or complaints.

Corporate America has made this response all too typical. Indeed, it is reflected throughout this book. Very few of the women I spoke with would agree to allow their real names to be used. In some instances, when they criticized their employers, or revealed personal details of their own lives, their concerns were understandable. But even women whose questions or comments appeared the most innocuous were afraid to disclose their identities. One reporter at a major national newspaper, for example, had recently had a child and had decided to work part-time as a result. She was happy with her "deal" and had begun to question the time demands of an institution in which people worked ten- to fourteen-hour days routinely. Although she knows many other women — and probably many other men — share her concerns, she was nonetheless unwilling to come out publicly and suggest that perhaps professionals need to consider working a few hours less a week.

Women's unwillingness to allow their names to be associated with a book that illuminates the problems of the workplace is, of course, not the real problem. What is, is their fear, sometimes justified, sometimes not, to openly talk about and act on their complaints in the workplace. Women do not keep totally mum about the problems described here. In private conversations with one another they will share their complaints. Similarly, they may also speak out at meetings and seminars outside of the workplace. But it is only when such private or sheltered conversations become part of a more public conversation within the workplace or society — when private knowledge becomes public knowledge — that collective action for change is possible. But creating this kind of public conversation has become more and more difficult, not simply in the workplace, but in the larger society as well, because the rules that teach women how to retreat from the exercise of voice have also affected their behavior as citizens of the nation as well as of the corporation. Many professional women I talked with had become so individualized that they had totally opted out of the political process and did not engage in any kind of political activity that would help bring about change in the regional or national political arena.

For some, the generalized depoliticization and privatization of the Reagan years, combined with the messages of their own employers and equal-opportunity feminism, seems to have stifled all recognition that they could help themselves and other women through political action. Over and over again, I asked the women I interviewed, as well as women to whom I have lectured in colleges and professional organizations over the past several years, whether they vote, whether they belong to any women's or other political group, whether they have ever written a letter to a congressional or local or state representative to register their support of care-related programs that would make their lives easier — like national parental leave legislation, more money for quality childcare, health care, or education. Many women do vote. But too many don't bother to. Very few are active in political organizations. Nor do many even take the five minutes necessary to write a letter or make a phone call in support of care-related legislation.

All of this reflects the despair and or apathy so many feel about political action. Because our government provides almost no programs — apart from Social Security — that help *all* citizens deal with their many human needs, women, like many other Americans, consider government beneficence to be no more than what Emerson once called a "trick." When it comes to government aid, we don't just have lowered expectations, we have disappearing expectations: we look to either our employers or the ideology of self-help and self-management as the only solution to our problems.

This solution, however, is only part of the problem. After years of begging corporations to be kinder and gentler, we have not advanced as far as we could have and should have. After two decades of self-help we ourselves still feel helpless. As one professional told me, learning to "manage one's time more efficiently does not, after all, add another four or five hours to the day." Unfortunately, when we confront these realities, we do not tend to reexamine our ideas about the potential of government; we tend instead to retreat into resignation, apathy, or anger. When someone suggests that there may be collective solutions to our individual ills, we may dismiss them with the oft repeated insistence that "no one can really make a difference," or with the claim that a phone call, letter, vote, or other political activity is "only a drop in the bucket." And even taking the five minutes involved in making one's voice and preference heard may not seem to be an ordinary act of citizenship but rather an extraordinary amount of futile work.

What is perhaps saddest is that some of the few women who were the most politically aware and sensitive said that because of time constraints, they had chosen not to be politically active. Maureen Kennedy says she was "a fighter" in her college days and was involved in a number of feminist organizations. But she quickly discovered that she can't belong to those organizations and do well in her career, too. "I don't have a moment in my day now. If I wanted to help women get better childcare, it would cut into either my family or my career. So I decided not to do that."

Perhaps the most illustrative case is that of scientist Helen Faulkner. Extremely articulate and progressive, Faulkner is from South Africa and has seen one of the worst systems of discrimination at work in her native land. Moreover, of the ten years she has spent working at a large scientific institute, Helen Faulkner says that the first five were dedicated to an incessant battle with a male professor who "hired me because he was appreciative of my talent, but who was, on the other hand, very jealous of my success."

Faulkner's problems arose when she was denied tenure. First, her superior rejected her request, and then, after a protracted political battle in which she managed to gain overriding support, the decision was reversed. Throughout the three-year ordeal, Faulkner says, it was her husband's support that kept her going. For her, as for so many men, her family has been a haven in a heartless world. "If I hadn't been able to go home to my husband and share with him my experiences and hear him telling me, 'You're worth more than this,' I would have been crushed. The same is true of my children. Without the soft, gentle, warm children, I might have been broken."

Faulkner says this fight has made her much harder, but she nonetheless recognizes the need to support the people who work in her lab. "I feel about the people in my lab the way I do about my family. I want them to feel good, and I want to get to know them. I feel mutual love and respect makes people maximally productive, although that's not why I am close to them.

"I don't think the definition of a successful woman precludes relationships," Faulkner adds, conceding, however, that the time demands of a professional career do tend to interfere with relationships. "In the competition to prove myself, the only thing I absolutely have to do is turn out top-quality work. That's the driving force. So I don't think it's at the expense of relationships. Career does sometimes interfere as one becomes more and more successful and the profession places more demands upon one, so that you get busier and busier. And that's where the time issue creeps in." There's a trade-off in human contacts, Faulkner says, not because success means that one has to be like a man, but because time constraints inhibit social interaction.

What has really suffered is political activity to help others. Having lived in and traveled extensively through other countries that have implemented progressive family- and work-related social policies, she knows that it is possible for the state to play a positive role in helping employees solve both their personal and professional needs. Faulkner is exactly the kind of bright, aware, and sensitive woman upon whose competitive advances many early feminists pinned their hopes for progress in the care agenda. Faulkner does not reject that agenda — at least not personally. But she explains that she has made a very conscious decision to sacrifice activity in its service to the demands of her career.

"I tend not to make an issue in general of the male/female thing," she says candidly. "I don't belong to any women's groups. I tend to think doing it by example is the most worthwhile way of doing it." On the other hand, she recognizes the problems women have in the United States will change only if women together engage in collective political activity. "I feel disappointed in the United States on work-family issues. I feel disappointed that in a country like this, it's a privilege of the rich to have their children adequately taken care of. I think the situation has become so serious that the only way it's going to be solved is politically."

Such political action, she knows, may depend on the leadership or participation of women like herself. But she is simply not prepared to provide it. "You know," she elaborates, "one of the products of a high-powered commitment is selfishness. Whereas when I was a graduate student, I was active on a whole number of issues, both political and personal, I am not for this period of my life."

She has made, she says, a deliberate choice between career and citizenship. "Absolutely. I think that the sacrifice is one of social interaction and social commitment." Although she says she hopes that will change, she has no plans to alter her priorities in the near future.

What Ethel Klein observed in her book *Gender Politics* seems to be true of a number of professional women: "People with a strong sense of personal competence are most likely to engage in direct action, because they believe their efforts can be instrumental. Yet successful people can also be more reticent to acknowledge discrimination. Having effectively handled their own lives, they favor individual or conventional political efforts rather than collective action to solve problems."[15]

The simultaneous resurrection of the ideology of success, coupled with the integration of women into market society has thus done great damage to one of transformative feminism's central political insights — "the personal is political." In the context of the mass political movement out of which it grew, this progressive slogan directed women toward an exploration of their personal lives viewed through the prism of a political analysis of patriarchy. Although it advocated an intense scrutiny of our personal lives, it did not, however, intend to substitute subjectivism or narcissistic self-involvement for political action. Indeed, because the political was so deeply embedded in the personal, transformative feminists recognized that political change had to be coupled with personal change if women's lives — and the society in which those lives are lived — were to be significantly transformed.

Ironically — and through no fault of the transformative feminists who developed and fought for change within both the personal and political spheres — women's very liberation into America's major institutions has subverted the highly political, collectivist core of this crucial feminist insight and project. By withdrawing women from both a rich personal life and a political life, corporate America and equal-opportunity feminism have borrowed from the subjectivist ethic of the human potential movement and directed women toward a highly narcissistic definition of self-fulfillment.

Rather than amplifying the political with the personal, corporate America and equal-opportunity feminism have reduced the political to the purely personal — to personal advancement and career. As we have seen in the previous chapter and will see in those that follow, many women have been taught to believe that their very success in moving ahead in their careers is a political act. Such career advancement may well be a political act — if it is supplemented by participation in a political movement for the good of the majority. When it comes to be seen as a substitute for such action, the personal, in fact, subverts the political, and in the process personal fulfillment may actually erode.

In many respects, the women I describe in this chapter have made great strides. They have good jobs, and most of them enjoy their work. Although their incomes and promotional possibilities may lag behind those of a minority of elite, white male professionals, they earn excellent salaries and are regularly promoted. In short, these women are faring far better than the majority of women and men in our society. Their accomplishments are a great victory for the women's movement. Indeed, the fact that professional women have advanced as far as they have is a direct result of centuries of collective struggle.

But if women want to advance their caring agendas — as well as themselves — through the glass doors and the glass ceiling of corporate culture, collective action is the only solution. No matter how successful heroic individual women are at changing things in their offices, units, or labs, when it comes to affecting broad institutional norms and activities, the power of any lone individual is severely limited. Although the American success ethic and its companion philosophy of the power of positive thinking would have us believe otherwise, we learn the lessons of reality every day when we go to work.

Only together can women make a difference. But over and over again, the women I spoke with revealed that they had been taught to eliminate the very idea of collective action from their imaginative vocabulary. The only possibility most could imagine was adaptation or exit.

The tragedy is that these are not real solutions. For the past decade we have obeyed the injunction that we should play by the rules and not rock the boat — proving that we are as committed to marketplace imperatives as men have always been. And yet, according to most reports, no matter how much we sacrifice to the marketplace, male employers still view women, as a recent report by the consulting company Catalyst stated, "as having less career commitment than men . . . and as less likely to take the same initiatives and risks as men in the company."

Although some would say that this demonstrates that we must

work even harder at emulating men, I would argue the contrary: we have to work harder to fight for what we want — as women who care as well as compete. Women have slowly begun to sow the seeds for change within the structures of corporate America. Our very presence in the marketplace is testament to the power of sisterhood. We have also changed the nature of the social and political debate in our workplaces and in society. So-called work-family issues are now hotly discussed in corporate boardrooms and in Congress. Many corporations have set up "human relations" offices designed to improve interpersonal communications and create a more sympathetic environment. Many hire work-family consultants to discuss childcare, elder care, and parental leave benefits. Although most of these departments and consultants do not challenge the corporate bottom line, and some serve simply as window dressing, other programs and efforts are more sincere.

What we must do is take advantage of any corporate openings and press from the bottom to the top of the corporate hierarchy for change. We must add our voices to those of personnel and human resources directors and staffs as well as outside consultants and become a lobbying force from within.

Similarly, we need to reconsider the strategy of exit. Exit is, of course, a form of protest, but an extremely ineffective one. It leaves the field entirely open to men, or to those women who have abandoned care or who have purchased their way out of their caring dilemmas and who have little sympathy for those who can't do the same. What is perhaps more unfortunate is that exit denies women the power they could, in fact, wield as a force for change both inside and outside the workplace.

The fact is, our marketplace society, if pushed, is more amenable to change than we believe. We may not be able to break the "iron rules" of the market, but if women join together, as they did over two decades ago, we may be able to round off its sharpest edges and do the important work of taming the American marketplace. Through national legislation that establishes and enforces our entitlement to be cared for and care for others, as well as company policies that acknowledge these entitlements, we can begin to push those doors open that have already been unlocked and force our jailers to unlock still others.

What is clear is that if women do not begin to act collectively for change, they will continue in the paradoxical position so many of us are in today. We will be both locked in and locked out, and the market will continue to turn our own very important dreams into hopeless utopian fantasies.

Chapter Five

THE CRISIS
OF WOMEN'S WORK

THE ROOM is standard medical modern with buff-colored walls, large plate-glass windows, a blackboard, and gently humming fluorescent lights. About fifteen men and women in their late twenties and early thirties — some dressed in requisition white, others in surgical green, some in street clothes — sit on aluminum scoop-backed chairs around a long conference table. Chatting amiably, they occasionally reach for red-and-white containers of Chinese take-out food and refill their plastic plates.

These doctors and nurses (the latter all female, the former not quite equally divided by sex) at the Hospital of the University of Pennsylvania's Medical Intensive Care Unit meet periodically to discuss the medical/caregiving issues that unite, perplex, anger, and, at times, separate them. After an hour-long discussion, the men and women in the group begin drifting back to the center of the unit, where ten patients hooked up to a baffling array of ventilators, IVs, catheters, and digital monitors lie in varying degrees of semisuspended animation as technology takes over the processes of life their bodies have abandoned.

Pat Wallace, a clinical nurse specialist, and two female residents, Judy Carpenter and Judy Glickman, linger behind, talking. Such a conversation is all too rare among female doctors and nurses — these women are talking about their interactions with their patients, their dealings with one another as superiors and subordinates, and, most importantly, their relationships with one another as newly liberated women who have moved into one of the rougher neighborhoods of the masculine universe — competitive, technological medicine.

I have come into their world to find out what has happened to women who have entered high-powered male professions. And to determine, as well, how women's liberation has affected those who continue to do women's traditional work.

As we sit around the table, I am, at first, the traditional interlocutor, the outsider who intrudes temporarily in someone else's routine. But quickly I become a catalyst, inadvertently creating the opportunity for these women to relate not only to me but, through me, to each other.

An observer might imagine that because we are all women, such moments are not the exception but the rule; that female nurses and physicians are bound to one another by the very masculineness of the setting in which they work; and that, unlike the traditional male doctor and female nurse, they help and support one another. It might also be assumed that these women are united against discrimination and unfair rules, that they are staunch challengers of notions of hierarchy that would divide them and critics of the practices that would turn them against the kind of affiliative, relational work women have done for centuries.

But the story I hear contradicts all these comforting assumptions.

"There are times when I wonder about my choice of career," says Judy Carpenter, a twenty-eight-year-old resident. "Times when I think I should have become a nurse. I like being a supportive person, rather than a controlling, decision-making person. I like the relationships I see nurses having with patients because I know that's what makes patients get better. We all know there's more to getting better than diagnosing and giving medication and performing operations." But, she explains, "I don't have time to relate to patients as people." Indeed, her fatigue has become an almost permanent feature of her gaze.

Her worries about relationships with her patients and colleagues are long-standing. "They begin when you're a medical student," she recalls. "You're not a real doctor, but residents are asking you to act like a doctor, and that means giving orders to nurses who are usually more experienced than you."

"The thing that bothers me so much," says Judy Glickman, a twenty-eight-year-old intern who plans to go into psychiatry, "is the undertones of an adversarial relationship between doctors and nurses. We all have our jobs to do in taking care of patients. I don't think my job as a physician is any more important than theirs as nurses. But I don't think most physicians understand that, because they don't understand what nurses do. Communication and collaborative skills are not taught in medical school."

"Yes," Judy Carpenter agrees. "I remember my husband's chief resident warning him because he was being too friendly with the nurses."

Pat Wallace smiles. "It's funny," she says, "because what I notice is the difference between how male doctors treat you as women and the way they treat other men." As a woman, she is clearly on their side, but the doctors' medical training has taught them to ignore such signals from other women. "What they tell you in medical school, before you go into the hospital, is that as a woman you're at a disadvantage dealing with other women; that male medical students and doctors have an easier time dealing with nurses because they can flirt with them. But as a woman you can't do that. And so you come in here on the defensive. You're insecure. You have to establish your authority. You can't ask for help because nurses will lose confidence in you."

Would they? I ask Pat Wallace. "Of course not," she says, smiling at the absurdity of the idea. "Our common goal is the care of the patient, not boosting our egos. As long as the patient remains at the head of the list, I don't care how many questions are asked."

"But that's not what we learn," Judy Carpenter reiterates. "All I was ever taught about nurses in medical school is what a resident once told us: you'd better get along with the nurses because if you don't they can *hurt* you."

In their long overdue discussion, these women are grappling with an unexpected and unwelcome paradox. More women than ever before have been liberated to move into professions traditionally reserved for men. When women moved into the marketplace, many of us believed, we would teach American society to recognize that economic exchange and the accumulation of wealth are not the only human imperatives. Care is also a fundamental human imperative that must be obeyed by all of humanity, not just half of it. Thus, we hoped to teach men to value caring, to share in women's caring work in the home and workplace, and to support truly care-centered programs in the political arena.

That's because most women have long recognized that without care there is no life, no such thing as human society. Caring and being cared for is the common link between people who share "membership in a common humanity that not only loves, competes, aspires, wins, consumes and gets promoted, but suffers and gets sick," say Patricia Benner and Judith Wrubel, authors of *The Primacy of Caring.*[1]

While caring, in and of itself, does not, in fact, require total self-sacrifice and abnegation, it does, as Nel Noddings, author of *Caring: A Feminine Approach to Ethics and Moral Education*, observes, involve a "move away from the self" and a commitment to act on behalf of another. That commitment involves different levels of intensity. It may be, says Noddings, a deep immersion in the problems of someone extremely close to you, or a less acute sense of responsibility toward those whom we've never met. "Even with those close to me," Noddings explains, "the intensity of caring varies: it may be calm and steady most of the time and desperately anxious in emergencies."[2]

No matter how tempered or intense, the empathy that is a prerequisite of caring, as the great psychiatrist Heinz Kohut has written, "is the accepting, confirming and understanding human echo, the psychological nutriment without which human life, as we know and cherish it, could not be sustained."[3]

But in our society, the very project of human caring has been compromised.

We see this in the collapse of our social contract, in the mean-spirited debates about social spending that dominate recent political discussions, in the rise of infant mortality and childhood poverty, the health care crisis and plight of the homeless and elderly, as well as the laments of working parents who want to have more time to care. But there is nowhere where we see it more clearly than in what has happened to women's attitudes toward traditional caring work.

Over the past decade, the marketplace has invaded what has traditionally been the public, caring sector of our society — the caring professions of education, social work, and nursing. The policies of the Reagan and Bush administrations have unleashed us as economic actors and attempted to deregulate those institutions of society concerned with the provision of goods and the accumulation of wealth. While they have injected bottom-line concerns with profit and performance into all the caring professions, our public policies have increasingly limited us as caring actors, regulating ever more tightly the provision of care. This deliberate starving of the caring professions has exacerbated their traditional low pay, poor working conditions, and limited opportunities for advancement.

At the same time, more and more American women have been encouraged to embrace the very marketplace values that have always denigrated care. New female images of success, like their masculine counterparts, preclude work in the caring professions. "If I were to say I wanted to become a nurse or an elementary school teacher," says a freshman at Wellesley College, "my professors and fellow students would think I was crazy. To them it would be like saying I wanted to be a janitor."

"People look at you and ask, 'Why would someone as intelligent as you become a nurse? Why didn't you become a doctor?' " a nurse at Boston's Beth Israel Hospital recounts. "I always turn to them and say, 'and aren't you glad someone as intelligent as I became a nurse and is here to take care of you?' But those kinds of comments get to you after a while."

The fact that there has been an exodus from the caring professions and that new recruits are not entering them is thus far more than a result of pecuniary calculation. The market has invaded women's attitudes toward care — imbuing us all with America's traditional suspicion of altruism and its emphasis on radical individualism.

"The entire premise of the pick-yourself-up-by-your-own-bootstraps ideology is that you are responsible for pulling yourself up — you don't need someone to help you," says Christopher S. Allen, a professor of political science at the University of Georgia. "In other industrialized societies, the knowledge that in a lifetime everyone will need help from others, and assistance from the government in getting those needs met, is deeply embedded in the social fabric. It can be measured, for example, by the way that money is spent on health care and other human needs. In America, our idea of progress is not that government will help people meet such needs, but that we can somehow banish or find the ultimate cure for those needs."

Until recently, America was able to undervalue caring work, while simultaneously ensuring that caregiving was widely available. This was because women provided this essential social service. "If we consider the labor that makes all human life possible, even in market-dominated societies, we mainly find the labor that women are obligated to perform: bearing and raising children, keeping house, and managing effective social relationships," says sociologist Diane R. Margolis. "Those labors have become the women's work that is never done. They remain obligations, tied to the circle of human relationships and fueled by human propensities to create emotional ties."

Today women still comprise the majority of those in the caring professions. We are 97 percent of the nation's nurses; 97 percent of its childcare workers; 73 percent of all its teachers (but 97.8 percent of its pre-K and kindergarten and 84 percent of its elementary school teachers); and 68 percent of its social workers.[4]

Our traditional women's work has always been denied respect. But over the past several decades, it has suffered from three interconnected trends: most significant has been the severe erosion of fiscal support, resulting from the Reagan and now the Bush administration attack on the public sector; the market's invasion of the caring professions; and some American women's overvaluation of high-powered professional work.

Ask anyone in the caring professions, anyone who has recently left caring work, or the young people who might be contemplating such a career, and they will tell you that one reason the caregiving professions are unattractive is that caring has become too expensive.

During the 1960s and 1970s, educational requirements for the caring professions were less stringent, and government funds were available for scholarships, research grants, and student loans. With lower costs for higher education and tuition help available, young people could get a relatively inexpensive education and still survive on the modest salaries prevalent in the "helping professions."

But throughout the 1980s, funding for students seeking higher education was cut, and what little remains has come under constant attack. At the same time, the costs of higher education have escalated. Today, a future caregiver can expect to pay between $9,000 and $10,000 a year for an average program, and up to $21,000 a year for a program at a top-notch college or university.

Moreover, the nation now imposes much higher educational demands on its caregivers. In nursing, three-year diploma programs are being phased out and hospitals are increasingly seeking candidates with four-year degrees for entry-level positions. Today most teachers, social workers, and nurses must have master's or Ph.D. degrees to advance in their professions. But the financial assistance they need to pay for this higher education is no longer forthcoming. In 1989, President Bush — the so-called education president — proposed about $441 million in new educational programs, but he cut and consolidated others, making no allowance for inflation. The United States ranks thirteenth out of fifteen industrialized nations in the percentage of overall spending devoted to education. As a representative of the National Education Association put it, "We're pretty disappointed with his proposals. His budget is even worse than his predecessor's."

The much publicized tax revolt that has swept states like California and Massachusetts has also affected all caregivers who work in the public sector. Citizens' refusal to pay higher property taxes — which in many states fund the public school systems and local social services — has meant that public employees' salaries are sharply limited. Fiscal restraint has also deprived caregivers of the kind of job security that was a traditional compensation for low wages and lack of status.

When the Commonwealth of Massachusetts passed its famous Proposition 2½ in 1981, about 10,000 teachers were laid off. Over the next few years, the state allocated aid to Massachusetts cities and towns and earmarked education funds for poorer communities and school systems, who were able to rehire a great many teachers. When, however, the state began to suffer its well-publicized fiscal crisis in 1989 and 1990, education was once again hard-hit. School departments began to lay off dozens of teachers. In order to keep their jobs, many have had to change specialties: a math teacher may be forced to switch to science, a Spanish teacher to physical education. And even then, a pink slip may await them at the end of the year, a cruel reward for years of dedication.

As wages have been depressed, work loads have increased. Nurses today carry caseloads that include higher proportions of acutely ill patients, and they need far more education to deal with the medical technology used to treat them. Schoolteachers are expected to serve as moral guides to students whose families or communities have abandoned the job. Social workers have far heavier caseloads as their role in protecting the young and the elderly from abuse and neglect has expanded.

As the demands of those in need have grown dramatically, the imperatives of the marketplace set the priorities in caring professions that are increasingly administered by economic managers and whose judgments are governed by bottom-line concerns. According to Burton Gummer, a professor of social welfare at the State University of New York at Albany, for administrators, policy makers, corporate and political leaders, "the concept of effectiveness, or how well something is done, pales next to its companion idea of efficiency, or how inexpensively it's done."[5] The idea that the goal of caring is to help others develop, to empower them, or to change the social context in which they live has been supplanted by competitive, bottom-line goals.

The kinds of comments that political leaders make about education illustrate the general ethos that orders priorities in all the caring professions. "A better-educated citizenry is the key to the continued growth and prosperity of the United States," said participants at a recent national summit. "We must have an educated work force, second to none, in order to succeed in an increasingly competitive world economy."[6] Although leaders refused to allocate any more funds for education, they nonetheless sought to achieve "the maximum possible return from our investments in the nation's education system," and President Bush declared that we need "tougher standards and a results-oriented system."

Our health care system is now increasingly dominated by for-profit hospitals and health maintenance organizations owned and run by large hospital corporations. Like most of those who manage private corporations, their managers are far more preoccupied with the maximization of short-term profit than the long-term provision of care. Similarly, private insurance corporations and corporate-influenced government managers now dictate how and when care is to be delivered and to whom.

Given these attitudes about caregiving, it is not surprising that young people today take the same bottom-line approach in making their decisions about potential careers. Incurring between $40,000 and $80,000 worth of educational loans to enter a field like child-care, where the average annual salary is $12,000 to $15,000, simply does not make economic sense. Average national starting salaries for nurses were approximately $23,488 in 1989. Average beginning salary for nurse practitioners was $28,698, while the average maximum for an experienced R.N. was $35,330. A teacher with fifteen years of experience and a master's degree averages $31,315 a year;* a social worker with an M.S.W. who works in a public service agency may make $25,400. "Caring professionals may have complied with unrealistic demands before the advent of the women's movement," says Diane R. Margolis. "But things are changing. Now, because there are more occupational choices for female professionals, teachers, nurses, and social workers are a lot less likely to go on sacrificing when the communities around them reject even the most minimal sacrifices themselves."

Many feminists had hoped that women's entrance into the marketplace would combat, if not revolutionize, society's attitudes toward the caring professions. They had hoped to expand women's

---

*According to the American Federation of Teachers, salaries have more than tripled since 1972. Unfortunately, however, when adjusted for inflation, they have actually risen by only $68 since that year.

job opportunities and grant greater respect and financial reward to women doing traditional caring work. But, as we shall see, this has not happened. In part this is because American society, in the Reagan and post-Reagan era, has been increasingly resistant to nonmarket concerns. But I am convinced that the current crisis also has its roots in the ambivalent attitude toward caring and the caring professions displayed by equal-opportunity feminism and many individual women.

Women committed to the struggle for formal equality with men have always had a complex relationship to women's work — from mothering to women's work outside the home. Many feminists have consistently fought for greater respect and remuneration for women's work. In recent years a number of feminist researchers and scholars — Jean Baker Miller, author of *Toward a New Psychology of Women*, and Susan Reverby, author of *Ordered to Care: The Dilemma of American Nursing*, among others — have written extensively about the important social role of women's nurturing, empowering activities both inside and outside the home.

But these scholarly studies have generally been overshadowed by a more popular tendency among women to adopt traditionally male attitudes toward "women's work." Many women now view women's work outside the home merely as an extension of women's work inside the home. And to them, liberation involves an escape from the "constraints" of both the former and the latter. "Because our society has undervalued women's work, a crucial component of that work — giving of one's self — has been distorted into the demand for endless self-sacrifice," says Isabel Marcus, a feminist scholar and professor of law at the University of Buffalo. "While many advocates of equal rights for women recognize the need to revalue work in the helping professions, they have generally identified with male definitions of power, status, and significant activity in the world. Rather than fighting to transform the cultural context that imposes such conditions on women's work, these women — while giving lip service to the idea that women's work is 'important' — have embraced male models of success and seem to believe that success consists of being a leader, not a follower, in traditional male fields of employment."

As social observer Barbara Ehrenreich points out, most social debates in the United States have focused on the lives and problems of those middle- and upper-middle-class men and women who had the greatest chance of becoming leaders rather than followers.[7] This has been no less true of feminism than of any other social movement. Taking the experiences of this male elite as her point of departure, Betty Friedan defined important work — work that demands "energy, initiative and ambition" — as work in traditionally male fields of employment. Although she did not specifically target the caregiving professions, the demeaning language she used to describe caregiving in women's maternal work could easily be construed to tar all nurturing with the same negative brush.

Throughout *The Feminine Mystique*, women's nurturing activities are associated with passivity and narcissism. They are, to use Friedan's words, "parasitic," "trivial" pursuits. If women were to prove they were not "useless," they would have to begin their "journey away from home," leaving behind "an immaturity that has been called femininity" to achieve a full human identity." For Friedan, the path to this full human identity traverses the peaks of the masculine landscape, where women could work in areas that "demand initiative and energy," competing to become Einsteins and Fermis, Edisons and Fords.[8]

Echoing these themes in an essay in *Woman in Sexist Society*, Doris Gold declares that women are generally involved in "busy-work," and that women's education in the home and helping professions "leaves many with vague talents and no skills."[9]

Some American feminists have also failed to emphasize the value of caring work in their theories and public discussions because they, understandably, fear that any widespread attempt to revalue women's caring work will be manipulated by conservative forces. Many believe that making compelling arguments about the human need for care, our mutual obligation to care for one another, or women's historical insights into caring and caregiving will be used to impose the duty to care on one half of humanity and one half only. Women will, therefore, be dragged back into

the home, once again to be confined to domestic slavery of "sub-
servience" in the caring professions.*

They do not redefine caring on their own terms. Instead of fighting to improve the conditions in the caring professions, and working to revalue caring in the society so that men and women share
the obligation to care, they either avoid the subject, defend women
against the obligation to care, or bypass the whole dilemma by
concentrating on helping them move into traditional jobs in the
masculine marketplace.

No wonder, then, that many women who were proud to be engaged in women's work felt that mainstream feminism was — and
sometimes still is — hostile to their interests. Observes Joan Lynaugh, an associate professor of nursing at the University of Pennsylvania, "For many feminists, nursing and other caregiving
professions were part of the problem. Those feminists who were
seeking some kind of parity with men saw these activities as part
of the social body that had accommodated to the dominant, white-
male value system. That's why, in the early days, so many nurses
felt very put down by feminists. And for a long time it meant that
many nurses didn't seek much affiliation with the women's movement and its goals."

Our inability to liberate women's traditional work from patriarchy's firm ideological grasp, as we have tried to liberate ourselves
from its occupational constraints, has resulted in a profound division within feminism and among women. Aside from those important transformative feminists who value and act upon the
caring imperative, women's caregiving work has become a negative standard against which we measure our progress. Our progress, that is, is charted in the distance women have traveled *away*
from caregiving work, and *toward* traditional male activities and
preoccupations. In the process, women's professional options have
been, paradoxically, narrowed.

For example, in her book *Remaking Motherhood: How Working Mothers Are Shaping Our Children's Future*, Anita Shreve

*European feminists have often criticized their American sisters for their at-
titudes toward care. Many have felt that American feminists failed to value wom-
en's caring work for fear of a conservative backlash and thus did not do the
important work of acknowledging and revisioning care.

interviews nineteen working mothers and asks them about their hopes for their daughters. Only one of them considers motherhood as an option for her daughter, and none considers a career in women's work to be something worthwhile or important.

Jayne, a forty-one-year-old architecture critic, is representative of these new and improved female values. "My girls assume they will always work. . . . I've found in my experience that women who have careers have greater self-esteem than women who stay home and don't have work. I also think one's expectations are important. If you grow up thinking you'll be a doctor, you won't be a nurse. You'll be a lawyer maybe, but you won't be a paralegal."[10]

In her best-selling how-to manual *Women Who Love Too Much*, Robin Norwood, whose work has reached millions of women, advises us to look out for "number one" and to avoid caring too much — either for the men we love or for anyone else. Rather than viewing a commitment to caring in the helping professions as the basis for positive forms of human interaction, Norwood equates caring with neurosis and emotional weakness. "Having received little nurturing yourself, you try to fill this unmet need vicariously by becoming a care giver." She writes, "In general, we become care givers in most, if not all, areas of our lives. Women from dysfunctional homes (and especially, I have observed, from alcoholic homes) are overrepresented in the helping professions, working as nurses, counselors, therapists and social workers."[11]

And, of course, *Working Woman* magazine — the bible of equal-opportunity feminism — runs frequent articles attacking caregiving work. In its July 1988 issue *Working Woman* catalogued the twenty-five hottest careers for women and warned them away from the ten worst. At the top of the *avoid* list were nursing, teaching, and social work.[12] In another article, entitled "Great Transformations," four immaculately dressed professional women were honored for abandoning the teaching profession. "Consider them profiles in career courage," writes Beverly Kempton. "Each of these four women abandoned the teaching profession to embark on a career alien to her background. They moved on, but they did not abandon their former selves. Over time, their teaching skills evolved into management skills, forming the bedrock of a new career. The risks were great, but the rewards even greater: excite-

ment, money, challenges, opportunities. Today these career chang-
ers are proof that disciplined adventurers — be they teachers or
bankers — can do the same."[13]

In a recent Hers column in the *New York Times Magazine*,
feminist Letty Cottin Pogrebin joined the assault on caring. Referring to accounts of marriages and engagements in local newspapers, she applauded "women's professional progress and growing
autonomy." "Today's announcements present brides who are lawyers, doctors, corporate vice presidents, financial analysts, marketing managers, bankers, management consultants, business
owners, computer specialists, editors, psychologists, curators, ath-
letic coaches, veterinarians, and chefs. (Nurses, secretaries and
teachers are few and far between — mirroring the shortage of
nurses, secretaries and teachers in the labor force.)"

According to Pogrebin, it is when women enter male professions
that they can be equal to men. "Wedding announcements also
proclaim the new reality of male-female equality. He's a radiolo-
gist, she's a cardiologist. . . . He's at Citicorp and she's at Bankers
Trust. In other words, they are peers. They share common interests
and workloads, understand each other's tensions and dreams."[14]
Apparently nurses and doctors, teachers and stockbrokers,
whether the caregiving partner be male or female, are incapable
of this kind of understanding and empathy. To be together, we all
have to be the same — elite professionals in formerly male occu-
pations.

Given this social context, it is not surprising that equal-
opportunity feminism has had such a negative impact on the caring professions and on those women who have always done caring
work. Let us look more closely at what has happened to women's
caring work.

Although mothering is not a "profession," as such, it provides
the ground for women's work. Once the majority and the norm,
full-time mothers are now a frequently ignored and undervalued
part of the country's work force. This is, in part, because the
media, which shape our ideas, focus on what's new, and what's
new in our culture is that an unprecedented number of American
women are remaining in the work force after having children.

But the media also reflect the prevailing view that "real" work is something that, by definition, goes on outside the home. The marketplace is the "real world"; the family and community are not. The woman's role as nurturer in the latter arena has long been undervalued — especially by men. But today, many working women and promoters of equal-opportunity feminism seem to have incorporated this disparaging attitude in their own think- ing — viewing the twelve million American women who devote their energy, creativity, judgment, and organizational abilities to child rearing and housework as "wasting their lives," "doing noth- ing at all," or as "just mothers."

Such prejudices (and slights) disturb many stay-at-home moth- ers. When Priscilla Howland, a forty-one-year-old mother of three, introduces herself at a dinner or cocktail party, she says she rarely volunteers that she is a full-time mother. Howland, who was a teacher before she had her daughter Amanda eleven years ago, did some substitute teaching in between having her children. But when her son Silas was born in 1985, she decided she simply didn't want to divide herself between two worlds. While she respects the choices of mothers who decide to work outside the home, she says not everyone understands her career choice.

"My friends who stay at home and I try to bolster each other's confidence. We assure each other that what we're doing is impor- tant. But today, a lot of people who work don't respect women who stay at home with children."

Susan Shattuck exchanged a high-powered career in broadcast- ing at CBS for full-time motherhood because she could not tolerate the lack of support and understanding for women with children in the world of network news.

Shattuck's career experience has made her extremely aware of the sacrifices as well as the rewards of full-time mothers. "First there's the financial risk," she says. "In today's economy, having only one income means you have to compromise a lot. Although we do have some savings, we have no college fund for the kids. And although my husband has sacrificed some of his career am- bitions to be with his family, he often has to work long hours.

"But I think the greatest risk for someone like me, who's had an exciting professional career, is the problem of being seen by people in the working world as not valuable. I encounter this all the time — particularly from mothers who have jobs outside the home. They think you couldn't work if you wanted to, that you aren't interesting, that you have nothing to say. All you do, they think, is eat bonbons all day and watch soap operas."

"As a result, for a lot of women, being a full-time mother just isn't a legitimate choice that a woman can consciously, happily make even if she can afford it," says Amelie Gelfand, a thirty-six-year-old mother. "I think a lot of people feel that women who stay at home do it because they can't succeed in the male world and still have a family. People feel you've chosen a lesser of the two worlds. And that's very unfair."

Of the classic caring professions, social work is an important example of what has happened to women's work in the workplace. Social work emerged in the late nineteenth century to deal with the problems of a rapidly industrializing society trying to integrate immigrants, rural Americans, and blacks into an increasingly urban marketplace. Because so many newly urbanized Americans suffered from the effects of poverty, racism, disease, and social dislocation, social workers concentrated not only on individual change and adaptation, but on social reform as well.[15]

According to Elizabeth Mulroy, director of the Human Services Management Program at the Boston University School of Social Work, "Fighting for social change has distinguished social work from psychology or psychiatry. Social workers have traditionally had a utopian view and been advocates for the disenfranchised. Our goal of social work is to empower the powerless and their communities to create a better world."

There have always been divisions within the profession over the best way to effect change — by focusing on individual therapy, or by dealing with the social context. But in the 1970s, many social workers began to pursue a strategy that led them away from broad social change. After gaining the individual licensure necessary to set up private practice and be reimbursed by third-party payers (the government and private insurance companies) for their services, these social workers began to adopt a fee-for-service model, eschewing work in social agencies in the public sector.

With the 1980s, this trend increased, and today it has become harder than ever to attract people into the public service agencies that once formed the core of the profession. "It's far more difficult today," says Mulroy, "to stay the course in public service agencies in an era when caregiving and social care are so devalued." Not only is there a dearth of qualified social workers in these fields, but many of those who remain are loath to engage in political activity to encourage a more equal distribution of social resources.

What happens when competitive concerns drive women's professional goals and their definitions of self-esteem? Forty-three-year-old Terri Davis provides a case study not only in the crisis of caring in general, but in the trends in her field over the last two decades. The native Georgian has driven through the city to meet me at my hotel in Atlanta. As we sit down to a late lunch, she apologizes in advance for any lapses in clarity. She was up half the night with her baby boy, she explains.

As she talks, however, it becomes evident that late parenting is only one of the pressures that burden her. It seems that the model of both professional and personal liberation she has chosen has become, instead, something of a prison.

Before I am even able to ask Davis preliminary questions about her background, she describes her major preoccupation — money and success. "Social workers serve, they don't make money," she announces abruptly. "That's been part of my growing up and my changing and being more open and free. I've learned to get for myself, and I've been surprised to see how successful I could be as I've been building my practice. I've felt more and more pressure to produce and make money."

Somewhat taken aback by her sudden transition to what she calls "moving beyond the ethic of service," I ask her to backtrack to her professional beginnings. She willingly obliges. Terri Davis became a feminist in college and started an abortion referral service. As a VISTA volunteer, she worked in community organizing. Then she enrolled in social work school and, after graduation, worked for a social service agency where she "earned next to nothing." After three or four years, with no savings and a failed marriage behind her, she came back to Atlanta, remarried, and became much more businesslike.

"When you grow up as a woman," she says, "you do for and

take care of. You make sacrifices. I lost that. I am much more oriented to getting for myself and being a success.

"Before, I would have worked for an agency and made twelve thousand a year, working up to twenty thousand a year. But that doesn't feel good. It feels like being taken advantage of."

What feels good now, she says, is "getting for myself. I think I feel the way a man feels. There are things that have to be done to the house. There is money I have to make. There is my son, who has to go to private school. There are demands on me, and I know that my husband does not have the potential to earn the kind of money I do. I feel pressure to produce. I don't have a choice. So I have to market myself, sell myself. I take on all kinds of speaking engagements all the time to keep up the numbers of people I'm going to see."

Davis insists that in her practice, and in her mothering, she is caring and giving. But she has redefined the content of caring in her work. Her therapeutic task, she says, is to help her women clients resolve, as she has done, their conflicts and guilt about "getting for themselves." Most of the people she treats have been raised to be traditional women. They are now successful, and feel guilty about it. "They're doing a lot at work and at home. They can't feel good about hiring a housekeeper. They haven't gotten to the point where it's okay not to do everything they were raised to do. Part of my task as a psychotherapist is to help them get rid of the conflict and feel good about themselves and enjoy their success."

Although, in theory, there seems little wrong in helping women unburden themselves, Davis seems less than reassuring as a role model. In the course of her moral journey, she seems to have discarded care, relationships, and community, layer by layer. During her college and graduate school years, she explains, she thrived on relationships. Now she has few friends. About the only group she has time for is a network of female psychotherapists who view themselves as businesswomen. They meet monthly to share resources, discuss insurance problems, and perfect the market strategies that will assure a steady flow of business. As she talks about her life "before" and "after," Davis describes her transformation.

Before, she saw herself as a member of a social movement and
a profession that emphasized the role of culture and social change
in personal transformation. Now, she believes that changing individuals is the most important thing she can do. As for her participation in the feminist movement, "I am grateful I was part of
the women's movement," she concludes. "It was at a time when I
needed to have support. With all the women I was involved with
we were strong enough to do what we needed to do. But I've internalized that. I've gotten stronger and tougher. I'm an asshole
of sorts," she says with a kind of bewildered pride. "I'm really
masculine. And I don't need the support and validation of the
women's movement or any movement like I used to."

Before, she cared; now, she feels she can't afford to. "I feel that
I should care more than I care now about those issues [women's
roles and social change] but they're not a priority for me. The
priority is dealing with me. I don't have time for that now. I don't
have time to be educated, I don't have time to know what's going
on in the world."

Before, she would have described herself as a caregiver, a person
in the profession of providing service. Now, she is a "businesswoman," and she looks upon the social problems that arise in the
world as just so much more business.

Although Davis is certainly not typical of all social workers,
many of whom have remained in the most demanding, least respected, and poorest paid areas of their profession, she is representative of a new breed.

"Today," says Elizabeth Mulroy, "those who aspire to work
where they are valued by the public tend to go into the private
sector or private practice, because there you are considered to be
more like a psychiatrist who is working with more prestigious individuals and groups and making money at it. You're living in a
competitive world, and competing with the professional elite.

"But working for the Department of Social Services or the Department of Public Welfare is considered to be caregiving to those
on the bottom social rung. In the era of the New Federalism, those
folks are considered to be at fault. We're back to blaming the
victim. If they're substance abusers, homeless, or poor, it's because
they haven't tried hard enough. And if you're a social worker and

you're working with those kinds of people, then you haven't tried hard enough. You're defined by those whom you serve, and if you serve those people, the public considers you to be as much a loser as they are."

In the teaching profession, the demoralization resulting from society's refusal to respect caring has reached an all-time high. Because of cuts in education budgets and taxpayer revolts, money for education is dwindling and teachers are being laid off in great numbers. Those who remain at their posts shoulder more and more caring responsibilities but get less help from parents and communities as they try to fulfill them. "It's overwhelming, what we're asked to do," says Mary Futrell, a teacher in Alexandria, Virginia, for almost thirty years and president of the National Education Association (N.E.A.) between 1983 and 1989.

Futrell and other teachers have become increasingly disheartened by the problems children bring with them to school.

Futrell tells story after story about the tragic condition in which children live today. There was the child who returned home from school to find out his parents had moved away. Teachers had to identify the social services that helped him until he found his family again. The child who never spoke out in class without putting his hand in front of his mouth. When Futrell told him to keep his hand down, he wouldn't; he was too ashamed of his rotting teeth. Or the child who used to hoard her snacks from school because she had no food at home.

"Today you have to spend time talking with kids. You have to put aside being a teacher and try to be a mentor or friend," she explains patiently. "For many kids school is the only stable corner in life, the only place where they get a kind word, or get treated with respect. The only place where a child knows that someone cares."

Although their caring duties have expanded, Futrell and many other teachers report that the public does not value or even understand the extent of the nurturing work they must do. "We now spend sixty percent of our time on the caring components of our job. But teachers are not judged by how they care for children, they're only judged on how they teach children to perform. No one seems to appreciate that you can't just give a child lessons."

Instead of valuing caring and appreciating the need to care for its caregivers, teachers feel what they receive from society is often only criticism. They are criticized because schools — not society — are not doing their job educating and caring for children. "People simply don't think about what it means to shoulder more and more burdens. We have to feel good about ourselves, if we're going to make children feel good about themselves." More and more of them are leaving the field and it's hard to find women or men who want to go into teaching. "A lot of people just don't want to put up with this and why should they?"

In the next five years, the nation will need 1.3 million new teachers. To ensure an adequate supply, school systems would have to hire 25 percent of all those students now in college graduating classes. In 1988, however, only 9.2 percent of all bachelor's degrees conferred were on college students in teacher education. Moreover, minority teachers are in even shorter supply. In 1980, minorities made up 12.5 percent of the teaching force. Today, 10 percent of all teachers and about 30 percent of all students come from minority groups. By the late 1990s, 33 percent or more of all students will be minorities. But, if current projections hold, because of low pay and status, fewer than 5 percent of all teachers will come from minority groups.[16]

"As a result of the civil rights and women's movements," says Futrell, "doors of opportunity that were closed thirty years ago are open today. So these social movements have had good outcomes and negative ones — for us. The problem is that nurses, teachers, and social workers are crucial to the community, but they work for poverty wages, and they're subject to constant criticism."

Why then, Futrell asks, would anyone want to go into teaching, particularly when society has not helped her or him to understand the value and challenges of the job. Futrell adds that recruiting minority women is even harder than recruiting middle- or upper-middle-class white women because companies who want to kill the proverbial two birds with one stone — hiring a minority as well as a woman — are especially aggressive in seeking female minority candidates for corporate positions with higher salaries.

Futrell speaks from a national podium, but teachers at the state and local level are no less eloquent about society's abandonment.

In Florida, Ann Smith, a forty-six-year-old veteran junior high school teacher, works in Daytona Beach. Ten thousand new teachers will be needed each year for the next decade to keep up with the state's growth. But both Florida Governor Bob Martinez and his mentor, President George Bush, are determined to keep education spending down.

Everyone wants schools and teachers, Smith says with frustration, but no one is willing to pay for them. And no one seems to understand the complexity of the teacher's job. "Everybody has gone to school," Smith observes, "so everybody thinks they could teach school. When you talk to parents, they don't understand why schools don't run better. People say, you only work ten and a half months a year. They think we get off work at three-thirty or four. People just don't understand that you need the summers to educate yourself, nor do they understand that you're not finished in the midafternoon. Today, because so many women work outside the home, you can't even begin making parent contacts until after six or seven at night."

Add to this the fact that teachers are inhibited from caring too much. Because there has been so much attention on child abuse, Smith relates, teachers have become prime targets of false accusations. "Teaching is a nurturing, caring profession. But today, it's dangerous to touch a child," Smith points out. "We're recommending that teachers not touch kids. That's a crying shame because some of these kids don't get any affection at home, so where will they get it?"

Teachers like Smith feel they are constantly under attack by a public that complains about the quality of education but does not bother to educate itself about what teachers really do. "Ten years ago, you'd have very few kids with learning disabilities. You didn't have that many kids who couldn't function and didn't know right from wrong. Today I have a class with a majority of kids with severe discipline and learning problems. These kids need individual attention, and I'm only one person. And I can't even imagine what's going to happen when we have to deal with all these crack babies who are not even in the system yet."

What Smith worries about is the tendency to practice defensive — rather than caring — teaching. "We are criticized because children aren't doing well on test scores. When you're constantly barraged with the accusation that your kids aren't doing well, and you have to get their test scores up, you start dealing defensively. You start worrying about documenting how you tried to get scores up rather than dealing with each child's individual needs."

In the scramble to address the cognitive needs of today's children, teachers feel that the public is embracing the wrong "solution" to the crisis of education. For example, some of the latest proposals for education in America would essentially turn public schools over to the business community. This "solution," caregivers insist, will not enhance but jeopardize caring because business's competition-oriented definitions of performance will dominate what will soon become the educational marketplace. And they will punish, not reward, teachers.

"In Illinois," says Lee N. Betterman, the president of the Illinois Education Association, "the Illinois Manufacturing Association has put forth a proposal to help the schools. The problem is it's vicious and punitive to teachers." Teachers whose only compensation for low pay and poor working conditions has been job security would lose that benefit under this proposal. "Business wants to do away with all teacher protections — tenure, seniority, security. I see a role for business," Betterman insists, "but this is not it."

What Betterman and others propose is a partnership, rather than a directorship, for and with business. Employers, she says, could donate equipment, like computers. A bank could give space for a classroom. Business could work with teachers to bring preschools into the public education system, thus solving a societal and corporate need for childcare. "This is not what business wants," Betterman says regretfully. "They do not want to be adjuncts and work with teachers. They want to be alternative educators. And this will not work."

The crisis in education has been considered a political, economic, or pedagogical crisis. But for this society, it represents a moral crisis of major proportions. "Morality isn't only about fairness and justice," says Harvard professor of education Carol Gilligan. "It's also about care and responsibility. What's happening in education is the disconnection of one generation of adults with one generation of children. A citizenry that is not interested in education has basically turned away from the future."

"The subliminal message that's sent to kids that are taught in school buildings that aren't well maintained, that do not have equipment that is up to date, whose classes are too large, is that you're not important," argues Rosanne Bacon, president of the Massachusetts Teachers Association. "And when parents sit around the dinner table each night and the conversation they hear is, 'I'm not going to pay more taxes, I don't care what it's for,' the message that they get is that school is not important and what they do at school is not important and the teachers who teach them don't matter."

Not surprisingly, many children hear this message and do what the adult world considers important, which is consume — toys, clothes, records, and sometimes drugs. Consider the implications of the name of the largest toy chain in America — Toys R Us — sociologist Diane Margolis suggests. If society is telling children that they are what they play with, caring for others may easily become meaningless.

The crisis in contemporary nursing offers perhaps the most devastating example of how America's traditional attitudes toward caring, combined with many women's new goals, have affected the caring professions. There are approximately 2.1 million nurses in the United States and, as of January 1988, 585,597 physicians. Despite the range of their responsibilities and the almost four-to-one ratio in favor of nurses, their important work is rendered all but invisible by the nation's obsession with medical heroics.

The fact is, nurses are the backbone of all hospitals, where 70 percent work. Physicians, on the other hand, are transients in the hospital system that they have dominated in the twentieth century. They admit patients, diagnose disease, devise treatment plans, and check to see that they are carried out. (Surgeons, of course, use hospitals as their workshops.) During an average hospital stay of five days, a patient might spend less than an hour with his or her physician.

In academic medical centers and most community hospitals,

doctors in training — usually called residents or house staff —
carry out the physicians' directions. They execute the diagnostic
and therapeutic regimen, order lab tests and X rays, monitor or
prescribe medication, check on results, and report to the attending
physician. Depending on their education program, they rotate in
and out of particular units, monthly or bimonthly.

Nurses take care of patients 24 hours a day, 7 days a week, 365
days a year. On units where physicians are on monthly or bimonthly rotations, nurses who specialize in a particular field —
psychiatry, critical care, pediatrics, or oncology, to name only a
few — remain year in and year out. While physicians in training
may be unfamiliar with particular machinery and generally do not
know the staffs of other hospital departments that work with their
own, nurses assure safety and continuity of care. Nurses, particularly those who work in hospitals, have developed a wide and
essential repertoire of technical knowledge and skills that enables
them to use complicated medical technology to detect and prevent
life-threatening events.

Moreover, in their dealings with patients, nurses focus not on
"disease," but on what Patricia Benner refers to as "illness — the
human experience of loss or dysfunction." To do this, nurses do
more than make sure the doctor's treatment plan is carried out.
They also assess a patient's basic needs and do for him or her
what the patient cannot do alone. In the modern medical universe,
this may mean helping the patient breathe, eat, turn over, and
eliminate, as well as helping with informed decisions pertaining to
his or her care and treatment.

Care involves working collaboratively with other caregivers —
social workers, occupational and physical therapists, and nutri-
tionists, as well as physicians — when the patient is in the hospital.
It involves teaching the patient how to care for himself or herself
after going home, and making sure it is safe for a patient to leave
the hospital — by arranging for visiting nurses or home health
aides and instructing family members in patient care. Finally, of
course, nurses help family members cope with a patient's medical/
emotional problems.

"Without nurses," professor of nursing Joan Lynaugh states
succinctly, "it's not safe to be in the hospital. If a hospital is open,

there are nurses in it. What nurses worry about is that distance between a patient's needs and his ability to take care of himself. Nurses fill in the gaps. Nurses are there to make sure that being in a hospital does not kill patients."

Ironically, whenever popular culture deals with the medical system, the important role of nursing is almost always trivialized or ignored altogether. On the other hand, the depiction of physicians — from Dr. Kildare to Marcus Welby to the doctors on "St. Elsewhere" — has always been far more favorable and equally unrealistic. On TV and in movies, physicians linger devotedly at their patients' bedsides and show interest in the intimate details of their lives. Nurses, meanwhile, make an occasional bedside appearance to take a temperature or monitor a heartbeat. Indeed, when television does give nurses equal time, the portrait is generally unflattering. Aaron Spelling Productions' recent prime-time TV series "Nightingales," which was killed as the result of a protest from American nurses, focused on a group of sexually promiscuous nursing students who were more interested in attending their exercise classes or seducing senior physicians than in caring for their patients' well-being. On an episode of "St. Elsewhere," a head nurse became so addicted to drugs she could not perform her duties. And when that series finally reckoned with feminism, it was again at the expense of nursing: a nurse who finally decided to assert herself did so by becoming a doctor.

The same imbalance is evident in bookstores. Numerous mass market books chart the intricacies of medical education and health care and describe the experiences of individual physicians. Nursing books, however, have been ghettoized in the textbook departments of academic publishers; as a result, the public rarely glimpses nursing's serious contributions to health care. And most news stories about health care totally ignore the fact that nurses are also health care experts and legitimate sources for insight, analysis, comment, and information.

Nurses' negative public image, low pay, lack of autonomy, and poor working conditions have combined to create one of the worst nursing crises in American history. The supply of registered nurses has doubled over the past three decades. But the spread of AIDS, the growing population of older Americans with chronic health

problems, the ever more complex needs of hospitalized patients
(what nurses refer to as the acuity level), and the fact that nurses
are now frequently asked to take on tasks that used to be assigned
to pharmacists, technicians, and nurses' aides have created a
greater need for nurses at the bedside.

In the hospital sector, the average community hospital R.N. vacancy rate jumped from 4.4 percent in 1983 to 11.3 percent in
1987. The vacancy rate for all hospital nurses doubled from 6.3
percent of budgeted positions in 1985 to 13.6 percent in 1986.
Moreover, this failure of supply to meet demand is even more
serious in nursing homes and in the ambulatory care sector.[17]

This shortage of qualified nurses has had a negative impact on
quality of care available to those in need. Hospitals in every part
of the country have had to limit elective admissions. Emergency
unit departments and intensive care units have been eliminated or
have only limited beds available, and in nursing homes, restraints
and drugs are used to make up for lack of direct care by staff.

And if nursing, like teaching, is having a hard time retaining its
professionals, it is having an even harder time recruiting new ones.
As the demand for nurses increases, fewer and fewer high school
graduates are choosing nursing each year. Between 1983 and
1985, the number of students registering in two-year associate
degree programs dropped by 12 percent and in baccalaureate programs by 8 percent. Fewer and fewer hospital diploma schools
exist, and some major nursing schools attached to universities have
closed.

By 1995, experts predict that the total number of new nurses
graduating annually from all types of nursing schools will drop
from a high of 82,700 in 1985 to 68,700. The picture for the next
century looks even bleaker. Because of the aging population (the
number of Americans over sixty-five will increase from 12 percent
of the population in 1986 to 17 percent by the year 2000), the
introduction of new diseases, and the increasing complexity of
technology and medical treatment, even greater numbers of nurses
will be needed. While there seems to be increased interest in nursing, the supply will simply not be there unless this trend is aug-
mented and continued.

The nursing crisis has been exacerbated by our society's preoccupation with the health care bottom line, which increasingly denies nurses not only the monetary reward they deserve from their
caring work, but the time essential to all caregiving activities.

In 1983, for example, the federal government instituted its Prospective Payment System of Diagnostic Related Groups (DRGs),
setting fixed fees for procedures for Medicare and Medicaid patients. Third-party payers — insurance companies and preferred
provider organizations — followed with attempts to decrease the
average length of hospital stays. Because hospitals now get a fixed
fee for a patient's stay, they try to cut down on costs in order to
maximize profits. One way they do this is to heap more nonnursing
tasks on nurses, who represent 20 percent of the costs of a patient's
stay. Another is to curtail the length of that stay. Patients are now
in hospitals for a shorter period of time. They do not, for example,
enter the hospital for a day before an operation. They are sicker
while they are there, and sicker when they're discharged. Because
caseloads are heavier and patient turnover more rapid, many caregivers have come to feel that the greatest reward for their work —
seeing the healing, empowering, life-enhancing benefits of human
interaction — is now denied them.

Because of this, many nurses find their jobs frustrating. I first
met Peggy O'Malley, a forty-two-year-old nurse, at a seminar at
Boston College's program on Women in Politics. When the group
of about twenty women began to discuss what has happened to
women over the past twenty years, a woman spoke compellingly
and with great disappointment about women's attitudes toward
those who have remained in hospitals, social service agencies, and
public schools doing traditional caregiving work. When I asked if
I could interview her at greater length, she enthusiastically agreed.

We met at O'Malley's small but comfortable apartment on a
noisy main street in Cambridge. She escorted me through a living
room and small bedroom to an old-fashioned kitchen that she had
painted in vivid primary colors. As O'Malley made tea, she described what, for her, had been a very important life decision —
to give up a career in research and consulting to become a nurse.
After graduating from Emmanuel College with a degree in

sociology, she worked as a VISTA volunteer and later as a researcher at Apt Associates. In her early thirties, Peggy O'Malley decided to change careers and went into nursing.

"Nursing," O'Malley explains with fierce pride, "provides very great challenges and very immediate satisfactions. You interact with people in almost every kind of way that human beings can interact with each other. Verbal communication is important, and so are other forms of contact. You have to be able to analyze people's situations and diagnose their problems. You have to work very hard in a very short period of time, discovering who a person is and what they need. And you do this with other people, with whom you share a great sense of camaraderie and collaboration. Nobody does nursing by themselves, which is very different from medicine. But if you don't work together in nursing, then quality declines."

Ten years ago, O'Malley chose nursing because of its commitment to caring. Ten years later, she is even more dedicated to that central aspect of her work. "Twice, since I've become a nurse, I have been extremely ill and in the hospital," she says. "I learned that the surgeons were brilliant and I wouldn't have survived without them. But it was the nurses who made me well. Knowing how that caring affected me made me incredibly eager to get back to nursing."

Now, when she goes to work, O'Malley says with evident distress and frustration, she is constantly deprived of the time nurses need to care. "When I entered nursing," O'Malley explains, "you might have had a caseload of five or six patients. One might be in for a day or two before surgery; one or two might be very sick; and one or two might really be on the road to recovery, and you could see the benefits of your care. In those days, if there was any downtime, you captured that valuable time to go into patients' rooms and talk.

"Today, if there's any downtime at all, the nurses are at the nurses' station talking to each other. That's because there is so much pressure to get people in and out of the hospital quickly that there's no point in getting involved with someone for that short a period of time. Also, people are so sick and their medical demands so intense that you don't have time to go in and sit down and find out who else in the family is stressed; how the person is coping with the changes in their body from being ill or having had surgery; whether they need social services; what is really happening. The whole system is becoming so depersonalized that it just cuts off how much you're allowed to care. And if you aren't allowed to care, then there are an awful lot of other things you can do for a living.

"I like staying in these units," says Peggy O'Malley of her decision not to move out of bedside nursing into a more socially acceptable area like administration or teaching in a university school of nursing. "I went into nursing to take care of patients who end up in the hospital. But sometimes I look around me and I have to ask myself, I'm forty-two, why am I still here? Am I the oddball? Is there something wrong with me? Am I a failure? I don't buy that argument, but it's hard not to ask yourself such questions these days when most of the discussions I have with nurses are not about how to improve the profession but simply to convince them to stay in it."

Ironically, the loss of job status that Peggy O'Malley and many others find so disheartening has been exacerbated rather than alleviated by women's freedom to enter male-dominated professions. "You tell people you want to be a nurse," says Liz Darling, a twenty-four-year-old nurse at Cambridge's Mount Auburn Hospital, "and they think that all you'll do is empty bedpans for the rest of your life. They wonder what's wrong with you — why didn't you choose to become a doctor?"

Of the almost 590,000 physicians in the United States, 92,718 are women. In 1989-90, women made up 36.2 percent of all those enrolled in medical schools. This means that nurses work with more female physicians than ever before. While many nurses say that female physicians can be easier to work with than men, the fact that she is a woman does not mean that a physician will be more collaborative, less authoritarian, or more willing to listen to and recognize a nurse's expertise than a male doctor. Most nurses insist that it is a physician's training on the job, not sex, that determines how he or she relates to nurses.

Given their training, physicians gradually distance themselves from the primary group of "subordinates" with whom they work — namely nurses, says clinical nurse specialist Patricia Wallace at the Hospital of the University of Pennsylvania. "In the beginning, they're more sensitive to shared gender, what it's like to be a woman — any woman — in a male-dominated field. They'll ask you what you think about things and inquire about the nursing issues involved in patient care," explains Wallace, who's been a nurse for twelve years. She finds, however, that this openness and shared concern fades once women have been socialized into the medical system. "After a while, women physicians start to develop a mind-set that nurses shouldn't be sought for their opinion. They become more desensitized over time."

And so, with no way to communicate about the issues that divide or unite them, the female physicians become part of a "closed circle" that excludes nurses. "It's like the closed circle that physicians travel in when they make rounds," Wallace says. "They don't allow nurses in, and to us that is distancing, nonconfirming behavior."

It is not too long before I experience at first hand the way that some of the women physicians who are allowed into that closed circle may keep nurses in their place. When I visit a neonatal intensive care unit (NICU) at a major urban medical center, one of the first nurses I meet is Jane White. She has spent the past five years tending the low-birth-weight babies whose ranks are swelling in the neonatal care units of hospitals that serve inner-city populations. The day I visit, White is in one of three small rooms that make up the NICU. The three babies in her care are all black, all born prematurely because their mothers were either on crack or were too poor or uneducated to get adequate prenatal care. As the thirty-three-year-old nurse monitors the equipment that keeps these babies alive, she explains their histories. One tiny boy was born at twenty-five weeks and weighed 1,723 grams. Now, seven weeks later, he is still struggling for life. His mother, she says, probably free-based cocaine to get rid of him. "That's real common today. Women who can't pay for abortions free-base because they know it causes the placenta to break away from the uterus so they'll lose the baby."

As we talk, alarms constantly interrupt our conversation. Another newborn in an adjacent isolette ceases breathing every few

minutes, causing the bell on the apnea monitor to sound in warning. Each time, White quickly surveys the equipment, checks the
baby, and then reaches inside to tap him on the back till his
breathing resumes. "Breathe," she urges. "Come on, breathe."

While we are speaking, a team of physicians on rounds enters
the room. Led by a female attending physician who is new on the
staff, they assemble by the tiny boy's isolette and begin to discuss
his case. Jane listens intently. The female physician decides that
the baby should be "weaned off the pressure" from the ventilator
that controls the amount of oxygen that comes into his lungs, the
number of breaths he takes per minute, and the pressure needed
to keep his collapsed lungs open. She orders a decrease in the
amount of pressure that the baby gets with each breath.

White, who has lived with this baby for weeks, argues that he
will not be able to tolerate the adjustment. She explains that the
baby has been very sick over the weekend. The female attending
physician pays no attention. A resident writes out the order and
the respiratory therapist changes the equipment setting. The physicians then move on to the next room and the next case.

About ten minutes later an alarm sounds. The baby has indeed
responded as White predicted. First he turns blue, then his heart
rate drops. White goes to find a resident. "The baby is turning
blue," she says as they return. To stabilize the baby, they must
now take him off the ventilator and inflate his lungs manually with
a hand-held respiratory device. When he is finally out of danger,
he is put back on the ventilator — with the original pressure.

Jane White looks at me with grim satisfaction.

"A lot of times a physician will take a nurse's opinion into account, or make changes that do work," she says, trying to repress
her anger. "But this time, I knew it wouldn't work. I knew how
sick the baby had been over the weekend. She paid no attention
to my opinion at all. This whole little episode didn't have to happen to prove that he couldn't tolerate what I knew he couldn't
tolerate all along."

No matter where they work or what their title, nurses explain
that their situation has not necessarily improved since women have
entered the medical field in greater numbers. Claire Fagin is dean
of the University of Pennsylvania School of Nursing, one of the

best schools in the country. A nurse for forty years, she has written books on her clinical specialty, pediatric psychiatry, headed professional organizations, served on corporate boards, testified before congressional panels. And yet, she is still confronted with the question — whether it is spoken or not — "Why is someone as intelligent as you a nurse? Why couldn't you be a doctor?"

As we sit in her comfortable beige office at the University of Pennsylvania, she describes a typical scenario, one that occurred when she was awarded an honorary degree at the Medical College of Pennsylvania. The sixty-two-year-old dean sat on the platform in a lecture hall filled with eager, young medical students — almost half of whom were women. A member of the medical school's board introduced her, cataloguing her achievements. But, Fagin recalls, as she stood in front of the audience, she anticipated the reaction of the medical graduates in the auditorium. "They look at me, hear my accomplishments, and they see my face and think, not that I have been rewarded by time, but that I have been cheated by time. 'If only she had been born later,' they think, 'she could have been a doctor.' "

Because Fagin has encountered this new female perspective over and over again, she decided to address it head on. "It's so prevalent that when I got my honorary degree, I decided I had to deal immediately with what I knew would be their major assumption, which is that if I were choosing a career today, I would choose to be a physician. And so I told them the truth. Unlike many women in my generation, I had parents who scheduled my life very carefully and had decided early on that I would be a physician, following in the footsteps of a very successful aunt. But when I was in college, I knew I didn't want to be a physician." Fagin explains that she has never regretted her decision to be a nurse. "Nursing, caring," she says, "is indeed powerful and has been consistently rewarding."

The idea that caring is an act of assertion, strength, and affirmation, of course, contradicts all of our comfortable notions that caregiving work consists of little more than nodding sympathetically, emptying a bedpan, writing letters on a blackboard, or diapering a baby's bottom. In nursing, and all other caregiving fields, a complex combination of skills, both emotional and intellectual, is required.

"Teaching," says Mary Futrell, "is not just making lesson plans, picking up supplies, and writing on a blackboard. Teaching is helping young people get a better appreciation and understanding of themselves and their society so they can feel good about themselves. You have to motivate children to help them want to learn."

Teachers in public schools teach parents, not just children. Nurses are preceptors to nursing students, who come to gain clinical experience in hospitals during their years of nursing education. As highly skilled diagnosticians, they teach doctors, informing them of a patient's condition. "We teach doctors a lot about the psychosocial issues that are our focus," says Leslie Buter, a nurse at Boston's Beth Israel Hospital. "A perfect example is a conversation I had with a young doctor today. Doctors are always wanting to cure people. That's how they measure their success. If they can cure somebody and get them out of the hospital, that's good; but if someone gets sicker or dies, that's a failure. We don't consider dying a failure. Nurses don't feel that death is a nursing failure. We always have a function to perform, even if a patient gets sicker or is dying. We want to help people die with respect.

"So today, I was talking with an intern who was having difficulty giving a ninety-two-year-old terminal patient morphine to help him get through the last stages. He thought he was failing. To him, morphine was a last-ditch medication that meant giving up. And I had to help him understand that making this man comfortable with morphine was just successfully helping him to die with some peace."

Perhaps the least understood aspect of caring work is its empathic component. In the sociological and psychological literature devoted to emotional and organizational development, empathic interactions have been either ignored or misunderstood. Psychologist Judith Jordan and her colleagues at Wellesley College's Stone Center for Developmental Services and Studies believe this is because women's experience and women's work have been undervalued by the men who have dominated both research and theory in these fields.

Empathy, that classic female trait, has suffered because of this. "Empathy," Jordan comments, "often has been construed as a mysterious, contagion-like, and primitive phenomenon or has been dismissed as a vague and unknowable subjective state."[18] Those who manifest empathy are said to be engaged in a process in which they surrender their individuality to others and lose themselves in someone else's identity. In a society that values separation and "individuation," such activities arouse suspicion rather than admiration.

In the popular imagination, empathy is considered a simple, intuitive act, requiring only that you be a good listener. Empathy, many similarly believe, requires no more than reaching out a hand so that another human being can grasp it, or opening one's arms so that you can enfold someone in a comforting embrace. But empathy is far more difficult and complex. It is the attempt to put oneself in someone else's shoes, to stand in them, walk in them, and feel their pinch. It is hearing the different emotional or cultural language another speaks in his or her terms, without translating it into one's own. It is acting on another human being's behalf, doing not only what you want for another, but ascertaining what the other wants and needs. And it is learning how to *be* with another when you can no longer *do* anything to solve his or her problems.

This involves cognitive skills. It involves patience and it involves courage: in our *doing* culture, the *being* of caring is not prized, because to be with someone is deemed to be "doing" nothing.

To conceive, then, of caring work as an instinctual merging with the other is to ignore the discipline and knowledge required of those who engage in all empathic work. It is to ignore the fact that while women's work in the home and caregiving professions may have helped us develop empathic skills, empathy is difficult — sometimes impossible — even for many women.

To increase support both within and outside of their professions, leaders in all the caregiving fields are trying to elaborate models of professionalism that improve caregivers' status, without compromising the heart of their work — care. In the process, they are creating some exciting experiments that put transformative feminism's values and ideals into practice.

Leaders in the field of caring theory and practice recognize that some misguided attempts to "professionalize" their fields could easily jeopardize the activity they most value — caring. Professionalism, as most people define it, is a masculine, market-driven concept that generally precludes caring. Indeed, the hallmark of the typical male professional has been his rejection and repression of caring impulses. To the professional, people, things, and events aren't supposed to matter — particularly if they endanger what is really *supposed* to matter: the bottom line of money, status, and power. In many instances in the business world where professionalism has been defined and refined over the years, even concern with producing a decent product isn't supposed to intrude on what's really important. As Alfred P. Sloan, the former head of General Motors, once candidly stated, the goal of General Motors is "not to make cars, but to make money."

Caring professionals reject these ideas in principle — and what's more, they have found them to be ineffective in practice. Thus, the majority of caregiving professionals today agree that the invasion of the market into their traditional spheres of interest has compromised, not enhanced, the provision of high-quality care. And so they are trying to develop new, relationship-oriented, caring models of professionalism that also "keep the marketplace in its place."

At Boston's Beth Israel Hospital, Joyce Clifford, vice president of nursing, has developed a model of nursing practice that gives nurses greater control and authority both over their work and within the hospital. This restructuring of nursing practice is called primary nursing. Just as a patient has a doctor — who is accountable to the patient and his or her family — so, too, each patient has a primary nurse who determines the patient's nursing treatment plan and is available, twenty-four hours a day, to provide continuity of care. Primary nursing is embedded within a system of collaborative, rather than competitive, practice with physicians and other hospital staff.

Patricia Benner also promotes this kind of care-centered expert nursing practice as she travels the country, teaching nurses what, she says, they already know how to do — care for other human beings. Benner works with nurses at a variety of hospitals, helping them articulate the essence of their nursing practice. Her seminars are tutorials in care. They help nurses understand that their demoralization and "burnout" is not a result of "caring too much" — as is commonly argued — but of a society that cares too little. The solution is not to care less but to "account for what counts" by struggling to make hospitals and the health care system itself responsive to human needs.

Nurses are also defending care by setting up cost- and *care*-effective programs that treat those citizens our society has abandoned. In Denver, Colorado, nurses at the University of Colorado's School of Nursing have opened up a nurse-run community center for AIDS patients, the Denver Project in Human Caring, that delivers care more efficiently and at less cost than many in-hospital programs. In New Jersey and Dallas, nurses are giving primary care to America's homeless. In Philadelphia, they have set up outreach programs for low-income teenage mothers. Nurses help mothers secure adequate health care for their newborns and infants, encourage mothers to finish junior high and high school, and teach them how to avoid getting pregnant a second or third time. And throughout the nation, nurses are trying to provide community-based alternatives for the chronically ill and for elderly Americans.

It is the idea that human beings are the center of our world that is the essence of these experiments in caring work. This does not mean that caregivers do not have to deal with the costs of their services, nor that they can be inefficient in their delivery, warns Elizabeth Mulroy of the Boston University School of Social Work. It does, however, mean that caregivers have to concentrate on care rather than on cost. "Today, with the business gloss of the eighties, many schools have gotten into a more administrative mode that tries to bring systematic analysis to social agencies. Individuals trained in business and public policy are taught to be concerned with efficiency and the market above all else, and they are now supplanting people who have been trained in social work.

"That's why," says Mulroy, "our mission in the Human Services Management Program is to really educate social workers who want to practice in the community and the nonprofit sector to develop programs and systems that are efficient, while empowering and serving clients."

Although these experiments in caring work are, I believe, some of the most powerful examples of transformative feminism at work, they face tremendous obstacles. The resistance comes not only from a market society that is hostile or indifferent to care, but from some female caregivers themselves, who have been so influenced by our emphasis on the bottom line, power, and independence that they have come to "identify with the aggressor" and try to elevate their status by denigrating care.

Indeed, it is a testament to the extent of the social transformations of the past twenty years that so many women are now part of the very public to whom caregiving professionals must explain the importance and content of caregiving work. Today women as well as men must be convinced that caregiving is essential to the health of *every* human being and to human society. Without such widespread public acknowledgment of the value of care, caregiving professionals know that the public will never reward their work with the respect it deserves, more men will not be convinced to enter the caregiving fields and share in caring work inside the home, and political representatives will be unwilling to spend the money necessary to provide high-quality services and keep professionals in their respective fields.

Most importantly, we need to value care not only to save the caregiving professions, but because we must protect, defend, and expand this human activity upon which we all depend. By abetting the market's invasion of the caring professions and encouraging so many women to fear caring, our society has certainly succeeded in unleashing us as economic actors. But our cultural obsession with the regulation and restriction, rather than the provision and broadening of quality care, ignores the fact that human beings are also caring actors, and has turned care into an increasingly scarce commodity.

If we are all to get the kind of care we so desperately need, some women, along with the majority of men, have no choice but to stop fearing the bonds of care and renew the societal discussion many of us tried to begin two decades ago. The question is not just how can we grant more respect and reward to professional caregivers, the question is, how can we all — men and women alike — join them?

Chapter Six

IS SISTERHOOD POWERFUL?

WHEN MODERN American feminists began organizing to change the world of work, they focused not only on expanding job opportunities for women, and on the caring work women performed in nursing, teaching, childcare, and social work, but on their support and service work as secretaries, flight attendants, and in the ever-expanding service sector of our economy.

Their indignation and sense of injustice was fueled by the not-so-hidden injuries of patriarchy. Feminists illuminated the central role women played in the economy and in society. It was women's domestic work and support roles that helped make men's accomplishments possible. Yet, men had rendered women's work invisible — ignoring and/or denying the importance and complexity of their contributions. Where women were recognized, it was often in the most trivialized, sexist, and insulting fashion — as in the famous airline ads that featured shapely young flight attendants who invited male businessmen to "fly me" to their destinations. Feminism's task was to secure greater societal acknowledgment of women's role, more respect, less discrimination, and improved financial remuneration.

Feminism addressed the problem of women's work in two sometimes contradictory ways. Transformative feminists sought to make women's invisible work visible. In research studies, books, magazine and journal articles, scholars, journalists, and activists described the history and development of women's work. Their insights and critique helped lay the groundwork for contemporary struggles for more egalitarian work relations and specific reform goals like pay equity. Their message was that sisterhood could be powerful only if it was based on collective action — forming unions, creating working-women's organizations, and lobbying for fair employment legislation.

While many equal-opportunity feminists rhetorically supported these goals, their strategies for change often emphasized personal rather than collective advancement. The problem of women's work would be solved when enough individual women went into previously male-dominated fields or management and professional positions in traditional spheres. When women did the really important work of society or managed other women, then they would develop and project a different institutional voice that couldn't be ignored. Of course, women — albeit fewer of them — would continue to be secretaries, flight attendants, and other kinds of service sector workers. But as women replaced men in positions of power, their female subordinates would benefit from sisterly solidarity of a trickle-down sort on the theory that women in supervisory, managerial, and executive positions would be better bosses than their male counterparts and predecessors.

The conviction that women would never oppress other women because they themselves had experienced oppression was an article of at least some feminists' faith. (Why, after all, should poor and working-class women, who would never make it to the top of a very narrow pyramid, root for their upper-class sisters if those women were going to behave much like men had in the marketplace?)

This idea that the oppressed, once liberated, will automatically wield power differently than their oppressors is a myth shared by many groups struggling to free themselves from bondage. It has, for decades, motivated third-world liberation movements. It has informed the belief that Jews would be constitutionally incapable of dehumanizing and mistreating their Arab neighbors once they had entered the Promised Land. And it has been an animating force among blacks, who could not imagine that they would be capable of the same kind of racial prejudices whites have exhibited for so long.

Oppression, the oppressed often believe, denies them power but simultaneously confers upon them a kind of mystical, moral superiority. As if an acquired trait, passed from generation to generation, the oppressed carry within them the goodness and virtue their oppressors so manifestly lack. Under oppression, these qualities are recognized only among the oppressed and systematically denied by their oppressors. Once oppression is removed, however, these capacities will flower.

This myth of the generalized moral superiority of the oppressed does not often stand the test of reality because, as feminist psychoanalyst Jessica Benjamin so eloquently states, the oppressed often "remain in love with the ideal of power that has been denied them," and thus replicate that behavior when no longer in bondage.[1] That is perhaps the most pernicious consequence of oppression: deprivation does not, in fact, breed kindness, gentleness, and generosity in all those who are oppressed but, rather, often brutalizes the human spirit.

Nonetheless, the myth of moral superiority continues to be a powerful force for maintaining collective identity and motivating collective action. It persists among all oppressed groups, including modern feminists. Thus, many liberal and even more radical feminists believed that even within status hierarchies that assigned greater privileges and pay to professional than support-staff jobs, women would appreciate the complexity of the work their female subordinates performed and acknowledge the contributions they made to their employers and society. Women would act as mentors to other women who wanted to advance. Female employers would fight to help women workers improve pay and working conditions — particularly in the areas of childcare and parental leave. Women rising from the ranks would, in short, remember those they had left behind.

To find out if cross-class as well as intraclass solidarity has been the rule, I spoke with dozens of women in the traditional service sector of the economy — concentrating on the flight attendants who now serve an increasing number of female business passengers and sometimes even fly with female pilots; secretaries who work for women bosses; and workers involved in two recent labor disputes who sought the help of feminist directors of their companies.

In choosing my examples, I have selected instances that illustrate the paradoxes of these two definitions of liberation. Thus, the working women — and some working men — I have spoken with have all been involved in collective organizations that have helped them improve their working lives. What we see from exploring the lives of these women in so-called subordinate positions is that feminism has clearly had a positive impact on millions of those who are still doing support and service work in our society. Within the ranks of women workers, sisterhood has indeed been powerful. The women's movement has helped women value their contributions and join together in unions and other collective organizations to reduce overt forms of sexual discrimination in hiring, promotions, and pay, to challenge common practices of sexual harassment, to demand pay equity, and generally educate the public about the value of their work.

But amidst all these much discussed achievements and changes there has been surprisingly little assessment of the impact of some women's career success on others. Our attention often goes to calculating how many different bodies now occupy the seats of power traditionally reserved for men and ascertaining how those women who now sit in them fare when compared to men. Media and public discussions and analyses do not, however, spend as much time asking whether those women exercise their different voices and act in a different manner when in positions of power. Nor do they often question their accountability to those women whose interests women in positions of some power claim to represent.

Evaluations and assessments of how women at the top relate to their female "subordinates" and other less fortunate women are few and far between for several reasons. First, many assumed that women would be accountable to and act on behalf of their women "subordinates" as well as other women less fortunate than themselves. Second, many women have understandably focused more on how the vast numbers of men in power treat women, rather than on how the relatively few women in power relate to women under them. In our society, which tends to deny class realities and conflicts, it is not surprising that many middle- and upper-middle-class women take little heed of their working-class counterparts. Women have also feared that public disclosure of less than model sisterly behavior would provide ammunition to an ever vigilant enemy all too eager to reverse the gains of centuries of struggle.

Many women, I believe, have also been reluctant to pursue such assessments because — whether consciously or not — they have been loath to uncover any practices that would undermine the myth of moral superiority some have come to cherish. Jessica Benjamin argues that feminists' unwillingness to consider women's participation in relationships of domination and subordination with men stems from the fear that "the onus of responsibility will appear to shift from men to women and the moral victory from women to men."[2]

In spite of those fears, it's important to look at how women are really faring in a world in which at least some women have a good deal of power over others. When we explore how they wield it, we discover that neither biology nor oppression is destiny. When women are integrated into a corporate culture or hierarchy obsessed with wealth, status, and power, they are often unable — or unwilling — to treat their subordinates with more respect than insensitive male "superiors." Women workers often report that their employers do not care about them and do not try to understand their invisible work as much as they could or should. What's more, women often add insult to injury by using feminist ideology or appeals to feminine solidarity to disempower subordinates. Many female managers or executives expect their subordinates to support *their* professional struggle to advance simply because "women should stick together in their battle against men." These professional women, however, do not always return the favor and support women workers in their own struggles to improve their working lives.

The situation of the nation's 90,000 flight attendants (86 percent of whom are female) illustrates the dual impact of the women's movement on women's work. Because of transformative feminism's collective emphasis, flight attendants have indeed come a

long way. Because of their workplace organizing, they now experience a greater sense of self-esteem and sisterly solidarity. Nonetheless, they often still feel undervalued and even demeaned in
their interactions with a "business class" that includes a growing
number of women.

The women's movement, as Susan Bianchi-Sand, president of
the Association of Flight Attendants, explains, has had an incal-
culable impact on her 28,000 members. The forty-three-year-old,
eighteen-year veteran remembers what it used to be like to fly the
nation's skies. When she began her career in the late sixties with
United Airlines, she was fired because she decided to get married.
In those days, flight attendants were called "stewardesses" and
viewed more as attractive accouterments — sex objects who served
meals, fetched blankets and pillows, and informed passengers how
to buckle their seat belts and scurry to the nearest emergency exit.

"Stewardesses" could not marry, be black, or have children.
They had to conform to stringent height, weight, and age standards (no heavy, short, or older women were accepted). Most did
not regard their work as a career but only as a job on which they
remained for no more than a year or two. The women's movement
helped change all that. Because feminism emboldened women,
Bianchi-Sand says, women have changed the nature of their work.
"Women's liberation has given recognition to women. It has given
women the impetus to fight within women's work, to fight against
discrimination. It has given us the courage to say that we are not
just a number, that we have some value. It has given us a voice."

After waging lawsuits and engaging in collective bargaining
throughout the sixties and seventies, "airline stewardesses" became "flight attendants" — a change of name that reflects changes
in the job itself. There are now many black flight attendants. Many
are married, and height and weight restrictions have been either
eliminated or relaxed. Pay has improved, and many flight attendants now work, on average, ten years or more in their careers.
They have also tried to deal with what Arlie Hochschild calls "the
commercialization" of their emotions.[3]

Bianchi-Sand's own position as one of three female members of
the thirty-member AFL-CIO Executive Council is testament to the
changes in the profession. Flight attendants and their organiza-

tions are working to explain their work to the public. "Our problem," Bianchi-Sand explains, "is that as safety professionals, we get little recognition. It's an uphill battle to get people to recognize that we're on the plane to save their lives." The airline industry makes it as difficult as possible to get this message out to the public. Airlines don't want passengers to be reminded that it's, in fact, risky to fly the nation's skies — particularly in an age when airline deregulation and cutthroat competition among owners has led to more and more safety problems. Any discussion of safety is thus opposed. Similarly, in an industry that is now ruthlessly competitive it will be increasingly difficult to make sure airlines do not solve their often self-engendered financial problems by cutting back on the pay and benefits of flight attendants.

Working women have demonstrated their intraclass solidarity in dealing with these problems. In one of the most acrimonious recent battles about the future of the airline industry and those who work for it — the strike against Eastern Airlines — flight attendants also point to the impressive solidarity women within the labor movement demonstrated. Those involved were struck by the outpouring of help from other women within the labor movement and women's movement activists during that strike. "Women's groups supported us, NOW supported us, and so did the public," says Bianchi-Sand.

"The sisterhood and brotherhood within the labor movement really surprised me," says Kathy Ward, who has worked as a flight attendant for the past twenty-three years. Ward worked in Queens, New York, on the strike and was in constant contact with members of other unions as well as her own during the long ordeal. "It was really enlightening to go to union and civic meetings and see the kind of support we got. We were acknowledged, and that made us feel very good."

The one group of passengers and the public that was not particularly sympathetic, Eastern strikers report, was the business class of fliers. And women were no exception. "A lot of business people take the shuttle, and they related more to [then-owner Frank] Lorenzo's arguments than to us. That was true of women as well as men," says Ward.

For women flight attendants, as well as all the other women

workers I spoke with, this represents the essential contradiction of recent female victories: feminism has helped them value their work, but our culture's obsession with definitions of success that focus on achievement in the masculine marketplace — on men's terms — teach women who abide by those marketplace rules to devalue the work of their working-class sisters.

This is the contradiction that Deen Leonard, a forty-year-old Eastern Airlines flight attendant, has struggled with throughout her eighteen-year career. A committed feminist, Leonard credits the women's movement with helping her learn to value her own work.

When she started out as a flight attendant eighteen years ago, Leonard tells me, she was like many other "stewardesses" who viewed their work as a temporary stop on a more exciting career journey. From a working-class family, Leonard regarded flying as a good way to get to travel. "At the outset, I was a little bit ashamed of what I did for a living. People would be initially fascinated when you told them what you did. That would last for about five minutes. Or they'd say the typical, 'Oh, you're a flight attendant,' and you could hear the tone of dismissal in their voices."

Her attitude changed when she became a feminist. "I learned that women are doing most of the work, invisible and otherwise, that is the underpinning of our culture. We get very little credit for it, and certainly not the compensation we deserve. We're very visible and yet we're invisible. Realizing that revolutionized my attitude toward my work." Leonard thus made the emotional journey from being a "stewardess" to being a flight attendant — a safety professional without whose skill people would not be able to fly.

"The pilots do the important work of getting us from home to our destination safely. Then they're out of the front windows. But if there is an emergency, it is up to us to expeditiously evacuate the plane — to deal with children, handicapped people — in the ninety seconds we have. People see us as service workers, which is fine. I have nothing against that label, but people need to know that when they go into a restaurant and eat they don't expect the person who brings their food to give them CPR, or deliver their baby, or pull them out of a burning wreck."

What people boarding airplanes are unaware of is the manifold activities that go on before they're on board — the safety checks flight attendants conduct to make sure the airplane is safe, coordinating with the flight crew, and conducting exit checks. That comes first. Then flight attendants review their stores of food and beverages, blankets and magazines.

As an example of the crucial but invisible difference she and her colleagues make, she cites the case of a flight attendant who was working for Eastern Airlines during a snowstorm in Denver. Some months earlier, a plane had taken off from the same airport with ice on its wings, and Continental Airlines had one of the most devastating crashes in its history. On this particular evening, one of the flight attendants on board noticed that ice had built up on the airplane and voiced her concerns to the captain. He ignored her. It was his job to fly the plane and her job to serve him, he said. To ensure the safety of the passengers, the flight attendant refused to fly under unsafe conditions and left the airplane. The rest of the crew followed. Management was soon involved; the plane was de-iced and the flight proceeded safely.

"This was a good example of what flight attendants do around safety issues," Leonard says. And a good example, she adds, of the invisibility of the role they play. "Because we don't want to cause passengers undue anxiety, all those negotiations took place out at the gate area, off the plane. The passengers never knew — and still don't know — what went on in that airplane that day. They have no idea the crew refused to take the trip and that a flight attendant probably saved their lives."

Leonard believes that, when they do have the occasion to understand flight attendants' work, many women are supportive and sympathetic. "If women are the least bit enlightened, they'll make eye contact or engage in conversation if there is an opportunity to do it." The women who seem the least so, she believes, are the ones Leonard refers to as "corporate women" — women who are so busy pursuing their own careers that they don't have the time, energy, or awareness to pay attention to the women around them.

"Unless they need something, you're hardly there," she says. "It's like they're trying much harder to shed the things that make us uniquely female and wonderful just to survive out there."

Leonard says she finds this is particularly true of younger women who have been the beneficiaries of the women's movement without necessarily having had to struggle like older women for the gains women now enjoy. "Sometimes we'll take hordes of female buyers in the retail business down to New York. The older women are pretty good. They talk to us. They're funny and sympathetic. But the younger women seem self-conscious, competitive. They seem to have made a determination to go after their sense of what the American dream is, to chase after what men have got and take that as their goalposts, and I don't think they're even aware of all the people who help them get there."

Flying with women pilots presents another example of the class dilemmas that liberation may highlight. In an entirely male-dominated profession, comprised mainly of pilots trained in the military, there are now a few female pilots. "I remember the first time I opened the cockpit door and saw a woman pilot sitting up there. First of all, they always wear pants, and this woman was in a dress and she was five months pregnant, sitting at the panel. And I said 'Oh my God, how happy I am to see you.' "

Unfortunately, says Leonard, women pilots and flight attendants do not necessarily share more than the common recognition of the importance of women's advancement in the workplace. "There's a real class barrier between flight attendants and pilots. Pilots get paid enormous sums of money. They think they're gods." Women pilots, Leonard and others say, can be good to work with and certainly aren't as macho as men, but they are often confused about their allegiances. Are they women first and pilots second, or pilots first and women second?

Reba Brenner, a forty-year-old flight attendant who's flown for twenty years — first with Eastern and now with the Trump Shuttle — has also observed the same social dilemma that Leonard describes. "They don't know where they stand," she says of female pilots. "When they're in the cockpit, they're in the men's seat, up front with the guys. But then, there are the 'girls' out there in the back of the airplane. This becomes particularly evident when we're on layover. They don't know where to go. Do they hang out with the guys or with us? If we're all going out together, the pilots and the rest of the crew, they'll come, too. Otherwise, they tend to stay by themselves."

Brenner says that female pilots are not necessarily any better — or worse — than male pilots. "Some are friendly. Some are typical pilots. We tell them our names. They tell us theirs. I don't know," Brenner concludes. "There's just a thing about pilots. They have this air about them. They're just sort of obnoxious."

Although Brenner says she feels gratified that women are now more of the business-class customers she serves, she has also been sometimes torn about how far she should go to serve them when they are insensitive to her presence and problems. Helping women with their garment bags, she says, may seem a trivial activity, but it presents a classic example of how much trouble she has resolving her work-related dilemmas regarding these women. "Some businesswomen come on board hugging these garment bags that are so heavy you'd think there was a person in them. You come up to her and want to help, and bam, she goes absolutely limp. Suddenly, she's totally helpless." As if she were a male weight lifter, the female passenger, Brenner says, may expect her to heft the heavy bag up into the storage bin on her own. "It's not at all like you're two women together, and you can both get the bag up there. They think they're better than you and you should do it alone."

Brenner was perplexed about how she should deal with this situation. At first, she tried to be helpful and do what was expected of her. "Finally," she says, "I decided I am not going to throw my back out because these women have heavy bags and are in too much of a hurry to check them. Now," she announces with some pride, "when they go limp, I start going limp. And we have to push together."

The recognition that women's liberation means that women must now "push this heavy bag together" is, in fact, a symbol of what working women want from those women in power whom they now serve. The flight attendants and other working women I spoke with took pride in their supportive and service work. Some wanted out. Most wanted to stay — but with dignity. What they ask for is what many feminists originally hoped would be a natural outcome of the liberation of all women. "As I travel so much in the context of my work, I realize that if it weren't for the work of all these low-wage so-called subordinates, this country would never keep going," Deen Leonard explains. "I have this visual image that I carry with me that this country is held up by the sweat and labor of all these people who have no recognition and no power and no money. It's just taken for granted by the people who walk on the top that these people below them are going to be there. They don't even need to think about it. People identify you by your work, and if they don't think your work is important, then you're not."

The invisible work and contributions to which Leonard refers are not just women's work, but working-class work. The persistent problems reported by women who work in such jobs highlight, therefore, not only intrasex conflicts, but class divisions. Although many feminists, of course, recognize the divisive power of class, much of mainstream feminism has tended to ignore these divisions. Like other liberal ideologies, it recognized the excesses of the rich and the terrible tragedy of poverty. But it has often assumed that women in the vast "middle class" would remain, somehow, sisters under the skin.

This belief that we are all part of an indistinguishable middle class whose interests are homogeneous and for whom harmony, not conflict, is the rule, is a central belief of American society, says economist Richard Parker.[4] This myth of the middle class holds that if we do not live in abject poverty or fabulous luxury, we can, by dint of effort, all share in the fruits of our affluent society. Women, of course, recognized that partriarchy had prohibited their full enjoyment of the fruits of this society. But liberation, many felt, would allow us all to participate fully in society, to run the great race of life and win.

This notion of a classless society has not only clouded our vision about economic realities, it has also precluded any larger societal understanding of the nature of the work performed by working-class people. With the exception of films like *Norma Rae*, or the more recent *Stanley and Iris*, and the depiction of their domestic problems in sitcoms on television, workers are absent from popular

culture, as is any depiction of their work. It is, therefore, compre-
hensible that neither most professional men nor professional
women recognize the importance of the supportive work done by
working-class women.

One of the main groups of female workers who hold our world
up with their labor is, of course, clerical workers. In 1989, there
were 18,416,000 administrative support workers in the United
States, 80 percent of whom are female. Of these workers,
4,010,000 were secretaries, and 99.1 percent of these workers are
women.[5] The feminist movement has helped to guide them toward
a much greater sense of self-worth and to the collective actions
that have grown out of a growing clerical working women's movement. As a result of feminist organizing, secretaries began to organize in unions and working women's organizations in the early
1970s, and to encourage male-dominated trade unions to focus on
and organize clerical wokers in offices all over the country. Until
this time, male-dominated trade unions, which had historically
organized in the manufacturing sector of the economy, had largely
ignored clerical workers' problems.

One of the first clerical women's organizations was 9 to 5 —
which gave its name to the 1980s movie about the secretaries
portrayed by actresses Lily Tomlin, Jane Fonda, and Dolly Parton.
These secretaries banded together against their sexist male boss
and transformed their office. The work of real-life secretaries, as
well as that of other feminist trade unionists, was instrumental in
integrating women's care-related demands into collective bargaining all over the country — making childcare, parental leave, leave
for sick children and family members, part-time and flex-time
work central bargaining issues in trade union negotiations with
employers.

Unlike the recent film *Working Girl* — a product of the radical
individualism of the 1980s which suggested that every secretary
with smarts and ambition should solve her work-related problems
by trying to become the boss — these working *women's* organizations argued that women should not try only to rise from the
ranks but, rather, should rise with them. This philosophy and the
organizing that emerged out of it resulted in major unionization drives at Yale and Harvard universities. Those struggles to

unionize clerical and technical workers resulted in two of the most successful and well-publicized unionization victories of the 1980s.

One of the things that prompted many secretaries to join these unionization campaigns was, in fact, the lack of cross-class solidarity among women in the workplace. Because feminism has encouraged women workers to ask for what they deserve, they have become more assertive in their workplaces. But many of the women whom they now work for have often not chosen to support their struggles. What is even worse is the fact that many advocates of equal-opportunity feminism have helped subvert their desire to even create a different female voice and behavior in the workplace by encouraging professional women to emulate their male counterparts in relationships with their clerical "subordinates."

As Rosabeth Moss Kanter explains in *Men and Women of the Corporation,* secretaries have always held a very special place in corporate life. A secretary's importance is directly related to the rank of her boss, not to the measure of her own professional skills. She is subject to a constant and arbitrary set of demands, which may include such personal duties as "cutting the boss's hair, dog-sitting while he and his wife are away on vacation, returning his wife's mail-order shoes, and providing homemade coffee cake at board meetings."[6]

Secretaries have fulfilled these duties because they are supposed to "identify their interests with those of their bosses," subordinating to his needs any desires for their own career advancement. To the extent that they do all these professional and "wifely" duties well, that they "learn the boss rather than the organization," are "timid and self-effacing," and make themselves "indispensable," they will be valued. But, Kanter observes, it is precisely because they do become indispensable that they cannot move out of the secretarial ghetto. Describing how male bosses have historically kept their secretaries in their places, Kanter explains that bosses stood in the way of the opportunities for the secretaries to advance because male superiors were not eager to lose indispensable female subordinates.[7]

In this excellent analysis of what happens to subordinates in a large corporation, Kanter talks explicitly about conditions under patriarchy, where men are the boss. Now that some women have moved into the corporate culture, however, the same rules still apply, although women must now enforce them. That's because these are the marketplace rules and many women who try to teach other would-be female bosses how to play the market game to win extol hierarchy, inequality, and traditional definitions of success.

Not surprisingly, one of the first women to address the proper relationships between female master and slave was Betty Lehan Harragan. In a section of *Games Mother Never Taught You* entitled "Avoid Personal Fouls," Harragan tells up-and-coming gameswomen that they must "divest themselves of all equipment that is normally associated with secretarial work. . . . The enduring, immediate association with secretarial duties is a typewriter, of course. The executive woman must develop an aversion to typewriters that borders on the paranoiac."[8]

She must also, Margaret Fenn suggested in her executive-success guide *In the Spotlight,* distance herself from the woman who uses that typewriter. Because "associations and friendships reflect managerial values, these imply a degree of social distance from subordinates."[9] Margaret V. Higginson and Thomas L. Quick concurred in *The Ambitious Woman's Guide to a Successful Career.* "Women," they wrote, "seem to have a special problem in this area. In the company cafeteria, for example, they will sit with other women — even if these women are on a lower job level — rather than join men who are now their peers."[10]

These lessons, reinforced by the corporate hierarchy, have affected even those women in the business world who are uncomfortable with such inequalities. "Women managers are not supposed to do anything their secretaries do," Helena Walzer reports from firsthand experience. "This was explained to me as soon as I left business school and went to work for a major bank in New York. One day when the secretary wasn't around, I sat down at her typewriter to address some envelopes I needed. A female supervisor came up and told me that I shouldn't be using the typewriter. I asked why and she told me it would compromise my professional image. I could use a computer if I wanted to, because managerial women always use computers. But to actually sit down at the typewriter, she said, would not be well looked upon."

In the bank Walzer later worked for, reinforcing distance

between secretaries and their bosses — whether male or female — became such a fetish that secretaries were banned from entering a newly constructed executive dining room. Thus they could not even accompany their bosses to lunches with clients whose accounts they played a major role in serving.

Because many managerial women have internalized the values of male power, women secretaries have learned — the hard way — that women in power are not necessarily their "sisters" and may even try to hinder their collective struggles for advancement. That was, says Kristine Rondeau, lead organizer and chief negotiator for the Harvard Union of Clerical and Technical Workers, what brought many of her members to the union. A feisty thirty-seven-year-old, Rondeau has fought to unionize Harvard for the past thirteen years. As we sit in her tiny office, in a warren of similar partitioned units that makes up the headquarters of the union in Cambridge's Harvard Square, she describes the dilemmas her members have confronted. "People in managerial and supervisory positions here either have interpersonal or empathic skills or they don't. And a lot don't. What's more, they aren't encouraged to. There's no one behind the scenes who is saying, let's treat people with kindness, or, create an environment in which there are as many options for people as possible. That's not happening, and women who are in positions of power are as guilty as men."

In fact, Rondeau says, Harvard's well-financed campaign against the effort of its workers was run by a woman. She helped conduct a vigorous campaign to defeat a unionization effort on the part of 3,500 employees, 83 percent of whom are female. And she encouraged female supervisors to convince workers that collective action on their part would be a personal and academic disaster.

Many of these supervisors, professors, and managerial women did not join the campaign. But others did, in part, Rondeau feels, because of their negative attitudes toward women's work. "Secretaries and their employers are both taught that if they do clerical work for very long, like more than a couple of years, they are somehow defective. There's something wrong with you. So many of the women in power around here share men's views that secretaries are part of the bottom line. You figure out what your costs are and try to cut them as much as possible." Or maybe, she suggests, the discrimination her members experience is a result of the fact that their employers simply don't think about them in a serious way. They dismiss support workers, Rondeau says, because they refuse to acknowledge that these women — and men — "have at least as complicated lives as any high-powered administrator or professor. They deal with all the big issues, like life and death and raising a child. I don't think that there are a lot more serious issues than that. But because a lot of secretaries don't aspire to more, we're supposed to be failures."

What Rondeau describes is a hidden injury not only of patriarchy but of class, and such injuries have never evaporated, because only the sex of those in power changes. At the turn of the century, for example, when secretarial work became the predominantly female occupation it is today, thousands of women left their farms and sewing machines to take their places behind desks where they labored on the newly designed and refined typewriters that appeared in the nation's offices. Viewing these changes in female labor, upper-class "ladies" disdained these new "office girls" whom they considered to be inferior.

In the early 1920s, middle- and upper-class women and working women clashed over the Equal Rights Amendment. Upper-class women sought passage of a bill that would eliminate the kind of protective labor legislation that millions of working women depended on for protection in the workplace. During that same period, as more women entered the professions, they were trained, feminist historian Nancy Cott points out, "in a professional ideology that encouraged professional women to see a community of interest between themselves and professional men and a gulf between themselves and nonprofessional women."[11]

In offices of universities like Harvard and those of other corporate employers, hope has not triumphed over either experience or deep and enduring class divisions. Many secretaries say their employers have improved the quality of their working life. But, they add, it depends on the luck of the draw — on which woman is your boss. For some, like Elaine Bonfatto, an assistant librarian at Harvard, working for a woman has been a rewarding experience. Her boss is interested in helping her advance, has a young child, and thus cares about women's relationships to their children and understands that Bonfatto may have aspirations beyond her current job.

But not everyone is lucky. Donna Andrews, who worked at Harvard, has had a number of secretarial jobs in which females were her supervisors and was disenchanted after years of frustrating encounters. When she took her first secretarial job, at the Chase Manhattan Bank, Andrews, like many secretaries, had an advanced degree — a master's in education. She did not consider herself to be a "mere" secretary, a "nonentity." Her boss — a vice president on her way up the corporate ladder — did not share this view. "She saw me in the same way that men look upon secretaries. A secretary is there to launch you, support you, to make your career easier."

Rather than recognizing and rewarding what Andrews felt to be her competence and ambitions, her boss considered her a personal helpmate and related to her the way a busy male executive might relate to his wife, to whom he complains about work-related problems. "I was there to take care of things quietly and competently. And to be a nonentity. She never solicited my opinion about anything. Instead, she gave me long lists of things to do, and when she added another role, it never occurred to her to wonder if it was too much. She was like a man."

This female boss seems to have resisted giving her discontented secretary any support until she absolutely had to. "I wanted more challenging work and felt I had the ability to do it. But she didn't want to lose a secretary. She didn't say to herself, 'Well, here's another woman in a male-dominated environment who wants to move ahead, let's help her do it.' Although she did end up helping me, she didn't want to have to do it."

When Andrews finally got a promotion to a junior managerial position, her new female boss, she says, was not much of an improvement. "I had expected her to be more supportive because she had worked her way up from secretary to management. But she expected me to pay the same dues she had paid. She simply emulated the behavior that would get her ahead. And since there's a general disregard for subordinates in corporate culture, she behaved the way men behave."

Indeed, when Andrews finally made it clear that she did not

intend to stay in her job forever, her boss told her she would never again hire a woman with ambitions.

Although Andrews describes herself as a feminist, she is careful to explain that neither of her female employers shared her political sympathies. These women were classic corporate careerists, not advocates of feminist ideology.

But as Sabina Hawkins, a secretary at a New England college, learned, even the feminist label may be misleading. After working in support positions for most of her adult life, Hawkins — forty-three — took a job there because she was told the college had an excellent program for employee advancement. And she applied to work for her particular female boss — a well-respected academic feminist — because she knew of the woman's reputation. But it soon became evident that, professions of egalitarianism notwithstanding, her boss seems to have felt she, as a professor, was more important and valuable than a lowly secretary.

And so Hawkins found herself saddled with the classic secretarial stereotype described by Kanter ten years ago. In the course of a normal day at the office, she gets coffee for her boss, types, fields phone calls, makes copies, and handles various other assignments. It is also common for her to be asked to perform tasks that were never part of her formal job description. She recalls, in particular, one fall day when her boss arrived at work with the family dog in tow. The dog spent the day tied to a tree in the college courtyard. When Hawkins's boss left that afternoon, however, the dog was inadvertently left behind. About an hour later Hawkins's phone rang; it was her boss. She asked Hawkins to please fetch the dog and bring it home.

Or, she told me as we talked in a café near her office, there's the time she had a bad cold and temperature and wanted to go home early. "My boss had an appointment for her son and insisted that I had to get three things done before I left. I wound up staying late and I was fuming. I didn't say anything, partly because I'm a timid person and partly because, as an underling, I could lose my job if I did."

The next day, Hawkins's boss raised the incident — not to apologize, but to express concern about Hawkins's performance on the job. "She said I should be getting more work done. I think she has

a case, because I am getting bored and tired. But I don't think she
realizes how much time it takes to do these non-work-related
things she asks me to do. For example, she was working at home
this afternoon and asked me to find out who in town she has to
call to get her pipes tested for lead paint. Now wouldn't it be faster
for her to do that?"

What really troubles Hawkins is the sense that her "dead-end"
job will be difficult to escape. Since her first interview with her
current employer, she has understood and abided by the cardinal
rule: you never tell a prospective boss you want to move up, because then they won't hire you. Her boss, she says, must realize
that she doesn't want to be a secretary forever, because she is
taking a course in administration. But, Hawkins says, her boss has
never once asked her about her future plans. She does, however,
often ask Hawkins to photocopy feminist papers to be circulated
to female colleagues — never asking if Hawkins would like a copy
herself. "She knows I'm an M.A. But she has never solicited my
opinion or offered to help. To me that's particularly significant.
One reason," she says, speculating on her boss's studied indiffer-
ence, "is that she doesn't want to lose me. But I think, finally, she
doesn't even think about what I want personally. She has a full-
time nanny and a friend who helps her, and I always think that
collectively we are her wife."

Hawkins believes that her boss's feminism is "lateral," a sense
of comradeship and concern only with women in similar jobs, with
similar prospects, if not similar titles. "There's no mentoring. I
think women on that level are having such a hard time surviving
that they don't even have the time or ability to help women up
who are under them."

Beverly Johnson, a black twenty-four-year-old Harvard secretary, is disturbed not only by gender issues, but by racial ones as
well. She, too, works for women bosses — doctors at the Medical
School. And she, too, has come to the conclusion that gender is no
protection against either classism or racism. "I have a B.A., and
I'm applying to graduate school next year. But these women are
not very helpful. They are very self-centered. They care about
women who are in the health care professions and women who are

other doctors. But they don't give a thought to what I and the other secretaries want from our jobs and our lives."

Johnson believes that these elite white women professionals also perceive her to be "inferior" because she is black. "You're not considered to have many aspirations in life if you're a secretary per se. But it's worse because I'm black. Maybe it's because I look younger than I am, but these women seem to think of me as a little girl. I find that they give me much more detailed instructions than they give other women who work for them. My boss will ask me to type a letter and then she'll add, 'and please date the letter.' Or someone will say, 'Oh, by the way, could you order some ball-point pens — that's PaperMate.' With white secretaries, they never give those kinds of detailed instructions. What's interesting is that I trained that white secretary. She comes to me to ask me questions when she has one."

Johnson says that her relationships with her female superiors changed only when they found out that she had been admitted to graduate school. "Before they learned this," she explains, "they never had time to speak to me. They talked to me about my plans and seemed to be astounded when I explained them. Now it's as if I have become a human being because I'm on their track. The other secretary in the office, however, is Hispanic. She is not on their track, and she's just considered another poor unfortunate."

In talking with secretaries like Sabina Hawkins, Donna Andrews, and Beverly Johnson, several disturbing truths emerge. Not only do some dismiss those who are considered to be permanently "off-track," some female superiors may use either their femininity or feminist ideology to disarm their female subordinates. Andrews explains that although neither of her bosses ever felt a reciprocal obligation to help her advance, they both appealed to her femininity and her feminist consciousness to get her to help them in *their* struggles, against men. Suggesting that they were comrades in arms in a battle against male privilege, these professional women implied that their victories would help pave the way for the women who were under them. In practice, however, the only benefit the secretaries got out of their bosses' promotions was the opportunity to work for a woman with a more prestigious title.

In some instances, working for a female boss may even be worse for a woman than working for a man. Sabina Hawkins prefers working for a woman, in spite of her boss's behavior. "There's just enough difference. Just that little edge. It would bother me to do some of these subservient things for a man. But it doesn't bother me as much to do them for a woman. I would feel more degraded with a man. With a man I would feel it necessary to resist."

But when someone like Hawkins — a quiet woman who cares about women's progress — is confronted with the same demands from a female boss, the illusion of difference is apparently beguiling. Sadly, through such interactions, feminism is reduced to rhetoric with little or no substance.

The female subordinates involved in these complex and confusing encounters often misunderstand the dynamic that controls their lives and, as a result, may give male employers more credit than they are due. Both Hawkins and Andrews attribute their bosses' behavior to some innate female flaw. Women, they insist, have trouble mentoring other women; rather than bringing subordinates up with them, they leave them behind. These women believe that men, on the other hand, are truly generous because they graciously mentor male subordinates and help them climb the ladder of success.

This notion concentrates so heavily on gender that it ignores issues of class. Yes, some men do bring other men along — but that is because the men in question are generally both of the same class and on the same professional, elite track. A senior partner in a law firm may indeed adopt a junior partner and guide him through the corporate hierarchy. Or a chief executive officer may identify an up-and-coming young manager and show him the ropes. But secretaries are not in the same kind of subordinate role as junior partners in law firms or managers in large corporations. By definition, they are off the professional career track.

And, in analogous situations, men and women in power tend to act in the same way. The executive in an auto plant does not, typically, reach down into the ranks of factory workers for managerial candidates. Physicians in hospitals do not often "mentor" lab techs. And, in spite of some secretarial workers' advanced educational qualifications and "close" working relationships with their bosses, they are no nearer the latter in status than the factory worker is to the factory owner. It is this difference in class, rather than in gender, that most frequently determines conduct.

This became quite clear when I talked with male secretaries working for both male and female bosses. Jonathan Spencer also works as a secretary at Harvard. He is from an upper-middle-class family and attended a prestigious Ivy League college. When he left school, however, he decided he did not want a fast-track career in investment banking or corporate law. Instead, he sought a low-stress job that would allow him to pursue his real love, art.

One of the first things Spencer discovered is that secretarial work carries far more stress and demands more skills than he had imagined. "It's not easy to do this job well. It's surprising how challenging it is. People underestimate how much decision making there is in clerical work. They underestimate how hard it is to deal with the conflicting nature of the demands, and the powerlessness you feel makes it even more stressful."

And a man sitting behind a secretary's desk does not receive any more power or respect than a woman. It is true, Spencer acknowledges, that his male boss is probably more reluctant to ask him to get the coffee or water the plants than he would be to ask a female secretary. But these minor privileges aside, he feels that his boss makes no distinction between male and female secretarial workers. "My boss is an old-school guy. He sees us as tools of his trade. He notices us most when we're in his way. He has no idea what I do. In fact, I think he thinks I don't do very much. He doesn't have much sympathy for how much work goes into the job. He doesn't see the need, for example, of taking a coffee break. If we're chatting for more than a few minutes, he's upset. The idea is that we're supposed to be seen and not heard, just like children."

Male secretaries may have the same problems as female secretaries, even when they work for female bosses, says Eric Ames, a thirty-three-year-old clerical worker at the Law School. Like Spencer, Ames came from a well-to-do background, but he never finished college. He realized, after a stint in the family business, that he just wasn't interested in earning a high salary and driving a BMW like some of his friends. "I guess I'm a committed under-achiever," he quips.

Ames does not feel he is "inferior" to men and women who do pursue fast-track careers — but he is well aware that his female boss does not share his view that there is more than one path to self-fulfillment. This high-powered woman, he says, views secretaries and clerical workers as inferiors who exist only to make her life easier. She is egalitarian in only one respect: she asks him to get the coffee. "In our office, no one makes coffee, we go out and buy it. She'll go by my desk and say, 'Here's fifty cents, would you get me a coffee?' She'll ask us to do personal errands for her in the Square, or go to the post office. It's just expected."

Moreover, his boss likes to be "the boss." "She does not like to be questioned any more than a male boss does. The other day I was doing a project that took me half a day to complete. I realized while I was doing it that it actually could have taken twenty minutes had I been able to do it my way. I mentioned this to her, but she insisted on my doing it her way."

The fact that Ames has made a nontraditional career choice and that his boss is committed to working herself up the traditional masculine career ladder makes things even more complicated. "As a man I'm treated as somehow less because I don't want to do 'more' with my life. I'm looked down upon because I'm not 'achieving' anything. It's really weird, because I'm a guy who comes to work without a suit and tie on, wearing a turtleneck and jeans. I don't want to make a lot of money and get a lot of status. And here's this woman who feels she has to wear conservative suits and who must work very hard to get ahead. And I look at her and think, my God, this woman is taking everything much too seriously — and she looks at me and thinks I don't take things seriously enough."

The relationship between secretaries and their bosses is admittedly a complex one. By its nature, secretarial work can often involve work performed with less autonomy in a subordinate position. Many secretaries may resent working for rather than with another woman, no matter how well they are treated.

I could not, for obvious reasons (the fear of reprisal and loss of their jobs), interview the bosses of the women and men I interviewed to obtain their version of the relationship. Other professional women, however, have recounted frustrating stories of trying to be sensitive, supportive employers to their secretaries to no avail. "I tried to work on a relationship with my secretary for over two years," an editor in a major publishing house told me. "I think I was very supportive and caring. But she just hated being a secretary and resented every little thing she had to do for me. Finally, after two years of trying to work things out, I felt forced to fire her."

Other female employers have explained that they have tried to create more egalitarian relationships in their offices but have been frustrated by their secretary's allegiance to hierarchical structures. A prominent academic told me that when she was awarded a prestigious chair and a larger secretarial staff to go with it, she tried to eliminate the degrading coffee-making, washing-up rituals her male counterparts considered acceptable office behavior. Her staff refused to allow her to get the coffee or wash out her dishes. They thought someone as important as she should not have to do such menial tasks at the office, tasks she pointed out that she does every night when she goes home.

In spite of the many professional women who try to create a more supportive environment in their workplaces, secretaries argue that the very structure of corporate institutions may defeat the best-intentioned employers. Although much of mainstream liberal feminism still encourages women to believe in the *Working Girl* myth that the way to solve workplace problems is through individual advancement, many secretaries recognize that they will spend their work lives behind the typewriter, not in the front office — if only because there aren't enough offices to accommodate all who would like to fill them. That is why so many have embraced a different feminist agenda — an agenda that prescribes collective action as well as a radical reconsideration of traditional American definitions of success.

"The idea that anyone with brains and ambition can become a boss has a number of flaws," says Kristine Rondeau. "Of course it does take intelligence to be a secretary. But the fact is that the vast majority of secretaries — even those with B.A.'s, M.A.'s, and sometimes even Ph.D.'s — remain secretaries or in secretary-like positions their whole life. And when they do, they can't rely on

successful people to represent them because you just can't take it
for granted that successful people will represent anyone but themselves."

Even more importantly, Rondeau asks, why is it that people who
aspire to rise from the ranks rather than with them are the only
ones in this society who are considered a success? "Whose idea is
it that secretaries want to be the boss? In our union, we personally
have spent a lot of time thinking about values. We want to be
rewarded and respected for our work. But we do not necessarily
want to be management. That's not to say that we have utter
disrespect for management or that we don't believe you need a
good salary to live on. But there are other routes to happiness than
simply looking out for number one and climbing to the top. Life
is a lot richer and more complicated than that."

Why some women workers have become skeptical of a narrow
definition of feminism that concentrates so heavily on individual
advancement and success becomes clearer when one examines the
conduct of some of the women who have attained considerable
corporate power. Equal-opportunity feminism and much of marketplace ideology, we recall, assured women that those who advanced the highest would fulfill their sisterly obligations not only
to women on their level but to the majority of women nowhere
near it, once they had attained such power. While some of these
women try to be responsible and accountable, too many — even
those who consider themselves to be committed progressives and
feminists — seem to have forgotten (or may feel forced to set
aside) that caring mandate on their way to the top.

The responses of two prominent feminist corporate and university board members to the pleas of striking female workers are
illustrative examples of this larger problem.

In August 1989, sixty thousand members of the Communications Workers of America (CWA) and the International Brotherhood of Electrical Workers (IBEW) went on strike against
NYNEX, the regional telephone company serving New York and
New England. The bitter, four-month dispute that ensued was
triggered by a management demand for health care cost shifting.
Despite earnings of nearly four billion dollars in the three years

preceding the strike, NYNEX wanted its employees to start paying hundreds and eventually thousands of dollars for their medical coverage.

NYNEX workers refused to make this costly concession; CWA and IBEW argued that shifting the burden of medical cost inflation from the employer to the employees would do little to contain costs at their source in the nation's crisis-ridden health care system. The unions urged NYNEX to join with labor in lobbying for a Canadian-style national health insurance program that would guarantee all Americans access to affordable health care while simultaneously controlling expenditures more effectively. In addition to calling for health care reform, the telephone workers also pointed out various short-term cost containment steps that would save the company an estimated $23 million within the framework of its existing private medical plan.

Of the sixty thousand workers involved in the strike, more than half were women who had another reason for walking off their jobs in protest. NYNEX also sought wage concessions in the form of a new compensation system that would discriminate against workers in lower-paid, predominantly female jobs. Instead of granting across-the-board percentage increases that would go into each worker's base pay (and thus be reflected in fringe benefit calculations), the company wanted to shift to lump-sum payments.

Under NYNEX's original offer, the first-year contract increase would have been 5 percent. However, the first $1,000 of this amount — for many women, their entire raise — would have been in the form of a one-time cash bonus that would not increase the rate of pay to which future percentage increases would be applied. Two female economists from the Institute for Women's Policy Research examined this proposal and concluded that it would merely exacerbate the existing gender-based pay gap between male and female telephone workers. According to Institute researchers Heidi Hartman and Roberta Spalter-Roth, NYNEX's proposed lump sums "would increase the base wages of lower-paid clerical workers (largely female) by a significantly lesser amount than it would the base wages of higher-paid mechanics and repair workers (largely male)." It should be viewed, they said, "as an anti-pay equity policy that would increase inequality between men and women in the telephone industry, as well as between typically male- and female-dominated jobs."

"For our members," says Donna Conroy, an outspoken local union president of CWA in Troy, New York, "the issue was pretty clear-cut. It meant survival. It was an issue we felt was going to make or break us in terms of our jobs, our self-respect and dignity. Most of the people in our local — and they're eighty-five percent female — felt this way. That's why they were willing to sacrifice so much for this strike. For many of us — a great many of whom are single heads of households — the economic impact of the strike was devastating. The stories were incredible. It was a terrible tragedy to individual families. People got their medical benefits cut off who had sick children. People were losing their homes. It was a testament to their sense of purpose that they were willing to go through this."

"As an employee I felt humiliated by the company's position," says forty-one-year-old Diane Stangle, who had worked for the company as a directory assistance operator for thirteen years in upstate New York. "It broke my heart. I couldn't believe what the company was doing to people. This town has twenty-two thousand people and NYNEX is the largest employer. It wiped a lot of us out." Her predicament, she says, was very difficult but, she admits, mild compared to what many other families suffered. "I have a son in college and I'm divorced. I had to pay for his tuition and books, for my housing and food, and I had no paycheck and didn't collect unemployment benefits for nine weeks. It wiped me out. It took all my savings. I had to cash in savings bonds. It was a terrible blow."

Because the strike had such a serious impact on women, a broad range of feminist groups, including the National Organization for Women (NOW), joined the unions in opposing NYNEX's wage demands as a threat to all women employed in the service sector. As part of the public education and outreach they conducted on this issue, union leaders contacted members of the NYNEX board of directors thought to be most sympathetic to the plight of female telephone workers. The first to be approached was the company's only female director, Elizabeth Topham Kennan, a noted medievalist and the president of Mount Holyoke College.

Kennan is among the small handful of women prominent in business, law, or academia who have been asked to serve on the boards of major corporations and who now sit alongside the more typical wealthy, white male directors who represent banks, insurance companies, and other large businesses. This development — even when smacking of tokenism — has been hailed as a victory for all women. In Kennan's own view, her position on the NYNEX board — and her directorships on a large Massachusetts bank, an insurance company, and an electric utility — reflect the significant contribution of women's colleges, such as Mount Holyoke, in preparing women for new roles in the world of work.

"Women have become important in America because of women's colleges," Kennan declared when she assumed the presidency of Mount Holyoke. "The first woman cabinet member in America was a Mount Holyoke graduate, as was the first woman elected governor in her own right. . . . Only here can women develop the strength and resilience to enable them to deal with the discrimination which still remains and with the cross-cutting responsibilities of family life which will always remain."

In a later speech on women and power that was reprinted and distributed by the Mount Holyoke chapter of NOW, Kennan elaborated on the special contribution that women themselves can make in the professions and in the decision-making positions in which they have traditionally been under-represented. Citing an academic study of influential women, she contended that "women who share with men an interest in power differ from men in aggression, in domesticity . . . power-motivated women are more magnanimous than men with a similar orientation. They tend to be highly responsive to human relationships *in every situation and especially in crisis*" (my italics).

Kennan noted that feminists have long hoped that women in power could make a "difference" but feared that they might become "ersatz men" instead. She urged her audience, the Junior League of Boston, to look closely and critically "at the women who exercise authority, and at their experience of it. Are their methods and motives in fact far different from those of men, informed more by a consideration of the effects of actions upon the lives of others? Are their decisions, their very wielding of power, shaped and tempered by characteristic attention to human relationships? How many of them . . . serve in a position primarily to make the world more hospitable for future generations?

"I suspect that the true radical potential of feminism lies in the individual women who are willing to make the sacrifice of self that is entailed in exercising authority," she concluded. "For these women, there may be occasional loneliness, as decision makers must always, in the final analysis, be lonely. But they retain the responsibility to strengthen, to listen, to understand, to provide for this generation and the next. Women in power have enormous potential: we have only to seize it."

In the first month of the NYNEX strike, Kennan herself was suddenly confronted with the opportunity to "seize" that potential and the responsibility to demonstrate that women in positions of power can make a difference, can listen, understand, be more responsive in situations of crisis, and base their actions on how they affect the lives of others.

Kennan received a two-page letter from the Communications Workers of America requesting that she meet with a delegation of telephone workers to discuss "the current destructive course of the company's labor relations policies as they affect women and all other employees. Female members of the IBEW and CWA, who are also NYNEX stockholders, want to confer with you about the company's position on health care cost shifting," the letter said. "They believe that you, as the only woman on the Board of Directors of NYNEX and president of a leading women's college, will hopefully be more sensitive to their concerns than top NYNEX negotiators (and other male executives) have been in the last few months of frustrating negotiations."

Specifically, the IBEW and CWA women, who represented tens of thousands of shareholder employees, wanted to explain to Kennan how the company's proposed wage and benefit give-backs would "drastically reduce their standard of living, force some to limit their utilization of health care, and put the families of female single parents under increasing financial strain." They hoped that Kennan might be sympathetic to such union objectives as improved "health and safety standards governing the use of Video Display Terminals in NYNEX workplaces," and "a ban on secret remote monitoring of operators and other workers — one of the most oppressive and degrading management practices currently in existence." Such measures, the CWA letter pointed out, would "greatly improve the working conditions in NYNEX's primarily female, lower-paying clerical and operator jobs."

Instead of a meeting with Elizabeth Kennan, however, the NYNEX strikers got the following reply, which read in its entirety: "I have received your letter of August 16 with its request to meet with me. Although I am, of course, interested in all matters touching NYNEX and although I understand the seriousness of medical issues in the United States for us all, the forum for solution of those problems in the NYNEX family is the bargaining table. For me to insert myself into those conversations would only be an interference with the normal process. I must, therefore, decline to meet with you. I have sent a copy of your letter to [a NYNEX labor relations official] and urge you to direct all further inquiries to him."

Female strikers were angered and dismayed by this response. Kennan's role on the board was to represent the shareholders by monitoring the performance of the day-to-day management of NYNEX. Since tens of thousands of union members are also shareholders in the company, they felt it perfectly reasonable to request a meeting with her and other directors to express their concerns about the direction of the company under its current management. Her refusal to talk with women strikers seemed a repudiation of her role as a responsible outside director and a publicly recognized women's leader. Kennan's stance on strike-related issues affecting women was seemingly no different than that of most male board members — fewer of whom were expected to meet with employees, listen to them, or otherwise respond to their appeals. In fact, while Kennan refused to act, one male board member whom strikers approached did play an important behind-the-scenes role in bringing the strike to a constructive end.

"It was incredible to us that Kennan — a supposed feminist — would not even talk to us and apparently didn't make any effort on our behalf within the board," says Conroy. "The most disturbing thing was that feminists like myself have for years criticized men on boards of directors for being insensitive, for not considering women's issues, and the poor, and for just paying attention to the sacred bottom line. And here was a prestigious woman, who claimed to be a feminist and talked a great game about how different women were in power, and when she had a prime opportunity to take a leading role to speak out on a major woman's issue, she wouldn't."

The NYNEX workers decided to press their case with Kennan in person. Buses carrying three hundred women strikers arrived at Mount Holyoke during registration week. Joined by sympathetic students and faculty members, the strikers rallied outside Kennan's home and office, demanding that she meet with them. The president of the college was nowhere to be found. Through her secretary, she issued a terse statement indicating that "if a small delegation from NOW, not connected to NYNEX, wishes to speak with me, I shall be willing to meet with them" at a later date. Her conditions for that meeting: there could be no strikers involved and no more demonstrators on campus.

This new rebuff puzzled strikers even more. Why, they wanted to know, would Kennan agree to meet with the generally middle- and upper-middle-class members of NOW, but not with the working-class women who were also supposed to benefit from having women like Kennan in positions of power on their board?

"I was shocked at her conduct," says Wilma Goodman, a thirty-year-old IBEW member from Troy, New York, who demonstrated at Mount Holyoke. "It was incredible to see how this woman lives, and how much she earns — she gets four thousand dollars more than I do — for just going to ten board meetings a year and that's on top of her Mount Holyoke salary. [Kennan makes $31,000 a year for attending these meetings, and after five years of service, qualifies for a pension at half pay.] A member of the board of directors at NYNEX has a responsibility to the employees of her company, who are also shareholders of that company. We had valid things we wanted to discuss with her. We are the ones who are making this company work. We generate revenue for it. I think of myself as a feminist, but women who do not understand what feminism is and who learn about this kind of hypocrisy are not impressed. When feminism is defined like Kennan defines it — as talk but no action — it sends the wrong message to women and to the world."

These concerns were relayed directly to Kennan, via a letter from the female strikers, that was presented to the Mount Holyoke president when the NOW delegation did finally meet with her more than a month later. In their new appeal, the strikers acknowledged Kennan's desire not to interfere in any way with the "normal process" of negotiations. They suggested, as an alternative, that she meet with them after the strike, when she would no longer be under any such constraints. In her discussions with NOW representatives, Kennan had appeared receptive to this idea and agreed to consider it.

In the end, however, she didn't even wait for the strike to be resolved before refusing again. "Upon completion of contract negotiations, I urge you to contact Richard Kingsbury, Managing Director — Human Resources — at New England Telephone Company," she said in a letter dated October 7, 1989. "It is not appropriate for me to intervene in administration matters, and I am sure Mr. Kingsbury will be helpful."

Without Kennan's help, the telephone workers went on to defeat NYNEX's demands for wage and benefit concessions. After a four-month strike, they agreed to a new contract with no health care cost shifting or lump-sum bonuses. But as of this writing, women workers are still pursuing their so far unsuccessful quest for face-to-face discussions with the only one of the company's twelve directors presumed to have particular sympathy for women's issues.

"Why Kennan would not make a statement to indicate that she was at least sympathetic to the strikers and concerned about health care issues is beyond me," Donna Conroy observes. "It shows that she is more dedicated to her position in the corporate hierarchy than to the women's movement. Or that she defines the women's movement as an elite of women getting ahead and the hell with those of us at the bottom. I'm a feminist. But to call yourself that carries some heavy obligations — like helping other women regardless of what job they have. You don't have to step over people to serve the corporation. There is some middle ground. And at some point you have to take a stand. It's just tragic that we didn't

have someone in a position to make a difference when we were
dealing with a major social issue like health care and compensation
for women."

I called Kennan several times for comment. Like the strikers, I
was never able to get through to her directly. Using her secretary
to shield herself, she refused to comment. "It's not looking too
good," her secretary informed me the last time I called. "There's
just no time in her calendar when she can talk to you."

Unfortunately Elizabeth Kennan is not alone as a feminist board
member who seems to have chosen the path of inactivity rather
than accountability. In the 1984–1985 Yale University strike,
leading black civil rights and feminist advocate Eleanor Holmes-
Norton also refused to speak out publicly on issues that directly
affected women workers.

Eleanor Holmes-Norton has always been a courageous woman
of great integrity. She gained her reputation as a civil rights and
women's advocate. Under the Carter administration she was appointed commissioner of the Equal Employment Opportunity
Commission and vigorously battled employers who discriminated
against female and minority employees. She played an instrumental role in placing the government on the side of those who had
suffered oppression for centuries. She later became a professor of
law at Georgetown University and was appointed one of sixteen
trustees of the Yale Corporation.

This particular episode illuminates the terrible moral dilemmas
that confront critics of any social and economic system when they
move from a position outside the system to one inside. Although
Holmes-Norton would not talk with me, she may have been greatly
disturbed and torn by her role. Certainly, the strikers who did
agree to talk about the episode spoke about her response to their
pleas for help with as much sorrow as anger.

The strike by members of the Hotel and Restaurant Workers
Union representing clerical and technical workers at Yale was a
strike about the classic feminist and minority issue of pay equity.
The union represented 2,600 white-collar workers at Yale, 82 percent of whom are women. "The central issue of the strike for the
many female and minority workers who waged it," says Lucile

Dickess, president of the union, "was that the university recognize us and the work we do and pay us for what we do."

"It was about respect and equity," says Annie Talbot, who served on the union negotiating committee and had, at the time, worked for Yale as a research assistant for five years. "It was about pay equity. We were fighting because women clerical and technical workers at Yale were paid at very different levels than male blue-collar workers. For example, a male truck driver, who needed only a driver's license to qualify for his job, was paid eight thousand dollars more than a female administrative assistant who had a four-year or sometimes even a master's degree and who was in charge of supervising students and running a whole department."

The strikers' strategy was to conduct not only a classic work stoppage but an education campaign, explaining the issues involved to Yale students and professors, the New Haven community, a national public, and the Yale board of trustees. Generally insulated from the decisions they make, board members, they felt, did not understand the impact of Yale's recalcitrance on the employees involved. Yale trustees did not live in New Haven, and so strikers approached them via telephone and letter to ask for face-to-face meetings. All, including Holmes-Norton, refused. So the strikers tried to meet with trustees wherever they could find them. Because Holmes-Norton had been such an outspoken advocate of women and minority issues, she was a particular target of education and activity (as were several other more liberal members of the board).

After going through the proper channels and failing to arrange a meeting, strikers went to Georgetown University where Holmes-Norton taught and followed her to several public events at which she was speaking. When strikers learned that she was going to speak at a dinner sponsored by the Women and Politics Program at Boston College, they decided to picket the event. Upon learning of the proposed protest, Holmes-Norton reneged on her commitment to appear. After protracted negotiations with the dinner's sponsors, she agreed to speak — if, that is, the protest was not on the college grounds.

After the dinner, two strikers managed to get onto the Boston College campus and, yet again, requested a meeting with

Holmes-Norton. She finally agreed to talk with them. At the meeting, says Steve Fortes, a young black Yale employee, she insisted that she was, in fact, supportive of their demands and said she was working for the strikers, but on the inside. She insisted that any public statement to that effect would compromise her ability to work within the system.

"She said, 'I salute you in your cause,' and she saluted us with her hand," says Fortes. "And then she explained that if you're a minority member of the board, you can't make too many waves. And then she left."

"I had two personal encounters with her," says Deborah Chernoff, another striking employee. "When she was speaking at a women's conference in Hartford, I managed to sit down with her for a short time. She essentially said she was our best friend on the Corporation but that we were naive to think that we could get things done through the kind of organizing we were doing."

Coming from a woman who had participated in two social movements based on nonviolent confrontation with power, this seemed a particularly odd argument to the strikers. "We asked her to make a public statement dissenting from the board's position and she declined. She told us that you needed to be part of the power structure to change it. We, on the other hand, argued that thousands of people had struggled to get people like her onto the Corporation and we asked what good it would do if she wouldn't speak out for us? She replied that we were naive.

"We, however, believed that a public statement affirming that there was indeed a legitimate pay equity issue involved would have helped us immensely, since the university consistently denied that there was any discrimination involved."

When Holmes-Norton once again declined to comment publicly on the issue, the strikers continued to appear at public functions at which she spoke. "My last encounter with her," says Chernoff, "was at an American Civil Liberties Union dinner she was speaking at in New York. Her talk was about how important it was to stand up for the little guy. We had purchased a table. Our aim was not to disrupt the dinner but only to plead our case. When she saw me, she seemed furious," Chernoff recalls.

Holmes-Norton never made a public statement expressing her

support of the strikers or disclaiming a connection with the Corporation's actions. Interestingly, she did violate her apparent policy not to publicly express disagreement with Yale's decisions when the university refused to divest in South Africa. At that point, she dissociated herself from their action.

"The whole incident filled me with distress," says Talbot. "I wouldn't be at all surprised if some Wall Street lawyer wasn't sympathetic and wouldn't be helpful. But she's a self-identified feminist. This was her issue. It seemed to us such a betrayal and an act of hypocrisy. Sometimes I hear about her speaking for some feminist event, and I can't believe it. Of course, having a black woman on the Yale Corporation could be a victory for women. But not if she doesn't do anything. And not if she won't come out publicly to fight for what she says she believes and say clearly which side she is on."

When I called Holmes-Norton to ask her to speak to me about the problems that confront women in power, her secretary — who fielded the request — called back with her polite refusal. He told me that she was too busy running for public office in Washington, D.C., to talk to anyone about anything other than the campaign. I was, therefore, unfortunately unable to ask her for her version of the Yale strike and her role in it.

The strike-related controversies surrounding Elizabeth Kennan and Eleanor Holmes-Norton both illustrate the limitations of a strategy that relies on women at the top of the corporate heap to bring about real change for those at the bottom. Women serving as corporate directors or university trustees are obviously at a disadvantage in shaping the policy of boards dominated by conservative male majorities. However, there are no formal, legal constraints on their speaking out publicly or consulting with shareholder constituencies. What seems to inhibit women like Kennan and Holmes-Norton is the pressure to conform to the unwritten rules of behavior for corporate directors. They have been admitted, in limited numbers, to what remains essentially an exclusive club, part of the "old-boy network." Perhaps their fear may be that they will not be accepted and listened to unless they play by the old-boy rules.

What they seem to forget is that they have not obtained these positions solely as a result of their individual career success, or professional or business status. The very fact that a black civil rights advocate adorned the board of the Yale Corporation or that a white feminist sits alongside insurance and banking-industry executives at NYNEX directors' meetings is the result of years of agitation for affirmative action at every level of the business and academic worlds. Movements of those excluded from corporate decision-making bodies forced corporations and universities to make governing boards more representative of the society at large. The presumption was that the newly appointed "representatives" would, in fact, represent something different. This means not just providing a black and/or female face for the annual report or, in Holmes-Norton's case, claiming to work quietly on the inside, but giving public voice to the concerns of the constituencies that, in effect, elevated them to director positions.

Many feminists would argue that political caution, cowardice, or hypocrisy on the part of isolated women in positions of power is the inevitable result of tokenism. Real institutional change benefiting most women rather than simply an elite would be possible, they say, if women occupied a greater proportion of corporate director and management jobs. In reality, however, those making initial breakthroughs must struggle to change the institutional and societal framework for themselves and those who will join or follow them. If they do not, there may be new players, but the rules of the game won't change, and neither will the outcome for their supporters in the stands.

In assessing the relationships between women in power and those under them, it is indisputable that some changes have been more than cosmetic. Women do not often sexually harass subordinates or use chauvinist language. They often try to be kinder and gentler. But when it comes to more substantive transformations of the workplace, women at the top often end up looking out for number one whether they intend to or not.

It is important to understand how and why this happens and what working women are doing to address issues of inequality in power, wealth, and status. My aim, in this discussion, has not been to reveal the unremarkable fact that women can be as callous, hypocritical, or unsupportive as men, but to cast light on the much larger and more important problem of accountability, responsibility, and collective action.

Women have been told to look upon women in power as role models. But what kind of conduct are they modeling? In a society like ours, where many are led to believe that the highest good is accountability to the self and one's own advancement, the very ideal of a role model who serves a broader moral and social purpose has been subverted. In this context, moreover, role modeling can foreclose the dimension of collective action and collective responsibility. We're supposed to identify with and support the struggles of women who get ahead, so that each one of us, as individuals, can one day be like those who succeed in the most conventional terms. The mutual obligation that women have to "push together" is overshadowed by their individual obligation to succeed — to be smart enough to get to the top and tough and shrewd enough to stay there.

But without a commitment to helping the ranks of working women attain both greater social standing and financial reward, the expansive ideal of sisterhood is reduced to a narrow sorority of elite women. And we will have journeyed into a world where women's task is not to transform power relationships but rather to replicate those that all too often prevail.

Chapter Seven

DOMESTIC DISTURBANCES

RELATIONSHIPS HAVE been the core of women's lives. Nurturing relationships has been our job description as gender. Tending to relational life has not only been an onerous obligation: it has enriched our lives and given us those feminine skills that make such a difference in our world.

If intimate relationships have been problematic for women, it is not because they are inherently oppressive. Although relationships certainly involve conflict, community and family have been imprisoning for women because of the patriarchal context that has defined women's existence.

One of feminism's greatest contributions has been to evaluate women's relational work. Feminist thinkers like Carol Gilligan, Jean Baker Miller, Nel Noddings, and many others have demystified male models of human development that conceal, rather than reveal, the importance of human relationships. As described by these women, the male model of human psychological and moral development posits an antirelational self. In mainstream psychological and moral developmental theory, the healthy human being is the person (read man) who is autonomous, self-reliant, and individuated. His life is a journey of disconnection, a collection of failed relationships. His developmental trajectory demands a slow shedding of relationships. First he must disengage from his mother. Then he must "kill" his father. From there he separates — definitively — from teachers and mentors so that he can become "his own man." He solves his moral and ethical dilemmas by divorcing them from a relational context, referring to abstract rules of equality and fairness that govern his decisions. Any hint of the need for care is considered a sign of weakness.

Unfortunately for men, women, and children, the end of this journey of disconnection, as Jean Baker Miller observes so aptly, is supposed to be attachment and intimacy — attachment with one woman and their children in the nuclear family. But after spending his emotional life alone, he is hardly equipped to relate to others and attain the exclusive intimacy that mainstream psychological theory considers the culmination of healthy development.[1]

Feminist thinkers have explained how activity in the marketplace, the playing field, and the battleground has impacted male definitions of development. And they have contrasted male development with female development, examining how women — indeed how all human beings — develop in a web of relationships, whether they acknowledge it or not. Just as feminist thinkers today revalue relationships, late-twentieth-century feminism itself was based, in great part, on a desire to preserve and enhance women's relational lives.

Women used to live in a diverse relational context of community, extended family, and friendship. But after the Second World War, American society became increasingly derelationalized. Vast numbers of middle- and upper-middle-class women were confined to newly constructed suburbs that uprooted community life as thoroughly as the trees and brush on which they were built. These "communities" lacked organic social centers — what social observer Ray Oldenburg calls neutral third places — pubs, bars, cafés, coffee shops where people could meet and socialize spontaneously.[2] All social encounters were scheduled. Transiency became a fact of urban and suburban life, exacerbating women's sense of isolation.

Women were increasingly dependent on nuclear families in which husbands commuted hours to and from work. When they returned home they were often too exhausted and almost always too divorced from their wives' domestic worlds to communicate. Women were forced to center their lives and aspirations exclusively around young children who could not possibly satisfy their mothers' interpersonal needs and older children who no longer required their vigilant attention.[3]

This suburban housewife syndrome provided the impetus for Betty Friedan's *Feminine Mystique* and much of the liberal feminist movement. Many middle- and upper-middle-class teenagers and young adults looked at their mothers and did not want to reproduce their seemingly empty lives. To escape solitude, loneliness, and the relational desert of suburbia, we would enter the marketplace. Our caring skills would enhance work, many of us thought, and working would enhance our ability to care at home. Work would remedy the relational scarcity that afflicted women, providing us with an ever widening circle of relationships. Many of us hoped we would gain professional self-esteem, and we were sure we would also gain relationships.

While work has, in fact, helped many women gain a greater sense of self-esteem and is certainly an integral part of any feminist caring agenda, the relational problems of women have not been solved by the marketplace. Not because work is inevitably antirelational, but because work in the American marketplace, as it is currently constructed, is. The "free" American marketplace does not value relationships. Relationships are considered impediments to profit, performance, and productivity. The only kind of relationships the market values are instrumental relationships: the kind that get you something — money, fame, power, status. Indeed, in much marketplace ideology there is no greater impediment to workplace performance than close relationships — with members of one's community, friends, lovers, mates, and children and parents.

Given the workplace context in which so many women now spend their lives, it is no surprise that women's relational lives have been compromised by the marketplace, just as men's have been for centuries.

Women's relationships have been affected in three primary ways. The incessant and irreconcilable demands of work and personal life have forced many women to retreat from caring both in the workplace and at home. A great many women have felt they have had no choice but to abandon the friendships and community relationships they have sustained — and that have sustained them — for so long. A number of women have found that the time and energy they've put into forging their careers has also robbed them of the ability to find and maintain relationships — particularly with mates and family. At a certain point in their lives, many women who had put relationships on the back burner discover they want and need them but that they are nowhere to be found.

Finally, many women who do have mates and children feel that their relational lives are unfulfilling. To some extent this is an accident of history. The men from whom women now seek intimacy have been socialized to fear it. Their sex is at a very different developmental point in its history than the female sex. But to some extent, their sense of dissatisfaction is a symptom of larger social problems. Women's entrance into the marketplace has not been able to stem America's destruction of the social context that sustains family and community. In fact, as we have seen, and will see, some women have even become aggressive advocates of the virtues of a derelationalized existence. Because of their lack of friendships, community, and collegial workplace relationships, many women are led to overburden their intimate relationships with expectations no human being — male or female — could ever fulfill. And the expectation that one's mate can be everything can defeat women and their efforts to change their own lives and the men they live with.

Vivian Alan is a woman who feels she has had to sacrifice some important aspects of caring to work. She and I meet on a cold winter night in January. Her husband, Jim, is sitting in the dining room, going over the homework of their eight-year-old son, Matthew. Twelve-year-old David is in his bedroom, huddled over his assignment. And six-year-old Jean is brushing her teeth and getting ready for bed. The dinner dishes have been cleared away. The sandwiches for tomorrow's school lunches are stored in the refrigerator. The children's lunch boxes are set out on the kitchen counter. In their rooms, clothes for the next day are already selected and stacked neatly on their dressers.

Such organization is essential, says Alan, a thirty-seven-year-old physical therapist, if she is to continue working full-time — as she's done for the past ten years — and take care of her family, too. "I have to be so organized to make everything roll in the morning. Everything for school has to be done the night before. The kids know they have to do it. We get our hair cut short so that we don't have to do anything with it. I don't want to fuss with my hair, with clothes, with makeup," she explains.

Her children have been in daycare since they were six or eight weeks old. Now, they're in after-school programs. "The most crazy time is coming home. Everyone is tired, hungry, and needs attention. It's always a debate, do I give attention right away or wait till everyone has eaten and then do it."

On the weekends, she says, she works harder than she does all week, stripping beds, doing laundry and a major grocery shopping. Her husband, who owns his own computer-consulting business, helps a great deal around the house but is often away. "Then I turn the organization way up," she says.

When she thinks about her life, Alan recognizes that she is "walking a tightrope." If one thing goes wrong, everything falls apart. "I wonder what it would be like," she asks wistfully, "to still be in my bathrobe and say, 'Oh, I think I'll have another cup of coffee.' " She also finds it hard to make more time for friendships. "I don't make friends except among people I work with or people whose kids go to school with mine." Socializing with other couples is rare — just one more complication, she says regretfully. "Getting up and going out isn't so attractive when you go out to work. It's just another scheduling problem."

Over and over again, whether they are single or married, with children or without, women say they can't find enough time for themselves, for their close relationships, or even for civility — the small gestures of politeness or neighborliness that contribute to the sense of community and neighborhood that has always been nurtured primarily by women. Women — particularly middle- and upper-middle-class women — used to have time, and men had stress. Men were the ones who had ulcers and heart attacks, drank too much, and died young. Women had time to support and sustain one another emotionally as well as to do the work that kept communities together. But now, because of a complex combination of factors, no one has time. Working women with families are burdened with what sociologist Arlie Hochschild calls "the second shift" — a job at work and another at home doing housework and childcare.[4] Professional women who can afford *au pairs*, nannies, and housekeepers, and women who are single or childless also say they have no time for social or spiritual lives because they now belong to a work world that has made overwork a sign of commitment and the key to "success" and advancement.

The sad fact is that some women have adapted so well to traditional masculine definitions of success and self-worth that they even become their own jailers. Psychiatrist Elizabeth Parker, when I spoke with her at greater length, described her efforts to reduce her teaching and patient load so she could have more time for both herself and her family. "I'm thinking about trying to be in the hospital but at a lower profile. But that's very hard to do," she says. "When you're not there all the time, and active, active, active, you lose something in terms of your sense of contribution and influence."

Moreover, it's hard to kick the work habit. "I've become just like a man," she says. "I come home, and I still beat myself over the head about my work. My seminar didn't go so well. I screwed up on this. Or I didn't go to the library. Or a patient didn't do well. When I feel like that, the kids and the house are no consolation. The problem is being a woman in a man's world. I've just soaked all this stuff up. It's all part of my being now. People look at me and think I've accomplished so much. But on a day-to-day basis, in my personal psychological life, if I feel I've screwed up at work, what I've accomplished the day before has almost no meaning. My standards are the standards of the male work world."

The standards against which she measures her success and self-worth also dictate a certain level of affluence. "There's a lot of pressure to keep the income up. A lot of financial pressure. First, our unwritten contract when my husband and I got married was that I could be a half supporter of the family." In addition, she admits, her own identity is very much defined by her role as an economic competitor. "My competitive spirit demands that I do as well as men." Upon reflection she concedes, "The quality-of-life issue is a big one. All this education, all this money, for what? If your quality of life is crummy what's the point of it all?"

But the male standards Parker has adapted to also impinge on her ability to find supportive relationships in the workplace. While Parker says she has a number of friends outside of work, the only people at work with whom she could imagine really sharing her personal concerns are female social workers and nurses. "Women doctors are few and far between. Occasionally there's a female colleague at the lunch table, but mostly it's a lot of male doctors. I always feel I have to keep my female issues and talk about my children to a minimum. I really do," she assures me. "Sometimes I talk about kids with male doctors my age who have children. But I can't do that too much."

In her view, it's also unacceptable to socialize too much with women in lower-status jobs. "Having lunch with the nurses and social workers is a different experience. But I can't have lunch with them too often. You have to maintain your place. And then, getting to know people, making connections is part of the lunch hour."

Attempting to juggle her own interpersonal needs and her ambitions led Elizabeth Parker to feel that she cannot afford to spend too much energy caring at work. "What I'm trying to do now is figure out how to maximize things I like and unload things I don't like." Teaching residents, she said, is one. "I really don't like teaching. It involves so much nurturing. I can't do that at home for my kids and my husband, and do it at work as well. I don't want to have any more parenting roles at work. I just don't want to deal with these overaged adolescents. I don't have the energy for it."

Some women find they no longer have energy for relationships with another group of "overaged adolescents" — men. According to a smaller group of women, workplace encounters with men have exacerbated long-standing anger and frustration at male behavior and actions. Janet Murray, a fifty-one-year-old professor, has been a lifelong feminist activist. After fighting against discrimination during her early years, she is now a tenured professor and works on a university faculty dominated by male scholars. She has also been married and divorced and, as a single mother, has had several unsatisfactory relationships. Because of all her experiences with men, she has essentially written them out of her emotional life.

"In my job, I see people who have status and power behave in ways reminiscent of schoolboys who have no self-consciousness or awareness," she states bluntly. "In the name of getting something done, they are insensitive and don't recognize the contributions of others.

"Often male conduct is excused because some guy who's a bastard in public is supposed to be nice and caring in private," she continued. "I just can't give a lot of credence to the idea that some insensitive guy is really okay because he's charming and tells jokes and gives good dinner parties and has his heart in the right political place. People excuse him because they say he has redeeming qualities, but he just can't express them in public."

Murray feels that most men are not changeable and that it's not really worth the effort to try. "I've had to conclude that most men in my age group are very limited. The possibilities for their understanding and being able to share in a meaningful way my world view is minimal." Murray does value the few male colleagues who do display sensitivity, although she adds that she constantly expects them to disappoint her. Moreover, she resents the fact that she must constantly demonstrate her appreciation of their support and understanding. "I sometimes wish I didn't have to always show these men how much I prize them and their sensibilities. I wish I didn't have to spend so much time massaging people. It seems truly a case of special treatment. I don't ever have to massage the women with whom I share this understanding."

For a variety of complex reasons, Janet Murray has decided to resolve the conflicts of caring in male/female relationships by living without intimate relationships with men. Most women do not choose this route. A more popular retreat from caring involves a widespread attempt to resolve the conflicts of caring by minimizing the importance of human connection. Frances LaBarre, a New York psychoanalyst, cites the case of a high-powered female executive who sought help in overcoming her fear of flying on the many business trips required in her job. "She was reluctant to go on airplanes because she didn't want to leave her young child.

Before she had her child, she would jump on a plane at a moment's notice, and she couldn't understand what was wrong with her. She thought this was a serious problem and that she should be able to leave her child without a second thought. She interpreted her anxiety as neurotic.

"As we explored her feelings," LaBarre continues, "it became clear that she was also reluctant to leave her child with a daycare provider. She would drop the child off at seven in the morning, get on a train and commute for an hour and a half, and then pick up her child at seven at night. She would find herself missing the child. And she didn't like the fact that the child was becoming too attached to the provider and sometimes didn't want to go home with her. But again, she thought this was kind of silly, that she was just being jealous."

Her patient had no sense that she had options, LaBarre points out. She felt that life was this way and that she had to deal with it. Instead of reinforcing that view, LaBarre tried to help her understand the value of attachment. And after four years of struggling with the problem, the woman finally decided to quit her job and take another one in a setting where she could work five minutes from home. But the outcome would have been far different for both mother and child if the woman had been counseled to adapt to the demands of her job rather than trying to change it or them.

That LaBarre's patient spent so much energy trying to learn not to care seems a direct result of a marketplace culture that extols the virtues of detachment. The idea that caring is the problem and the solution is learning how to be more distant is not only conventional psychiatric wisdom, it has also become gospel to much of the self-help industry — particularly what's come to be known as "the recovery movement" — that targets a discontented female audience. In countless best-selling how-to books like *Women Who Love Too Much* or *Co-Dependent No More*, messages that appeal to women's yearning for both independence and love offer few insights that would help women or men form and maintain caring relationships. Instead, current recovery titles tend to promote a kind of emotional survivalism that has become rampant in the late eighties and continues to flourish as we enter the early nineties.

The good news is that these books do place the individual in a world of relationships. The bad news is that relationships are not viewed as sources of sustenance, but as dependencies — addictions — that must be overcome. We are surrounded by people who are out to get us — by men who can't love or commit to us (or who actually hate us), by other women who need to control, rescue, or parasitically feed off us, by parents who have abused us, by children to whom we bequeath this legacy of relational destruction and deprivation, or by people who say they are caregivers but are really only "care addicts." Our goal in life is "recovery" — the never-ending process of learning how to recover from all these "addictive" relationships, so we stand on our own. Then, in a faithful copy of the male developmental journey, we can finally attain "intimacy."

Relationships in the world of the current titles that now fill specially advertised "recovery" sections in the nation's bookstores may be defined in male terms, but they are still women's primary burden. Instead of addressing men and helping them to love and care more, focusing on the causes of the tensions in modern life that lead to stress, anxiety, and addiction, or pointing the way to a larger, positive community that fosters care, popular culture now advises women how to love less and prescribes twelve-step programs that teach women how to be emotional survivalists. The endless struggle with the self may easily replace all other struggles — either between individuals or between a collective of women and the political powers that oppress them.

Although they proclaim a vision of human wholeness, what underlies recovery rhetoric is the masculine marketplace vision of relationships. Relationships are threats to independence, self-reliance, and autonomy. Thus, without ever acknowledging it, popular culture now ratifies the idea that healthy female development parallels a male model that views personal attachments and relationships as potentially threatening, distracting, and unnecessary.

But living without caring relationships does not tend to make women — or men — happy and fulfilled. That is why feminist psychiatrists like Jean Baker Miller, author of *Toward a New Psychology of Women*, report that they often see a new type of female patient, women who are suffering the effects of living and working without the benefit of supportive, human connections. "In the early seventies," Miller recounts, "I saw patients in their fifties and forties who had married young, had children, and suddenly realized what they had given up. They resented the lack of encouragement from spouses and families." Today, many of the women she sees in therapy are younger professionals, like the successful young lawyer who feels pressured to work twelve hours a day just to hang on to her job. Her marriage has broken up, says Miller, and nothing in her work or outside life is supplying her need for personal connections.

Without considering the consequences, a lot of professional women have thus embraced the male model of workplace success that equates success and independence. Then suddenly, when they have become established in their careers, they discover they want relationships but that they cannot find them or are incapable of nurturing them.

That is why Claire Riso has concluded that living life in the fast lane of masculine corporate culture is a "no-win proposition for women." A forty-one-year-old television news producer, Riso knows this from long and painful experience. For the past ten years she has been a producer for several of the biggest network news shows in the country. She worked closely with many of the stars who now dominate the media; she traveled all over the world, met fascinating people, and, she says, she has sacrificed a personal life in the process.

Riso has had a series of relationships with men, has no children, and has learned — perhaps too late, she says — that there is much more to life than thrashing through a jungle of office politics, scrambling to get a segment produced and on the air, seeing your name on the television screen, and basking in the all too transient admiration of colleagues or acquaintances who view you as a "success" because of what, rather than who, you are.

Riso finally decided she had gotten as far in the male workplace as she ever wanted to get. Although she continued to love her work as a journalist, she began to hate her job — and the professional persona she had to adopt to succeed in it. And so, two years ago, Riso took a significant cut in pay and left network news to work as a full-time freelance producer.

"There was no room to be myself in broadcasting," she states unequivocally, "no room to be a woman. The only women who succeed are either parodies of the masculine, superbitches who are ten times worse than any man, or parodies of the feminine, women who flirt or go to bed with men to get what they want. Women thought they would go into fields like broadcasting and change things. But in broadcasting women have become part of the problem. With only a few rare exceptions, women in senior positions at the networks are total bitches. They're real cowboys. One woman I know loved to be in a hotel in, say, the Philippines. She'd hole up in a hotel twenty-four hours a day, making phone calls to her sources. To her that was fun. Some of these women are like the Holly Hunter character in *Broadcast News*. That character was not a composite, she was based on a real woman who's really like that."

What these women end up with, says Riso, is a life without relationships — any relationships. They have no time for real friendships, no time for men, and no time for themselves. "You end up with a life that is very exciting, with a lot of ephemeral experiences in foreign countries but that fade as quickly as the nightly news. There's a lot of momentary comradeship, a lot of instant good feelings. But pretty soon you realize these people aren't really your friends, that there are no lasting relationships." That's what her colleagues found out, she says, when the networks began laying employees off. "People who built their lives around this false sense of camaraderie found that it was gone when they were out and that they had nothing left."

What was most troubling to Riso was the fact that she, like so many others, eventually became the character she had invented in order to succeed. "It's a hyperactive, hypercompetitive world in broadcasting. You have to create a protective shell that allows you to conceal yourself from the corrosiveness of the environment, and that's very damaging. A lot of women talk to each other about how we have to behave in that world. But after a while you become what you're behaving."

According to Riso it is all too easy to become addicted to the behaviors one is forced to adopt. "You get caught up in this idea of what it is to be a success. Everyone relates to you as being a producer of a successful show. The professional component becomes far more important to people than the personal one. People come up to you and ask you what it's like to work with this or that famous correspondent. After a while that becomes how you relate to yourself. The demands of the job make it impossible for you to have a relationship, because you're too busy or too tired. And it gets to be a vicious cycle. You have no relationship, no demands on you, so you keep working, and because you keep working, you have no relationship. Then when you get fed up, you're afraid to quit, because you have no relational life to fall back on. You're afraid that there will be nothing else there.

"You get caught up in this definition of success," she says bitterly. "You hate your job, you hate yourself, you hate your life. My shrink said to me once, 'I understand, Claire, you hate your lifestyle.' And I said, 'No, you don't understand at all, my lifestyle has *become* my life.'

"The problem is way beyond men," she says. "I made a Faustian bargain to get ahead. I remember the exact moment. I was trying to get a promotion at a major show at my network. I knew they wouldn't promote me where I was, so I took another offer where I would be made producer on a different broadcast. I knew when I took that job that I wouldn't have a life. But I thought at that point that it didn't matter."

Riso feels that in broadcasting men can at least have the form, the illusion, of a personal life without the content. But women, it seems, can have neither. "Most men in broadcasting are married to women who stay home with the kids. They're traveling two hundred fifty days a year, having affairs, running around, and the wives stay home. It's very hard to find a man who will put up with that."

The fact is it's hard to find a man at all. Not because it's so difficult to meet them, but because it's hard to meet the *right* one and to give a relationship the time and attention it needs to flourish. Says Riso, "Most of the men I met were intimidated by the kind of persona I began to project. I appeared completely in control. I seemed to be invulnerable. Most men want to condescend in a relationship. They don't like being around a woman who's smart and successful."

Even more enlightened men aren't willing to have a relationship with a woman who has no time to be with them. "Work has to come first in the job I was in. I could never make plans because I always knew I'd have to cancel them." Riso also admits that she was looking for the wrong kind of man. "I didn't tend to be attracted to men who were nurturing and noncompetitive, because those weren't the kind of men I was around. I wanted men who were strong and competitive and aggressive, because that's what I had come to equate with success. It's easy to confuse power with strength and intelligence. In the world of entertainment news, life is all about veneers, and I became a victim of what kind of man I thought a successful woman should be with." Thus, Riso suspects that she would not have been attracted to a gentle, nurturing man even if she had found one who was not intimidated by her position and success. "Besides," she asks, "why would that kind of man want to be with the kind of woman I'd become?

"I don't know," she reflects. "It's late for me. I may never have a relationship with a man that works. And that's why I worry about women today. Women don't realize these things until it's too late. So you're left dealing with the consequences of your early behavior. But I think women should start thinking about some new questions. Women should be less worried about getting to the top and more worried about what happens to them while they're climbing and, most importantly, what they're going to be like when they are at the top."

Riso does not blame feminism or men for her lack of relationships. But many women who find themselves alone in their late thirties and forties feel they have been burned if not by feminism at least by men — or sometimes both. Rachel Thomas, for example, has not had very good luck in her relationships with men. Her father was an alcoholic who essentially abandoned her; her graduate school mentor harassed her unmercifully; her boyfriend, during that period, insisted that they move to the West Coast, only to leave as soon as they arrived. When she was struggling to get tenure, Thomas was in a commuting relationship with another scientist who lived several hundred miles away. But soon after she got her tenured professorship, he decided he wanted to marry her and settle down. This meant that Thomas would have to give up the job she'd fought so hard to get, move in with him, and start from scratch.

"In all fairness," she says, "he tried to move where I was, but he couldn't get a job. It was bad timing."

Her refusal to move, she says, cost her a relationship she valued more than any other. "He married his graduate student and they now have two kids."

Although this happened ten years ago, it remains a source of great pain. "I was in love with him. It was a wonderful relationship. No relationship I have had since has ever been that deep." The pain is compounded, moreover, by frequent contact, for the two are still friends. And it is aggravated by the fact that Thomas feels he has gotten what he wanted, while she may not have made the right choices.

Indeed, as we talk, she reveals that moving away from her job and starting over "from square one" had not been her sole concern in deciding not to get married. "I felt I couldn't handle the relationship because I didn't have the energy to give it. I didn't know when I was younger whether I could handle having children, which he wanted."

Now, as a well-established professor of forty-eight, she says, her feelings about her work have changed. "For the first time in my life I feel that I have some emotional resources to have relationships which I never felt before. That makes the absence of relationships harder."

Furthermore, as she gets older, it's harder for her to find available men. "It's a problem to find men who can be with a woman who is powerful," she observes sadly. "That was one thing about my former lover, he was a very powerful guy, but he felt good about my being powerful as well."

Married rather than single men seem to fill her life. "When I was younger, my sexual liaisons came about at meetings and conferences. I'd meet a bunch of guys. We'd have some kind of relationship, and sometimes it would go on. But now everyone is married. In fact, most of the men I meet are onto their second wives."

Thomas's life is hardly over, but she talks as if her relational options with men have been foreclosed. "I don't see a pool of possibilities," she says frankly, "and that's a big part of my hope-lessness."

Her own self-development is the one thing about which she ex-presses optimism. "Throughout my whole history of relationships I was a victim. I looked for a powerful man who wanted a woman who was emotionally weak. I finally have gotten out of that. And that feels good. You have to come from a place where you don't need relationships to get one. That's required being alone a lot." Although Thomas enjoys furnishing and living in her house, she nonetheless feels her inner self could do with more work. "I still think that I could be stronger. I have a tendency to want to be taken care of. I could still exercise those muscles more."

For many complex reasons, the path Rachel Thomas has fol-lowed has led away from relationships with men and family. Dur-ing the early stages of her career, so much of her energy was spent fighting male prejudice that sheer emotional survival became one of her primary goals. When she finally felt more emotionally se-cure, her next task was to obey the rules of a profession that values only workplace accomplishment. Finally, the psychological theo-ries that helped her cope may also have affected her relationships. When she talks about fortifying her sense of self, of getting to the point where she does not "need" to be taken care of, or even "need" a relationship, Thomas echoes the psychological strategies that may defeat rather than enhance our ability to enter into and build caring relationships. Her fear of being a dependent victim has led her to define the need for care as a symptom of the neurotic patterns she is trying so hard to overcome. Yet, she seems so lonely precisely because she does indeed *need* relationships, as we all do. No one "me" can exist happily without a "we" to affirm it.

As Rachel Thomas finishes telling me about her life, she seems to sense that she has settled into sadness, and that her sadness has become a comfortable shelter. "Listening to myself talk to you, I worry that I have taken this too far," she concludes. "I can become emotionally committed to a life by myself. That doesn't hold open the possibility of being in a relationship again."

The cost of being deprived of care while they advance, try to maintain control over their work lives, or care for others is a theme in the conversations of many professional women. Because of both their personal histories and their experiences in the masculine workplace, some of these women seem to find it difficult to express vulnerability. They have become so self-reliant in their professional and economic lives that they have difficulty admitting their personal needs. They appear strong and powerful — qualities that have long been considered assets for men. They are, after all, the very attributes that have traditionally attracted women to men. And men, in turn, want to feel needed by a woman. This may be because they are intractable male chauvinists who want to dominate the "weaker" sex. But it may also be that men have been so programmed to fear their own vulnerabilities that they need permission to express their deepest anxieties and hopes. They need to know that they will not be scorned for these taboo feelings, and women who can themselves express their own interpersonal needs and vulnerabilities thereby give men permission to do the same.

Whatever the reason, they say that their careers in masculine institutions have encouraged distancing rather than intimate behavior. They gradually cloak themselves in an aura of independence and self-reliance that makes it more difficult for them to construct relationships with men. For them caring may not be a taboo, but it has become a scarce commodity, a nonrenewable resource that women who devote their lives to marketplace advancement can no longer take for granted.

For the majority of women I spoke with, the issue that preoccupies them is not the lack of caring relationships but the shortcomings of those they are in. Most have a mate and children, but they find that something is missing at the heart of their relationships. Today their liberation has allowed them to ask for it. The problem is that men seem unable to supply them with the kind of emotional support they crave.

"The buzzword is intimacy," says Deborah Mandel, a telephone worker who's been married for fifteen years and has three daughters and a son. She and her husband have been involved in an intense struggle about the nature of their relationship for the past several years. The problem isn't dividing the housework, it's figuring out how much of themselves they're willing to share with each other. "My husband and I have gone round and round on this issue. I think men really don't have an internal need, in the way women do, to pull things apart and look at them deeply. So, you can leave it at that, or you can say, well, is there a way for us to reach some meaning in the middle? Women have a really strong need to know that men are willing to do some of the emotional work on a relationship."

Mandel pauses and laughs. "I've given him books that stack up about this high," she says, raising her arms toward the ceiling. "They sit on his bedside table and they go nowhere. He'll read his computer books. He just doesn't seem to have this need to reflect about his world."

I ask if Mandel and her husband also argue about sex. She barely hesitates. "Of course, he thinks sex *is* intimacy and to my mind there's sex and then there's intimacy. Sometimes I think that for men sex begins and ends with ejaculation."

In her frustration with her marriage, Mandel expresses a great deal of anger at both female and male socialization. "I think women expect to get their emotional needs met by this one person. I have a strong sense that we all come to male/female relationships handicapped, disabled by the myth that we'll meet the one and only and then we will live happily ever after. That's how all the stories ended, and then the reality slaps us in the face, and we realize that this guy is really one-dimensional."

Although Mandel recognizes that male/female problems stem, in part, from forces beyond the control of either spouse, it is difficult for her not to feel angry at her mate for the shortcomings his socialization has instilled. "It doesn't feel to me that he is on a spiritual quest of any sort in his own life. He gets his rocks off on his job and his children, and there was a time when he got them off with me. There's less and less of that. But he doesn't seem to have many needs outside of the traditional need of being married, having children and family."

In a sense, the very contentment that women bring men, and that men experience in their work, may become a source of frustration for some of their mates. "He loves his job," says Mandel. "He's always gotten a great deal of satisfaction from it. In my opinion he doesn't have the closeness with his children that he should or the spectrum of friends I have. But he's happy as a pig in shit. Sometimes I wonder how it is he could move through life with all these women — he's almost fifty — and still have picked up so little from them."

Mandel concedes that the force of her anger against her husband increases when she sees how men act in the work world. "Right now, I am really furious about how women are being treated by the phone company," she says, referring to recent labor disputes in that industry. "I know that my husband is not to blame for the imbalance of power in this society. But sometimes, in spite of myself, he represents the species that's had control of things, and so he gets blasted for something that's not his fault."

In the final analysis, Mandel feels confused about how far she should push her husband and their relationship. "I know their socialization has kept men back, for sure. But then I wonder whose responsibility is it to teach them? I feel in so many instances that women are the ones who upturn the applecarts, who push the buttons, who get men moving on human relationships. When are they going to be motivated to move on human relationships on their own?"

On the other hand, she worries that she and other women will push too far and that men will feel like failures because, through no real fault of their own, they can't go any further. "We are much more evolved than they are," she says sadly. "I said this to my husband once. Maybe this is as good as it gets. That's the truth. It's not horrible. It's not fraught with all kinds of survival issues. My internal myth is that he has more to give, and that there's more out there we can achieve together. But maybe it's not fair for me to ask him to give all the things that I think he should give, because I really do love this man and maybe I'll just push him out the door because he will think he's such a failure."

At forty-five, and married for the second time, Susan Sullivan shares Deborah Mandel's yearnings and questions. We met about a year after she had left a high-powered job in one of the nation's largest high-tech firms. Her children are both in college, and she is worried about both her personal and her professional future. In describing her career as a marketing manager and her roles as wife and mother, Sullivan's personal and professional considerations appear to be inextricable. After years as a single mother of two children, she met, courted, and married her current husband, a physician. She moved from her hometown to his and left teaching to go to business school. During the first year of their marriage, she sent her children to private school. After she received her MBA she went to work in corporate America, marketing a new product line for a large high-tech company.

Things went well at first. Constantly on the run, she became a corporate jet-setter. Like the absent husbands so many women rebelled against in the sixties, she became too preoccupied to attend to the pleas for help from her son. In one year, this boy of twelve felt that he had lost his mother, to a new marriage and a new career; his friends, who were left behind when he moved; and the companionship of his sister, who was sent to a different boarding school. "He needed me more than I was able to be there for him," Sullivan realizes now. "There was a feeling underlying everything I did that that was true, but I crossed my fingers and hoped for the best. I tried to do it with quality time as opposed to quantity of time. And slowly, over the years, he just withdrew from me. I don't know how much of that was a boy's need to detach from his mother, or how much of it was that I just wasn't there for him and he got out of the habit of talking to me."

If she and her son lost each other during these high-pressured years, she now realizes that she and her husband never found each other. Both used the excuse of professional involvement to avoid the complex demands of building a marriage and uniting two separate families. "My husband was very busy at this time, too. When I started getting immersed in this professional challenge, he was in a new job, flying around. We'd meet in the Miami airport, or the Denver airport. It was very exciting."

The relationship felt like a continuation of their affair, not like the foundation of a marriage. When Sullivan's career goals changed and she decided to quit and do consulting from home, that "affair" lost its luster. Just when she needed a strong relationship, friends, and community, she had none. "I had no friendships because working all the time and never being home made that impossible. And I discovered that my husband was really uncomfortable with a wife who's trying to make him relate. He loves me best when I'm off doing my own thing, being a corporate manager. He feels uncomfortable when I'm probing, questioning, with him and myself. He wishes it would all go away. It makes me feel frustrated. I run the whole gamut of emotions — anger, sadness, anxiety. He's reached the pinnacle of his career. He's so highly developed in one area and so undeveloped in this other."

Like so many men, Sullivan's husband tends to withdraw when she presses him on emotional issues. And, like so many women, Sullivan knows deep down that his emotional disappearing act is not a deliberate rejection. He just doesn't know what to do, how to be supportive and engaged in the way his wife wants. "He's very uncomfortable with the way things are. It's very frightening and threatening to him. He used to know what his role was when we were both on the road. Now he doesn't know what to do, and he doesn't like it because he's used to knowing what to do and doing it."

As a result, Sullivan herself is ambivalent about what her next step should be. "I don't know what I want to do." She sighs as she considers her possibilities. "I could keep on doing consulting. But I'm not getting stuff I need from that. And I'm not getting stuff I need from the relationship. So do I go back into the corporate setting? That would deflect my attention away from the relationship more and give it balance."

When I ask her what kind of life she would like, she replies with the answer that I have come to expect — women's seemingly impossible dream. "I would like to work with people I like and respect. I would like to make something happen and get paid sufficiently to be well compensated. And I want balance in my work life."

Unfortunately, she says, she doesn't know quite how to fulfill these goals. Nor does she know how to feel about the void in her marriage. Just as she is trying to seek some balance in her professional life, she's also reaching for some balance in her expectations of the relationship. Like Deborah Mandel, she worries both about pushing too much and not pushing enough.

When I propose that she, like so many of us, may be trying to get her mate to satisfy all her emotional needs, she agrees. Perhaps, I suggest, she needs to create a sense of shared community with other women, neighbors, and acquaintances to ensure more relational variety in her life and put less pressure on her husband. The notion makes sense to her, but she also wonders whether her marriage still has unrealized potential. "In my head I have this model of how it could be," she says, leaning forward, her face beaming with possibility. "I can feel it. I can see it. There's a vision of the talking, the communication, the closeness. Wouldn't that be wonderful? Isn't that what we should strive for? How enriched life would be. I see it so clearly. To say that things are going to be like they are, and that I have to get other people to satisfy that, isn't that a shame? It all seems so possible and within reach."

When women talk about men today, their conversations often swing between resentment, frustration, and anger on the one hand, and optimism born of the hope that they can release some deeply buried feminine potential in their men, thus making them more expressive, supportive, and "intimate." Just as many women complain that some of their husbands want them to be "super-women" — traditional, nurturing females, and, at the same time, high-powered achievers in the work world — some women seem to want their men to be traditional, high-powered economic providers *and* gentle nurturers as well.

Whatever their individual hopes and dreams, the marketplace has added to women's confusion about how much they can and should expect from men. And this results in exhausting and often futile struggles about each sex's duty or capacity to care. It's no wonder, then, says clinical psychologist Sharon Gordetsky, that women seem to be taking out their frustrations on men and have little inclination to empathize with them. "Women who are feeling frustrated and disempowered are going to take that out on their husbands or children or anyone with whom they're in contact."

Gordetsky also reminds us that many women's belief that another woman could give them everything that men don't is a fantasy. "Nobody, not even in the best match, can get everything from another person. Women have used other women very well. But it's a myth that they can get everything from female relationships. In fact, lesbian couples often have some of the same problems men and women have. And women also get things from their mates and male friends that they cannot get from women."

Remember, Gordetsky advises, just as women have had to invent professional personas, men have had to invent themselves in the area of domestic responsibilities and personal relationships. And because men tend not to have close male friends, when they seek affirmation for their new roles, they turn to women. If women aren't there to offer empathy, prodding, and affirmation, who will men turn to when they are trying to change, who will guide them? Surely, not the masculine marketplace that encourages and promotes the values and activities that are now subverting all our attempts at getting and giving care?

Unfortunately, when it is suggested that women continue to care for and guide men, many feel so emotionally burdened themselves and so hampered by men's behavior in the marketplace and at home that the very idea angers and frustrates them. Although this response is certainly understandable, it may not help either sex in their efforts to cope with the demands under which we all labor. Because, like women, at least those more enlightened men I spoke with feel bereft and under attack both at work and at home.

If women's universal emotional demand is for intimacy, men's is for appreciation or credit. The recurring theme in my conversations with men is their sense that they don't get enough acknowledgment for their efforts to fulfill nontraditional parenting and homemaking roles.

Women complain that men want a "please," a set of detailed instructions, a "thank you," and a pat on the head for performing household chores. Why, women wonder, must men be politely entreated or rewarded for doing things that women do all the time without any fuss? But to men who have few role models in the domestic sphere, female mentoring and recognition are as important as male professional help is to women in the workplace.

"If you do things that are seen as typical female jobs," says Colin Greer, a social historian, "you don't get rewarded by the culture and you don't get rewarded by women, because no one feels that what you're doing is in any way out of the ordinary. The problem, of course, is that if you're a man, what you're doing *is* out of the ordinary.

"I remember when I first began to look after my son when he

was sick," Greer recalls. "It was a real triumph for me to feel comfortable doing that and for him to feel comfortable with me doing it. There was a part of me that wanted to be congratulated for this great leap we were both making, rather than having it be seen as simply part of ordinary life. Ideally, I think both parties should be congratulated for dealing with difficult things. Women want emotional support for moving into nontraditional areas. Yet by not acknowledging men for their efforts at change, some women are actually forcing men to enter into a domain of invisibility that women have occupied and are now struggling to reject."

Some men feel that, rather than providing encouragement, their wives or lovers subtly undermine their awkward but nonetheless well-intentioned attempts at self-transformation. Because women are accustomed to a certain standard of quality in the performance of child rearing and domestic tasks, they have little tolerance for men who do not do things "the right way" — i.e., their way. Thus, some men say (and women often confirm) that their wives are critical when they buy different products at the grocery store; when they depart from the nightly routine of putting a child to bed; or, as one father reported, when they dress a child for school. "Last week I was dressing my daughter to take her to nursery school," he recalled. "She pulled out a bright red jumper, a hot pink turtleneck, and a pair of raspberry tights. This outfit seemed all right to me. But when my wife saw her, her face fell. She didn't say anything to our little girl, but later she asked me how I could let her out of the house looking like that. Our daughter, of course, didn't care, but it made me feel like a total failure."

"Women are very critical of the way men do things at home," says Sharon Gordetsky. "We hear, over and over again, women saying, 'I can't trust him to do this. I can't let him pack the diaper bag, or get the groceries, or dress the kids because he'll do it all wrong.' "

Although this comparison may sound schematic, without realizing it some women may be mirroring in the domestic sphere the kind of behavior that is so typical of men in the workplace. At work men impose inflexible male standards on women workers and expect them to conform. You're not supposed to cry. You're not supposed to be too emotional. You're supposed to do things the way they've always been done, not the way you want it to be done. Because they have been confined to applying their talents to work in the home, many women have also developed firm ideas about how that work should be done. "Family has been women's area of expertise. But women have to let go of that control if they want men to learn how to do things around the house," says Gordetsky.

The men I interviewed are clearly in the minority. All said they were trying to shoulder more domestic responsibilities and share more fully in child rearing. They have been influenced to do so not solely by prodding from their mates but by their personal desires to be different from their own fathers. Men, not unreasonably, tend to measure their own progress against the image of their generally absent fathers, and they feel they have advanced eons by comparison. Women, on the other hand, measure them against a female standard and find them sorely lacking.

"There's a great deal of tension over how much I'm supposed to do around the house," says Eric Atkins, a thirty-six-year-old independent management consultant from Minneapolis. "We have a young son, and my wife, who is a writer, has not worked much in the two years since he was born. So I'm the major breadwinner. And the demands just never stop."

The family, Atkins says, needs $35,000 a year for a no-frills life — to pay the mortgage, buy food and diapers, and maintain two cars. Atkins puts in many ten-hour days, running from meeting to meeting, just to keep up.

When he finally gets home, he sincerely wants to share in the child rearing and domestic tasks. "I'm pretty aware of my father's failure as a parent. He was completely uninvolved and aloof from the parenting process. He was so wrapped up in his work, I don't think he ever changed a diaper in his life. The only time he ever tuned in to us was after he had two massive heart attacks and five bypass operations. Then he was more loving and emotionally open, but that came way too late, when he was sixty-five and I was twenty-five."

Determined to be different from his father and more supportive of his wife, Atkins tries to help at home. "It's true that my wife is the primary caretaker at home. But I do a lot of the legwork. I go shopping. I play with my son when I come home at night and she's cooking dinner. I do the dishes and give him a bath and put him to bed, and if he wakes up at night, I give him a bottle and then get up with him in the morning."

The exhausting double shift, however, is not his major complaint. "I never feel I get any credit for bringing home the bacon. Never! Even though my wife stays at home, she expects me to be some kind of superman, to do it all. I'm never doing enough."

From his wife's point of view, as Atkins describes it, he is somehow withholding the essential component to conjugal connection. She feels that he could, if he so desired, give that extra ounce of commitment, intimate energy, and emotional inventiveness that would make a crucial difference in how he performs what he now seems to see as his second job. As he describes it, his wife has become his judge and jury. He stands before her, convicted of being an emotional malingerer, a cheater, someone who has deliberately deprived her of the secret ingredient of himself.

"It affects the trust between us," he observes sadly. "I feel that I'm doing the very best I can do, and that's not good enough. I don't feel I get respect for making a yeoman's effort. Sometimes it just feels like a Herculean effort to get through the day, to earn a living. I guess I don't quite understand. There is a division of labor in our household as long as my wife is not working, but she doesn't seem to realize that, and so every once in a while things explode."

When he considers how hard it was for both him and his wife to adjust to the new responsibilities in their lives after years of freedom, Atkins does feel more positive about the marriage's chance of survival. More important, when he compares his own parental behavior to his father's, he feels that he has made more than superficial changes. "I'm one thousand times more involved in the daily life of my child than my father was with me. It's a revolution in behavior, not just an evolution." But the sense of sourness, of something being not quite right in the balance of expectation and demand remains.

"Being a father has taken a real toll in what I expected to do with my life. My professional development is null. As for work, I feel that I'm basically faking it. But there's not much appreciation of how hard it is for men like me, who have been programmed to get their sense of self-esteem from their careers, to make that accommodation. I know I'm no shining example of the 'new man.' I guess I feel that I'm just less demanding on my wife than she is on me."

Although many men still resist sharing household chores and child rearing with their mates, an increasing number, like Eric Atkins, are much more involved than their fathers were. Boston University professors Dianne S. Burden and Bradley Googins estimate that fathers devote almost twenty hours more per week to family responsibilities than do their nonparent male colleagues. Men today are spending far more time with their children than their fathers spent with them, reports Yale University psychiatrist Kyle Pruett, author of *The Nurturing Father*. They're transporting children to and from school, taking them to doctor's appointments, staying home with them when they are sick, and attending P.T.A. meetings. More fathers are also staying at home, either part- or full-time, and taking care of their children while their wives are the family's breadwinners.[5]

And, according to Burden and Googins, "male parents are as likely as females to report that they experience a lot of stress in balancing work and family responsibilities (36 percent of males and 37 percent of females). Men who experience the same family responsibilities as women react in exactly the same way as women, that is, with increased job-family role strain and depression."[6]

Joseph H. Pleck, of Wheaton College, has found major changes in men's domestic roles. For fathers with one child under four, childcare time increased "significantly" between the midsixties and midseventies. Between 1965 and 1981, the hours they spent on housework and childcare increased from 20 to 30 percent of fathers' total domestic work-time. Pleck also reports that fathers' inability to spend more time with their children is frequently cited in complaints about overwork outside the home.[7]

This is not surprising, given the fact that workplaces have increased, not decreased, time demands on employees. What's more, men also have a hard time rejecting the competitive, performance-oriented definitions of self-esteem that have long prevailed in the business world. The fact that so many women entering the work force have quickly adopted the masculine work ethic and definition of success has been confusing and disappointing to those enlightened men who had hoped that women would be more of a force for change. "In the labs where I've worked, women have come into positions of power over the last ten years," says Peter Bentley, a forty-four-year-old molecular biologist. "I was really hoping that the style of the department would change under this influence. But, as for humanizing or feminizing the lab, that just hasn't happened. The one woman who has gotten her own lab has bought the whole male model. She's very hard on her students. She's gotten rid of a lot of people who didn't come up to her standards. I think what's most depressing about this is that it validates all the myths that men have about how you have to act at work."

The majority of women who have not become male clones often have a hard time empathizing with men's difficulties in providing the emotional closeness they crave. They want an intimacy that men find not only hard to produce but even harder to define, and this makes some men feel that they will never be able to make their wives happy.

"The complaint is the usual," says attorney Ryan Richards, describing the conflict with his wife, a graphic artist, that seems to be at the center of his ten-year marriage. "I know she's right a great deal of the time. I find myself not talking, not telling her what's going on with my work. I'm a terrible perfectionist, and so I often grumble about my work and I think that turns her off. She seems uninterested in what I'm doing."

Richards and his wife have two children, and their attempts to do their work, socialize, and parent have led to what he describes as a "your turn, my turn" style of relating. "I take the kids. Or else she takes the kids. I am preoccupied by work and she takes over at home. Or then it's her turn to be preoccupied, and I take over. It's hard to figure out how to be together and do things together."

Like so many men, Richards says he has few memories or models of intimacy to guide him. "My parents are Irish Catholic and married very late in life. I cannot remember them ever touching or kissing. The moment we kids left home, they immediately got twin beds and separate bedrooms. The only way feelings got expressed in our family was through a kind of constant low-level bickering, or a persistent fussing over every little detail or plan. I used to think this was normal, until my wife — who's Italian and comes from a more expressive family — pointed out how odd it really is. In fact, whenever people try to talk about feelings in my family, my mother tries to shut everybody up, because it will ostensibly upset my father."

From childhood, Richards always assumed the role of peacemaker with his brothers; he also learned to escape the conflict and fussing. "I'm great at tuning out. I like to be left alone, and so I always try to leave my wife alone. I always figure that if I don't make demands on her, she won't make demands on me. But that never works. I just get accused of being withholding or rejecting."

Richards believes his difficulty responding to his wife's needs arises, in part, because of his tendency to mistake one aspect of his wife's personality for the whole. "When I met her, she appeared to be this high-powered person who had a great career. She was always traveling and racing around, and she was independent and not very anxious. She was the antithesis of the dependent, stay-at-home spouse. To me, given my background, that was very attractive. It seemed to suggest that both people could have their own separate lives, and there wouldn't be any problems making and sustaining a relationship. We had a lot of intellectual and political interests in common. And I thought the relationship would be built around those, rather than shared emotions or feelings."

Later, Richards was stunned to learn that his wife wanted more. "After we got married and lived together for a while, I discovered that what I thought was so, wasn't. My wife was unhappy and felt abandoned because I wasn't involved with her on a deep personal level. It wasn't that I didn't want to be, it was that I didn't even know I needed to be. When I learned all this, I felt surprised and bewildered. How could this person be so different from what she appeared? And I felt at a loss in dealing with it. I felt inadequate, unable to help. I didn't know how to deal with that part of her. I wanted the problems to just go away."

Richards says he's become more sympathetic and attentive since the early days of his marriage. Nonetheless, he knows that a deeply ingrained tendency to believe that the absence of conflict equals domestic happiness causes persistent problems, as does his belief that professional productivity and personal happiness are one and the same. "I'm constantly caught off-guard when my wife complains that she's depressed or unhappy. She's very productive and works hard, and because I have been so trained to feel that professional accomplishment is the measure of personal satisfaction, I'm always shocked that she can produce and be unhappy or depressed at the same time. I don't know if I'll ever be able to change that, or to feel adequate to deal with her emotional needs. Even though I feel I've changed a lot, it's still not a role I feel comfortable in. I just never know quite what to do for her in those situations."

Richards echoes the discomfort many men feel at living in an emotional world of *being* as opposed to a professional world of *doing*. Today, because women have learned to do for themselves — to earn their own livings, to be on their own during long periods, to take care of the parts of their lives that used to be tended by men — they want less doing and more being from their mates. And they are not timid about asking for this intimacy.

For some men, it may be too much. "My wife wants more than I seem to be able to give her," David Raphael says sorrowfully. The forty-seven-year-old film editor has been married twice. He and his first wife divorced after twenty years, and he is now married to a forty-three-year-old social worker. She has two children and he has two from his previous marriage.

The son of a remote father, Raphael worries about his own emotional limitations. He feels he has no models of even minimal emotional expressiveness on which to draw, and he berates himself for his inability to move in the direction his wife would like him to go. Yet he finds her level of demands and discontent almost unbearable.

"My wife is very energetic, very open. She wants a great deal of affection and reassurance. She says she wants intimacy, relating. She tells me that she can earn her own living, raise her own children, get sex if she needs it, redecorate the house for herself. She has a lot of friends, and she can get friendship from them. What she can't do for herself is get intimacy and closeness."

According to Raphael, the very thing he has the hardest time providing has become the crux of the relationship, the greatest sticking point between him and his wife. Raphael says his wife wants him to talk more about his work and wonders why he relates so few of the significant details about his day. But what she wants to talk about most, he wants to talk about least. "If I'm preoccupied by a big crisis at work, I want acknowledgment that something is going on, but after that I want to be left alone. I don't want to bring it all home and deal with all the nuances, because I do that at work. I am glad to talk about the actual tasks I accomplished or to discuss the impact of the things I do. But I don't want to talk about the struggle it took to get them accomplished."

She, on the other hand, often reflects in wonder at the "trivial nature" of the relationships he and other men seem to have with each other. Like many women who judge men's friendships from the vantage of their own, she feels that a friendship in which there is little exchange of confidence or sharing of feelings is not quite the real thing.

"Women want morals and manners, Edith Wharton and Jane Austen. Men want Jack London and Jim Harrison," says Raphael. But to him, relationships are less complex. He wants just what his wife gives him — a home, a companion, a sexual relationship, someone to help raise his children. But she wants more and feels cheated when she does not get it. "She accuses me of withholding, as if I can reach down inside and pull out these feelings she wants me to share. But I'm not comfortable talking about feelings. What's more, I'm not even sure they're there to share."

The couple recently saw a television show about poet Robert Bly's work about men. Bly contends that men's problems with emotional intimacy are a result of their inability to connect with their distant fathers.

"I got really furious after this show. My wife finally understood what I was talking about, but she would listen to Robert Bly and not to me. I'd been telling her this for a year and it didn't seem to matter. He said it in fifteen minutes, and it carried a great deal more weight."

Bly believes that if men are to become more expressive, they must confront their fathers. That may be a solution for some, but to Raphael, it seems impossible. "I can't imagine talking to my father about anything." The two men have never spoken about anything that really matters, and he is not confident he could break that barrier after so many years of silence.

"I don't think there is much hope for men of my generation," Raphael concludes bleakly. "I'm not sure I can accommodate my wife any more than she can accommodate me. I feel like a failure. I feel that I go home and get beat on for my deficiencies. It's bad for me, it's bad for her, and it's bad for the kids. I'm not sure it will end well.

"I think men like myself just lag way behind. We are not as highly evolved as women the same age. Perhaps my son will be better, or his son. But for me, the whole situation is pretty depressing."

David Raphael's hope that the next generation of men will be better than his own will not, of course, be realized unless men — and women — continue to change age-old patterns as well as their interactions. The question is not should men change, it is how should they change? What areas of transformation should they concentrate on? What should they ask of themselves and what should women ask of them?

According to social psychologist Robert B. Weiss, author of *Staying the Course*, a book about marriages that have endured, a man can be a lot to a woman, but the one thing he cannot be is a woman friend. What men and women should look for in and expect from one another — and work on in their relationships — is partnership. "A man can be a partner, an attachment figure, a companion," says Weiss. "Being a partner includes a lot of things. It includes helping get the business of life accomplished, giving a sense of assurance and security. But we must always remember that it's also necessary to be members of a community outside of a marriage."

Weiss cautions that women need a community of women and men need a community of men; no one can make a social world out of just one person. "Women need women friends and couple friends, a job and job-related relationships, as well as their mates. With their mates — and this is where men can change — both parties need to put energy into developing a relationship in a way that is congenial to it. They should be able to establish a partner-ship in which there is a division of labor that feels right for both of them. They should expect that there is always going to be irri-tation about that division of labor. They should be able to main-tain gratitude for what each does for the other, and come through for the other rather than banging each other over the head with increasing periodicity with 'I'm not sure this is the relationship for me.' Finally they should be able to feel that their life with each other is richer than it would be if they were not together."

They should not, Weiss warns, want the other person to be mir-ror images of themselves. "If you're trying to find someone who is the same as you — who thinks just like you do, always loves to talk about the same things you do, giggles at the same things you giggle at, that may be a problem. You can find people with whom that is true. But you should be able to enjoy being with the other person, which is not the same as being the same as that person."

That so many women want men to be that doppelgänger, that double, may be a reflection of our culture's narcissism and destruc-tion of community, as well as of women's understandable frustra-tion with men. As psychiatrist Arnold M. Kerzner explains it, "Over the past years, feminist scholars have done a great deal of research that illuminates the differences between men and women. The problem is, now that we've established how different men and women are, women say it's time for us to be equal. But men need time to catch up. We're trying, but women are using their own standards for what we should and shouldn't be, and we're not there yet. What's more, women no longer have the patience to be our emotional guides. But they're still asking, 'Hey, guys, what's taking you so long?'

"Look," Kerzner elaborates, "men and women are very differ-ent. They have millions of years of genetics and evolution sepa-rating them. It takes years to make the changes women want to make in men. And men really are changing. But the problem is you just can't rush empathy. Women are just ahead of us in that department because they have been caretakers and have had to figure out how to know what's going on in an infant and child."

Kerzner believes workplace pressures on women have exacer-bated a tendency that both sexes share — to misperceive and misinterpret each other's words and actions. In this case, women misinterpret men's reluctance to talk, to be empathic, as a failure of will. "Men's problems and their ability to solve them are not a question of willpower. It's a result of years of socialization that is not so easy to turn around," he argues passionately. "I don't know how we can ask women to be patient with us, but on the other hand, if you think being more open is subject to the power of positive thinking, then that's a recipe for failure."

Meanwhile, Kerzner worries that our culture's emphasis on intimacy ignores the important lessons of conflict and its resolution. "Over time, relationships grow from two things: from closeness and from men and women's ability to repair interactive errors. Good relationships are as much a result of how human beings cope with empathic errors as they are a result of empathic connections." Real understanding, he says, arises from our very disagreements. We can resolve them by extending ourselves, we become more tender, more sympathetic, more communicative, and happier.

Human beings have always had difficulty finding time to address and fulfill all the caring demands in their lives. Relationships between the sexes have never been smooth, and the United States has always been a society whose radically individualistic values work to defeat care. Although it is beyond the scope of this — or any other single book — to analyze and explain the relationships between the sexes, it seems that the market's intrusion into the realm of human relationships has not made them any easier.

Strategies that teach us how not to care or that transform caring relationships into burdensome ones have become increasingly popular today. But they do not stem our unquenchable thirst for caring. Women who are forced to retreat from caring in the workplace and community find that their interpersonal lives have eroded. They want to be cared for, but because they have no time to build a sustainable community of friends, relatives, neighbors, and co-workers, they say that even their professional and financial accomplishments seem unsatisfactory and ephemeral.

Women who put their careers first and relationships last find they, too, need caring. But they discover too late that caring is not something you can put on hold. Finally, our anticaring culture has

influenced the lives of women who do have mates and family by
making it more difficult for them to mobilize the empathic and
caring skills that might help them guide their mates and lovers
toward the intimacy they seek.

Given the intense pressures involved in balancing work and private life, we need support, affection, and affirmation from our
mates and lovers more than ever. We wonder why men can't be
more like women. Because we now measure men against a female
standard of empathy, we may become so critical of men that we
deprive them of the acceptance we want them to give us. They
won't talk about their inner feelings. When they do communicate
with us, the narratives they recount are written in a shorthand
that precludes the rich emotional portraiture needed to help us
identify with their concerns. When we contemplate their friendships with each other, we often argue that they are hardly worthy
of the name, that what they share with one another — work,
sports, politics, drinking — is not really worth sharing.

This dismissal of men's behavior, mode of expression, and
friendships may not, however, encourage the kind of changes we
say we want. What it does lead to is a sense of confusion and
frustration not dissimilar to that which women say they experience
as they try to conform to male standards in the workplace. At least
some more enlightened men say they have tried to alter old patterns. Judging themselves against their fathers, many feel they do,
in fact, live in a different world and speak — albeit awkwardly —
in a different voice and act in a different way. When they consider
the lack of cultural support for the feminization of the masculine
psyche, their efforts seem all the more heroic. Their employers are
encouraging them to be more, not less, consumed with work. Their
culture is obsessed with greed and consumption. It certainly does
not encourage compassion or caring. Indeed, even some of their
female colleagues may seem to embrace the masculine attitudes
and behaviors that other women complain about. Women, some
men feel, may not get what they want from corporate America,
but many at least have permission to ask for some of it — maternity leave, part-time or flex-time work, job-sharing.

Just as many women perceive that men in the workplace reward years of professional effort and commitment with escalating requests for more — more hours in the office, more dazzling on-the-job performances, more of a commitment to masculine marketplace values and behaviors — some men suggest that women, in the home, may now be doing the same. Not surprisingly, men are just as uncomfortable trying to become more like women as many of their female counterparts are trying to disguise themselves as economic men.

What all these pressures ultimately compromise is our capacity for empathy. Although all human beings are born with the capacity for empathy, it is easy to forget that that capacity must be nourished over time. Empathy is not a simple matter of being a good listener, nodding sagely at the right moments, or holding the hand that is placed in your own. To put oneself in another human being's shoes is hard work. It involves tolerance, judgment, and self-control. It is a cognitive, as well as an emotional, act. As doctors Kerzner and Gordetsky wisely explain, empathy cannot be produced at will, on demand — not even by women.

Feminist scholars have documented how most women learn to be empathic because of their central role in child rearing and their primary identification with their mothers. Empathy has been instilled in our hearts and perhaps bred in our genes. And yet, not all women are able to be empathic. Indeed, under adverse circumstances, some of the most empathic may have trouble caring for others. When one is harried, angry, frustrated, in financial need, and exhausted, it is difficult indeed to make the emotional effort required to pull oneself out of one's own shoes and occupy those of another.

Most men, on the other hand, have been cheated by history. The definitions of self-esteem with which they have been burdened have deprived them of an education in empathy. Having never learned to speak, read, or write the language of emotion, many have become emotional illiterates.

Adults naturally have a difficult time mastering a new language. Some, in fact, may never master it at all. With our help, others may learn, but haltingly. In many cases, men have been permanently handicapped. We may be angry at them and at the world that has produced them, but we can no more berate them for their limitations than we can an illiterate for not being able to read or a paraplegic for not being able to run.

Men need our help just as we need theirs. If we want them to learn to be more empathic and caring so that they can care for us, we must continue to challenge them. And we must care for them. Women seem to fear that if they once again dedicate themselves to caring for men, they will fall into a compassion trap from which there is no escape.

But we can care, without sacrificing ourselves. We can, for example, remind men that they must care for us in the workplace, if they want us to care for them at home. We can join them in gaining more freedom from work, so that we can have more time to spend with one another. And we can enlist them in the most important job of all — being empathic parents to our children and teaching them to be more empathic when they are adults.

Chapter Eight

THE ENEMIES OF
CHILDHOOD

WHEN MY older daughter was two and a half years old, our family was invited to Sunday brunch at the home of a friend, along with several other families. One of these professional couples had a daughter the same age, named Rebecca. When the two toddlers were introduced, my daughter eagerly approached the slight, dark-haired girl with an invitation to play. But Rebecca shyly hid behind her mother's leg, and my daughter went off to find more willing companions in the kitchen.

Sometime later, she and I returned to the living room, bagels and cream cheese in hand. Little Rebecca was hunched over the low coffee table, puzzling over a game she'd brought from home. As the box for the game explained, it was a Discovery Toy, appropriate for a child between one and three. The "Count and Contrast Puzzle" consisted of twenty sets of cards, with paired pictures of opposites and numbers designed to "strengthen math skills and help children understand the difficult concept of opposites."

Little Rebecca was applying herself to the game with the utmost diligence. Nothing less would do. The puzzle pieces were by no means easy to match. My daughter briefly gave it a try and then quit and looked around for a less taxing toy. But Rebecca grimly persisted, concentrating every ounce of energy and intelligence she

possessed on mastering what's known, in child development cir-
cles, as "readiness skills." When she had finally paired all the sets,
she took them off the table and, one by one, stacked them neatly
in the box. Only then did she look up and notice my daughter.

Immediately, she spotted a new problem to be solved — a small
blob of cream cheese smeared across my daughter's chin. Pointing
her tiny finger, she looked at me reproachfully and said, "Dirty."
I pulled out a tissue and handed it to my daughter, suggesting that
she wipe off her face. She dabbed absentmindedly at the corner
of her mouth. But Rebecca wasn't satisfied. "Dirty," she repeated.
My daughter looked at Rebecca as though she were a creature from
outer space. When I took the tissue and rubbed her chin clean
myself, Rebecca seemed immensely relieved.

At that moment, the little girl's mother walked in and started
gathering up her toys. I complimented her on her daughter's skill,
and she beamed with pride. "Yes, it's wonderful. She's doing so
well. She already has all her letters and numbers."

Then she said good-bye, and the two left the room. Rebecca had
not smiled once.

The "hurried child" is no new phenomenon in American society.
As David Elkind recounts in his book of that name, countless children in America's more affluent suburbs have long been subjected
to intense parental pressure to perform and compete during
their elementary- and secondary-school years.[1] In many status-
conscious, middle- and upper-middle-class homes, no expense is
spared to provide a heavy schedule of after-school lessons in everything from art to gourmet cooking. Academic achievement and
involvement in extracurricular activities are prized not as ends in
themselves but as tickets to the right colleges and universities,
graduate schools, and professions. Until the late seventies and
early eighties, however, even children subject to fast-track pressures in later years were relatively free of them during their early
childhood.

Today, all this has changed. At three months, an infant can be
enrolled in exercise classes especially tailored to his needs; at ten
months, it's time for her to master shapes, sizes, and colors; at

eighteen months he begins piano, or perhaps dance. For the three-
and four-year-olds, there is "skill training" — reading, writing,
and mathematics readiness — followed up by tests that can determine whether or not a child is "gifted" or just average. Elite nursery schools and private daycare centers now advertise their
academic excellence. And to make sure that children don't lose
their competitive edge when they get to kindergarten, there is the
option of holding them back in their preschool program so they'll
be bigger, smarter, and more advanced than their peers when
called upon to demonstrate their leadership skills the following
year.

The trend toward accelerated early childhood "development"
has become so widespread that it's already the subject of TV and
movie satire. In the film *Parenthood* an overanxious yuppie father
puts his firstborn three-year-old daughter through daily flash-card
drills and karate exercises. He scornfully dismisses any play that
seems to serve no apparent purpose and becomes so obsessed with
teaching his daughter that his exasperated wife is finally forced to
announce her intention to divorce him via a message scrawled on
flash-cards.

But the fact that younger and younger children are being turned
into clones of their workaholic, high-powered parents is no joke.
Nor is it only fathers who are overly preoccupied with achievement.

Traditionally, mothers have been the protectors of early childhood. But today, for a combination of personal, social, and economic reasons, both parents in many career-oriented, two-income
couples are making early childhood an endangered developmental
phase. As more and more women have come to undervalue feminine, nurturing qualities and to overvalue competitive ones, they
have also been told they should introduce adult standards of competition and advancement into the realm of early childhood.
Turned into developmental drill sergeants by the so-called experts,
they set increasingly unrealistic goals and then bestow rewards
of love and admiration if and when their children meet them.
Thus, in many families today children end up with the emotional
equivalent of two fathers and no mother because *neither* parent

is providing the kind of love, affection, and nurturing associated with the maternal role. Both mothers and fathers in such "two-father families" can become the enemies of childhood.

Attorney Erica Klein had her first child, Jennifer, when she was thirty-four. Although she and her husband were married in their early twenties, they decided it would be better to postpone having children until their careers were well launched. Erica finished law school and then went to work for Legal Services. Her husband got an MBA and landed a job in the marketing division of a large corporation. As they advanced, they also moved around — from New York to Chicago, then to Los Angeles, and finally back to New York, where Klein was hired by the high-priced corporate law firm for which she now works.

By the time Jennifer was born, Klein's extended-family situation was not unlike that of many cosmopolitan, upwardly mobile baby boomers who put off having children for professional reasons. Her own parents were too aged and infirm to help out very much. Her older sister had married much earlier and had children already grown up. Her husband, the oldest of four, had no nieces or nephews because his siblings, like most of the couple's professional friends, were either not yet married or married and childless. In the past, new mothers have reached out to family and friends for advice, but Erica did not have such a community to turn to.

The couple's apartment is cluttered with the most up-to-date books on child rearing. Burton L. White's *The First Three Years of Life* has a prominent place on the bookshelf, along with copies of Penelope Leach's work.[2] Catalogues of educational toys and natural-fiber clothing are scattered amongst copies of parenting magazines. Jennifer's small room is a veritable cornucopia of up-scale parenting paraphernalia, including dozens of children's books and educational toys.

Now two and a half, Jennifer completed her first Gymboree infant exercise class when she was only nine months old. Then she was enrolled in Rhythm and Glue — an introductory program in art and music. At the time of my visit and interview with her mother, Jennifer was about to begin a new, more "age-appropriate" art class.

Erica, who returned to her full-time job after a six-month maternity leave, says she sought out these enrichment programs because of her concerns about the family's full-time Hispanic baby-
sitter, Delphine. Although she knows that Delphine — who comes
to her home each day — cares for Jennifer with a great deal of
warmth and affection, Erica is less confident of the woman's ability to provide sufficient intellectual stimulation. "If I were home,
I'd experiment with fingerpaints and Play-doh," Erica explains. "I
know Jennifer's baby-sitter is very good, but I don't know if I'd
fully trust her to do that all the time. If it's not your child, you
may not want to put the extra effort into your day." So part of
Delphine's responsibilities include taking the child to her weekly
classes.

As Erica talks, Jennifer pulls out a container full of blocks and
assembles them into a multicolored train. Occasionally Erica in-
terrupts our conversation to question her. "Can you tell me about
the colors on the train?" she asks. At another point, she encourages Jennifer to relate a story about a dog she met at the park.
But Jennifer is uninterested, and Erica resumes her account of the
child's increasingly full schedule. Next year, she says, Jennifer will
attend a preschool two mornings a week. This will "give her more
opportunity to have different facilities and do more than she would
with Delphine," she says.

Erica also believes it's important for her daughter to attend one
of the city's best kindergartens so she can later gain entry to
the best private elementary and secondary schools, and then, of
course, to one of the best colleges. At four, Jennifer must be ready
to take the Educational Records Bureau (ERB) tests required for
admission to elite kindergartens. Erica pauses and laughs at the
idea of a four-year-old actually being tested for "readiness skills"
and interviewed for evidence of leadership ability. "You can't believe what goes on at some of these schools," she says. "I went to
one school for a group tour, and there was a five-year-old dressed
in a little Chanel jacket and a navy-and-black watch-plaid skirt,
with a little string of pearls around her neck." When she describes
the school itself, however, she grows more respectful. "It has the
best reputation in New York. It's got great facilities, and it gets
children into the best private schools in Manhattan."

When I ask Erica Klein if she thinks her age and professional status have affected her attitudes toward child rearing, she reflects for a moment. "Being older, you have a different perspective and concerns," she replies. "You have friends who've tried to have children and couldn't, and you realize how much more precious a child is. And then I guess when you reach a certain level in your profession by hard work and perseverance, I think that has some effect on your views. If I'd been twenty-six when I had her, I would have felt that she would be all right no matter what I did. And I wouldn't have read all those books and been as involved in every stage of her development. Because I'm older, I'm more aware of things. And if I were younger and didn't work, I would spend more time with her. But I feel bad that I don't have more time to be with her."

Under any circumstances, parenting is one of the most difficult and demanding challenges that human beings confront. It is a roller coaster ride of delight and anxiety, tenderness and anger, achievement and frustration, vulnerability and control, pride and guilt no matter how old you are when you have your children, no matter how much or how little contact you have had with children, no matter what kind of social support you have, no matter whether you stay at home or go off to work. But today, particularly for older first-time mothers who have spent their lives grooming themselves to advance in the workplace, the problems of parenting are particularly complex.

Because so many mothers who work full-time have had little recent connection with domestic life with children, they may view pregnancy, childbirth, and child rearing with great anxiety. Parents in the past had more extended family and community ties to help them navigate these new life experiences, and thus they were more apt to pursue homegrown, trial-and-error approaches to raising children. But many new parents today don't have the benefit of such informal and familial tutelage. If they have children — as so many do — in their mid- to late thirties, their own parents are often too old to help out; these grandparents may even be approaching the time when *they* need part-time or full-time care from their family members. Because many of these professional couples have spent so much time working and so little at home, they may not know their neighbors. Friends who became parents long ago, in their early twenties, can barely remember what it was like to care for a young child. And friends and associates who remain single or childless may not understand or sympathize with the new demands of family life. When I enthusiastically announced my first pregnancy to a colleague who had decided not to have children, she greeted my news with a testy warning. "I hope you don't expect me to listen to stories about your morning sickness for the next nine months."

Because of the limited availability of extended maternity leaves in the United States (and the even greater scarcity of paternity-leave time) and the escalating time demands on U.S. working men and women, working mothers often feel great pressure to return to work very soon after giving birth and must leave their babies with various surrogate caregivers. This limits their own interactions with their offspring and deprives them of the opportunity to observe and experience their children's natural rhythms. Thus their anxieties about parenting are heightened, and they have little chance to gain confidence in their own parenting abilities or to develop their own parenting style. Some become beset by the fear that they will make an irreversible mistake that will impair their child's ability to compete, excel, and succeed.

"My daughter was born six weeks early," says Rebecca Arnold, a thirty-one-year-old former partner at a major Chicago brokerage house. "I went from work to the doctor and ended up going into labor that same day. I don't think anything prepares you for being a mother. For the first six weeks I felt I had lost my identity. I felt completely isolated. I had worked very hard during my career, and so did my husband. We didn't know anybody in our neighborhood. It took me a year to make a community for myself. There you are with this baby. She's so fragile. You're responsible for her during a twenty-four-hour day that has no beginning and end. I felt totally inadequate. At work, I knew what I was responsible for the moment I walked in the door. At home, you never know what a baby's mood will be. Everything is always changing so fast, and they're so fragile it can be terrifying to think of all the mistakes you can make."

Many achievement-oriented parents also suffer from an almost survivalist preoccupation with the economic uncertainties of the future. In the immediate post-War era, until the midseventies, most middle- and upper-middle-class Americans felt that their children would live either as well or even better than their parents. The American dream of a car in every garage and individual home ownership seemed to have come true. If you were white, had a decent income, and your children went to college, they would enter a stable profession and thrive.

Despite the greater affluence of a small elite of multimillionaires, the eighties brought greater — not less — economic insecurity to the majority of Americans. Regional economic downturns can put professionals out of work in a matter of months. Younger couples starting out can barely afford the price of an apartment in most urban settings. Home ownership is totally out of the question for many. Government subsidies and loans for education have been cut drastically. Parents come to believe — quite rightly — that the world they inhabit is a ruthless contest for advancement in which only a few will win. "The government won't help you. There's no sense of community anymore. I have to make my pile and make sure my kid gets a good start, because it's every man and woman for himself or herself," one corporate lawyer recently told me.

Realizing that each succeeding generation of Americans is no longer guaranteed a better life than the one before, many parents search for services, programs, and techniques that will enable their children to get ahead by gaining a competitive edge earlier and earlier in life.

Professional women have a particularly difficult time adjusting to motherhood because the very behavioral traits that seem to serve them well in the business world can be just the opposite of those they need as parents. In the world of work, women are told they have to be competitive, individualistic, aggressive, and in control. But the qualities they have cultivated in their careers may be of little help with their young children. Mothering, like all caring work, demands much more than "woman's intuition." As Sara Ruddick, author of *Maternal Thinking*, says, maternal work involves protecting, nurturing, and training children. Although mothers are not inherently better than other people, their work involves, Ruddick points out, a distinctive kind of thinking which can lead them to be "reflective and generous."

That's because maternal thinking is strategic thinking, an effort to balance conflicting desires and claims. "In any mother's day, the demands of preservation, growth, and acceptability are intertwined. Yet a reflective mother can separately identify each demand, partly because they are often in conflict. If a child wants to walk to the store alone, do you worry about her safety or applaud her developing capacity to take care of herself? If you overhear your son hurling insults at a neighbor's child, do you rush to instill decency and compassion in him, or do you let him act on his own impulses in his need to overcome shyness? . . . Most urgently, whatever you do, is somebody going to get hurt? Love may make these questions painful; it does not provide the answers. Mothers must think."[3]

Throughout history mothers, of course, have combined their maternal work in the home with work outside the home. And today, no matter what class they are in, most mothers do work outside the home. Although they may not all have time to devote hours to reflect on their maternal work, good enough parents are able, nonetheless, to learn from their experiences and to reflect on them — most particularly about their failures or problems in parenting. Learning to do the kind of distinctive thinking involved in parenting work thus involves a process of trial and error in which parents learn from their failures or problems in parenting. They learn from *being* with their children as well as *doing* for, with, or to them. Relinquishing control and making mistakes are as important as, if not more important than, taking total charge and succeeding at all costs.

Introducing marketplace categories of control, performance, invulnerability, individualism, success, competition, and aggression into the parenting experience, however, can inhibit the process of learning the kind of thinking that helps parents develop and grow in their new roles. Being in total charge, fearing to make mistakes, needing to succeed at all costs makes it hard for parents. Those parents who, after years in the workplace, have internalized the need to be in total charge, never make mistakes, and succeed at all costs will have a hard time learning to relinquish control when

necessary, learn from their mistakes, and let their children learn
and grow at their own pace.

Similarly, the openness, inventiveness, and vulnerability that
good enough parents must summon in order to deal with their
children's constant and ever changing needs are the antithesis of
the emotional invulnerability one needs to maneuver in the marketplace. In the zero-sum contest of market exchange, vulnerability and openness are considered (however erroneously) to be
liabilities rather than assets and are taken advantage of rather
than praised.

"Because I try to be open and caring with my children, I find
myself constantly ill-prepared to deal with the kind of uncaring
behavior that goes on in academic debates," a professor of history
told me. "Before I had children, I could bounce right back after
being attacked by a colleague. Today, I respond quickly enough
and seem to defend my positions well. But I find I'm constantly
shaking inside. I just never feel prepared for it, and I think it's
because as a mother, I work so hard to be open to my children
that I'm unable to be as self-protective as I used to be. I'm no
good at turning myself on and off."

Unlike accomplishment in the workplace, maternal or paternal
work must often be its own reward. An infant never thanks you
for cleaning his bottom or for staying up with him all night when
he has an ear infection. A three-year-old doesn't express her appreciation after the birthday party you worked so hard to prepare.
And a teenager may bestow only a sullen scowl on parents who
sacrifice to send her to college. "When you work in an office, people tell you what a good job you've done," says Priscilla Howland,
a mother of three. "But when you do something with your kids,
they don't say, 'Gee, Mom, thanks.' So you have to be very self-
motivated."

"As a new parent, you spend the whole day alone at home with
a child, and there is no one to say 'Oh, you did that just right.
What wonderful verbal stimulation you've just given your baby.'
If you have two kids, and you've managed a sibling fight well, no
one tells you what a great manager you are," says Alice Digilio, a
reporter for the *Washington Post*. "Then," she adds, "as a parent,
you never get anything completed. When you've spent most of

your adult life working, you get used to starting something, finishing it, and getting satisfaction out of someone's response to it. At home you never finish anything. There's nothing that concrete you can hold up at the end of the day and say, 'I've done this.' Of course, at the end of the day, if your child hasn't killed himself, you pat yourself on the back and congratulate yourself, and you feel good if your child is healthy and happy. But that's very different from the kind of bouquets that are thrown at a successful person in the workplace."

Because professional life does not encourage the development of essential mothering skills, many women complain that they feel split between the kind of person they are supposed to be at work and the kind of person they want to be at home. Erica Klein, for example, explains that she often feels so divided that she needs to walk home from work at the end of the day just to decompress. Block by block she sheds her professional persona — the thick skin of the "ruthless litigator" — and prepares to assume the role of the caring mother. The emotional energy required for this daily transformation is certainly a contributing factor to the sense of frustration and fatigue experienced by so many working mothers.

"You're trying to be a nurturing mother, and then you go to work and have to deal with all these people for whom driving ambition is the only thing on their minds," says West Coast magazine editor Rachel James, mother of a seven-year-old son. "To deal with the kind of environments professionals work in today — where it's not acceptable to work just eight hours a day and then go home and take care of your family and where people have actually become suspicious of caring and nurturing in the workplace — you're always in conflict. There's no mutuality, no collaboration, no trust. Unless you're a Zen Buddhist, I don't know how you switch off at the end of the day. I would carry home all this defensiveness, prickliness, and short-temperedness with me at the end of the day. And then I would feel terrible about how it affected my relationship with my son. That creates a lot of wakeful nights, when you have to wait until everyone is asleep in order to think about things and try to put work into some sort of perspective."

Lacking sufficient support from their employers, family, community, or friends, women may frantically look for help elsewhere.

Many turn to the myriad products, services, magazines, books, and seminars generated by the nation's booming new baby industry. Aggressively marketed, these products — and the professional helpers who often come with them — promise to solve every parenting problem, soothe every anxiety, and assuage every feeling of guilt. But the baby business exists to promote one thing and one thing only — consumption.

"Shrewd, sharp, and poised to sell, the American baby industry need not ask whether it's a boy or a girl," observes David Michaelis, in *Manhattan, inc.* magazine. "Obviously, it's a consumer. While you are reading the next 16 sentences," he reports, "seven new consumers are being born; 14 new parents, freshly consigned to the tumbrel, are waiting for the blade to fall on their disposable income. By the end of the year, 3.2 million first-time parents will have joined the 15.8 million first-timers for whom baby goods and services have been annually cutting away from 23 to 30 percent of personal income since 1980."[4]

Pocketbooks, not parents, are the real targets of the baby business. "With two breadwinners who have established careers and fewer children per household, these 'achiever' couples offer a tremendous pool of eager prospects with checkbooks at the ready," reported *Marketpulse*, an industry publication. Or, as the director of the Juvenile Products Manufacturers Association proclaimed, "This first-birth thing gives us the greatest customer any industry ever had, and that is the first-time grand-parent who has been waiting for this child."[5]

In the eyes of the business world, babies are miniconsumers and parents are considered their "purchasing agents." The merchandisers' goal is to reach these purchasing agents with an appropriate sales pitch within the "critical buying period" — the first twelve months of a child's life.[6]

To promote consumption, the baby industry resorts to time-honored formulas that advertisers first developed in the 1920s. Stuart Ewen, author of an excellent study on the history of the advertising industry, explains that Madison Avenue long ago decided that the best way to encourage consumption was to encourage anxiety about the everyday activities of life. If citizens-cum-consumers were tutored in what Madison Avenue dubbed a "critical self-consciousness," they would soon begin to worry about things like bad breath, enlarged nose pores, underarm odor that few worried about before.[7] Advertisers, therefore, began to promote products not because of their particular merits — their ability to get dishes clean, vacuum a house, or do the laundry more efficiently — but because each product ostensibly solved a particular anxiety that Madison Avenue had recently awakened.

Since its early days Madison Avenue has perfected the art of creating insecurity about the "hidden dangers" lurking beneath the surface of daily life and about the consequences of failing to take preventive action to deal with them. A big business deal may fall apart because a client spies a ring around a busy executive's collar or dandruff on his shoulders; a dinner party can go awry if a guest discovers spots on the hostess's best crystal; an intimate encounter may founder on the rocks of vaginal odor. Hitherto, efforts to create and exploit such fears centered primarily on activities and relationships between adults. But with relationships between first-time parents and their unborn or newborn children so fraught with anxiety, birthing and parenting themselves have become the subject of selling campaigns.

Lessons on the do's and don'ts of childcare are supplied while mom is still recuperating in her hospital bed. When I had my first baby, the hospital provided new mothers with a packet of parenting material that included a special issue of *American Baby* magazine called "The First Year of Life." This 126-page dissertation catalogued everything that happens in the first year of life. Beginning with week one, a series of essays described every developmental event in a baby's first year. Each essay was accompanied by a chart that outlined the physical, sensorimotor, and intellectual/social tasks baby is supposed to accomplish. The focus was on detail — when infants first make eye-to-eye contact, bat at objects, listen to sounds, look and suck at the same time, carry two small objects in one hand, search for hidden objects.[8]

The magazine concluded with a section on "The Learning Experience: How to Be a Better Teacher to Your Child," by Dr. Burton L. White. White is the author of *The First Three Years of Life* and a leading advocate of the parent-as-teacher, child-as-student model of early childhood development. Drawing on research he initiated during the 1960s in the federal Head Start program, which was set up to help the children of low-income parents get a proper start, White now also promotes his ideas among real head-starters — upper-income professional parents — many of whom are already thoroughly obsessed with performance, competition, and control.

Reading all of this, mothers do, of course, gain useful information about the wonderfully mysterious little creatures to whom they've just given birth. But the intense preoccupation with performance objectives may awaken anxieties parents didn't even know they had. Rather than simply worrying about how their infant will learn to eat, burp, and sleep through the night, the first-time parent finds herself worrying about eye-to-hand coordination, small and large motor functions, or whether there's enough simultaneous looking and sucking.

As one new mother said to me recently, "I'm worried about whether my son is really bonding with me." Of the six-week-old she reported with evident anxiety, "I mean, I read that he's supposed to be looking at me more now. But he doesn't seem to be making much eye contact. Do you think I'm doing something wrong?" Indeed, the editors of *American Baby* themselves seemed to be aware of how anxiety-provoking their supplement might be: the editors warned that the developmental charts were "to be regarded as guidelines only. Many babies will perform each activity earlier or later than indicated."[9]

The publications of equal-opportunity feminism reinforce readers' proclivity to be performance oriented. In a column in *Working Woman* entitled "Your Success, Your Child's Success," professional mothers are given pointers on how to create high-achieving children: "When you're used to succeeding, you expect achievement from your child. Here's how to set high standards without exerting undue pressure."[10]

In another article, "The Managerial Mother," we meet professional mothers who kill two birds with one stone by designing their "quarterly plan for their families" on the same day they do their quarterly business plans. Indispensable in making these plans are the plethora of new age-appropriate, developmentally sound toys and books that the baby industry has produced for later purchase by new parents.[11]

Consider, for example, *Baby Talk: How to Help Your Baby Learn to Talk*. At first glance, it reads like a spoof. The authors, one assumes, could not possibly be serious about their array of language development charts; their hints about what parents can do to promote verbal facility in one- or two-year-olds (for example, "encourage word usage," "respond to your baby's gestures," or "let your child talk"); their "Baby Talk Dictionary" (with informative entries like "Brudder (bru'der)n. brother, syn. bobo, bubber, budder; Dada (Dah'dah)n. father, syn. addy, bobby, da, daddy, fodder, mompa, papa, poppy"); or the log in which parents can record all the relevant data about their baby's first words under headings such as "English Word, Baby Talk, Date Said, Meaning."[12]

But the authors of *Baby Talk*, Bruce Lansky and his "technical advisor," Michael Marastos, Ph.D., are very serious, and unfortunately they are not alone in their efforts to regulate and direct infants' earliest activities. In *Play with a Purpose: Learning Games for Children Six Weeks to Ten Years*, author Dorothy Einon encourages parents to monitor their children's playtime behavior in order to achieve "better value in terms of learning" and to pick up hints that indicate baby is ready to progress to the next lesson.[13] Other books bombard parents with advice on everything from the right and wrong way to tickle, how to hold their children, and how to play dress-up with them.

All place heavy emphasis on the type of educational toys that should be acquired. Brightly colored Judy Puzzles, for example, come with handouts that explain their "Puzzle Performance Objectives." These may include developing "perceptual discrimination by shape, size, color, direction, detail and design; practicing eye-hand coordination, problem solving skills, storytelling skills, developing readiness and concentration skills." Johnson and Johnson's recent series of "Child Development Toys" — rattles, rollers, bath toys, and balls — are now accompanied by a sixteen-page guide that enables parents to "learn to play" and helps them to help their children "get the most" out of each toy.

Elaborate printed instructions and developmental guides also accompany the products of a relatively new company called Discovery Toys. Discovery was started by Lane Nemeth, a former daycare administrator who was dissatisfied with the quality of toys found in most large toy stores. Like Tupperware products, Nemeth markets her wares through home demonstrations performed by a nationwide sales force predominantly of women who work out of their homes.

Sturdy, brightly colored, well designed, and fairly expensive, Discovery Toys are an appealing alternative to the shoddy, commercialized, cartoon- and film-inspired standbys like Barbie and Ken, G.I. Joe, and Rambo. But Discovery Toys carry a problematic message of their own that is, in fact, the company's motto: "Play Is a Child's Work."

Each box features a description of the toy inside and a rating for its age appropriateness and "educational value." To reinforce the company's message, members of the Discovery Toys sales force are called "Educational Consultants," not saleswomen or salesmen, and their job is not only to sell toys but to teach parents how to use them correctly. Their living-room presentations to potential "purchasing agents" include instructions on how parents can make proper educational use of their "quality time" with their children.

The same emphasis on the right and wrong way to play is included in exercise instruction given to infants and their parents in infant and toddler exercise classes all over the country. For example, there's Gymboree, a nationwide infant and toddler exercise service that started in California in 1980. As one Gymboree franchise holder explained it to me, mothers and their children benefit far more from Gymboree than from the untutored, unstructured play most engage in with their children at home or the playground. "The kind of play parents engage in at the playground is passive. There, mothers just watch their children play, while here at Gymboree they're active participants."

In these settings, being an active participant equals actively pushing your infant or toddler to do what he or she may be completely uninterested in doing. When I visited a Santa Monica, California, baby-exercise program called My Gym for Children, mothers were frantically trying to get their infants to perform the routines elaborated by the cheerful instructor who presided over the training. A group of mothers sat in a circle on the floor singing songs and doing programmed exercise routines while their infants crawled haplessly around the room — blissfully unconscious of the calisthenics they were supposed to perform.

In the middle of the hour, one mother of a child of perhaps ten months of age held him in front of a mirror and tried to get him to jump on cue. "Jump, jump, jump," she urged. The baby stood stock-still. "Jump, jump, jump," she repeated with greater urgency. He did not budge. "Jump, jump, jump," she said, her voice rising to a frustrated pitch. The baby stood, as if set in concrete. The mother edged back and looked at him with dismay. "Don't you want to jump?" she asked, her voice resonating with disappointment, her gaze crestfallen. Needless to say, the baby did not reply.

At the end of the class, another mother carried her infant to the front desk, where she cornered the instructor. In a parody of adult concerns, she wondered how she could arrange makeup classes for the infant. The instructor proposed several alternative class times as the mother's face creased with worry. "But that's just when she takes her nap," she said petulantly. I left them arguing about whether or not mother and daughter could get their money's worth.

Many of the mothers I spoke with at these classes did not originally come there to get value for money. Rather, they came seeking companionship. Because so many women work today, they have no maternal community in their neighborhoods, and they can't easily find that community on their block or at their local playground. Infant exercise classes represent a way to meet other mothers while doing something fun with their children.

While mothers do, in fact, meet other potential companions, the atmosphere that often reigns in these classes encourages competition as well as camaraderie. Because mothers are paying for play, they tend to expect more bang for the buck and may begin comparing their infants and toddlers with those of other participants. "Parents will come up to me and say 'He's not doing anything.' But I tell them if they stick with it, one day their child will get up

and do something," one Gymboree instructor told me. "Some kids
are doers and goers and some aren't. But the thing is, these parents
are paying money for the class, and they worry that, gosh, their
kids aren't doing anything." To encourage more action Gymboree
has, not surprisingly, developed a line of videos, tapes, exercise
suits, books, and toys that can help stimulate the right kind of
play in both parent and child.

That children learn through play is hardly a stunning new insight. Every good enough parent knows that play is not purpose-
less, that children need affection and encouragement to develop
and grow, and that learning is important. But what the new baby
industry does is take experiences that have always been in the
background of child rearing and bring them into the foreground.
This, in turn, transforms play from an integral, natural part of a
child's normal growth into a rarefied experience that must be com-
modified and then sold — at least to those parents who can afford
it. And so, like the hostess who lives in constant fear of spots on
the glassware, parents live in fear of failing to purchase the right
book or rattle, of playing incorrectly with their children's toys, or
failing to get their children into the right preschool or kindergarten.

"What is at stake here is the very nature of childhood," says
Harvard faculty member and pediatrician David Link. "The new
emphasis on achievement in parenting is tragic because it disturbs
the central element of play, which has to do with freedom and
spontaneity, not achievement and performance. Once you introduce the idea that there is a right way and wrong way to do things
in play, it's no longer playing. And once you inject consumption
into playtime, you kill spontaneity. If a kid is wearing a hundred-
and-fifty-dollar designer dress, or playing in a room that cost thousands to furnish, how do you think a parent is going to feel when
that kid happily smears chocolate pudding all over her skirt, or
cheerfully fingerpaints on the white wicker furniture?"

Moreover, what begins as a marketing strategy for products and
services becomes a wholesale market invasion into family life. The
emphasis on performance-oriented teaching rather than acceptance and caring does not end once mothers have gotten through
their children's first year of life. It becomes a way of life — a re-

sponse to the myriad problems, anxieties, and guilts that are inevitable aspects of the human experience of child rearing.

The choices that Audrey Wilson has made for her three-year-old son, for example, have been clearly influenced by the new concern with educational training in early childhood. Wilson, thirty-two, married a Nigerian student when she was in her late twenties and waited for several years before having her first child. When Benjamin was a year old, she went back to work at a computer firm near St. Louis. The couple needed the extra money, and Audrey needed the sense of independence working gives her. "I don't like to be dependent on anyone. It made me very unpleasant," she says.

At first Audrey was opposed to daycare. "I had an image in my mind of an ideal relationship between a mother and a child and that was one-to-one." So she hired a baby-sitter to come to her home. But when she found that she could not depend on the woman to turn up each day, Audrey placed Benjamin in the home of a well-educated Hispanic family-daycare provider.

When Benjamin was a year or two old, Audrey says, her priority was to find a warm, loving environment for him, and she is satisfied that his provider supplied just that. But by the time he was two and a half, she was more concerned about the development of her son's cognitive skills. "I think he needs more direction than he previously did. He needs more structured activities, things like cutting out paper figures, building things, being taught things in a storylike fashion, and he needs physical activities that are directed.

"If I were home, I'd be teaching him a lot of things. In fact I always think I could do a better job than anybody. Like, right now, I'm trying to teach him Greek mythology on a storytelling level. I think he could learn his ABCs but I haven't been that aggressive about it."

She has, however, become more assertive in trying to get his daycare provider to fill in the gaps of his early-childhood education. When Benjamin was twenty-eight months old, Audrey presented her provider with a list of things she wanted her son to learn. The first week, she felt he should master sizes, shapes, and colors as well as the seasons. Suggested lessons included material such as the fact that "bears hibernate and birds migrate south in winter." Audrey's provider valiantly tried to comply with her wishes. But the child, quite understandably, could not grasp abstract concepts more appropriate for a five- or six-year-old. "What's winter?" the little boy asked. "What's hibernate? Migrate? South?"

Instead of giving up on this kind of skill training, Audrey decided not to continue in such a low-key, family-daycare program, and enrolled Benjamin in an academically oriented preschool. She believes that this will help encourage the kind of independence and self-reliance that will enable him to function in an increasingly competitive world. "Life is structured, and school is that way. I'd like him to like school, and to have the discipline to do well in it. Life isn't easy. He's got to have a lot of discipline to get through it. It would be to his detriment if I stayed home and pampered him. His ultimate success in life depends on his ability to get through the institutions he has to live in."

Audrey acknowledges that her concern with teaching her son competitive skills at an early age is partly a result of her own feelings about the kind of parenting she herself received. "I was one of those kids who didn't get enough drive and direction from my parents, one of those kids who was taught to be interested in everything. But they didn't give me a very practical orientation, didn't teach me to think about how to make a living."

More importantly, she feels she must pay special attention to cognitive skills and structure because Benjamin, as a child of an interracial marriage, will have a hard time getting ahead in life. "I think it will be tougher for him because there are dangers for kids like Benjamin who come from racially mixed couples. There are very few people in authority and power who are nonwhite."

Audrey does believe that Benjamin also needs to develop social skills and the ability to relate to others. But she tends to view these skills instrumentally: "They are tools that will help him make it in the institutions he has to work in later in life."

Although Audrey Wilson and her husband are middle-class professionals, she exhibits a great deal of anxiety about the future. This is not simply because her son is black. Today's professional parents differ significantly from those who raised children in the fifties or sixties, when parents of means had far greater confidence that their children would be assured of a comfortable future as long as they received a good upbringing and a college education.

Today's middle- and even upper-middle-class parents lack any such certainty. Instead, they believe their children, as adults, will have to fight for what they want, and once they've gotten it, they will have to fight to keep it.

Like many other parents interviewed for this book, Audrey Wilson seems to view early childhood as a period in life lasting little more than two or two and a half years. Then it's time for toddlers to acquire the skills that will get them through life. Most parents who attempt to constrict early childhood in this manner do so out of a genuine desire to help their children gain self-esteem. But they define self-esteem almost entirely in terms of performing well, failing to understand that self-esteem develops when mothers and fathers express unconditional love and support, rather than bestowing it as a reward for performance.

Unlike parents of the sixties and early seventies, today's mothers are also far less apt to question the ethic of competitive individualism. Just as they believe it's never too early for a child to learn to read, they believe it's never too early for a child to acquire the other competitive skills needed to succeed. "I'm not very competitive," one mother explained. "That's my husband's domain. So he teaches Julie [four and a half years old] how to compete in things like the sports activities he does with her."

"People aren't trying to push their children for bad reasons," says T. Berry Brazelton, one of the nation's foremost pediatricians and experts on early childhood. "They want to make up for what they feel they aren't able to give their children. But this is not a child-oriented approach. It's adult oriented. And it's at great expense to the child. The effects may not show up right away, but they may show up later."

Brazelton refers to experiences he had in the 1960s, when one of the behaviorist B. F. Skinner's disciples, O. K. Moore, was also teaching young children to learn at early ages. "I had eight young patients who went through this training. They seemed to love it. They seemed to learn. They got lots of approval from their parents and grandparents." Unfortunately, the lessons didn't last. "The kids did okay in first grade. But they got into trouble in second and third grades. They couldn't generalize that kind of learning, and they depended on adult approval, not on something from within." All eight of them had problems. "I do not recommend adult approaches to teaching children to learn. It has to come from within the child," Brazelton concludes emphatically.

Parents don't become enemies of childhood only because of maternal anxiety; they often push cognitive development to assuage maternal guilt feelings. Many working mothers feel terribly guilty because they have to work either part- or full-time. They are troubled by the necessity of putting their children in daycare, and they are concerned about the quality of that care. The daycare provider may have a more limited educational background and thus seem ill-equipped to further a child's intellectual development. Or the daycare facility may be overcrowded and understaffed, as is all too common in many areas of the country. In either case, parents feel they must make the most of their "quality time" with their children by using it for "skill training" in order to compensate for whatever real or imagined shortcomings may exist in their child's daycare arrangement.

Amanda Emory, a forty-two-year-old mother of two daughters, says she feels extremely guilty about the quality of childcare her younger daughter, Becky, is receiving. Amanda remained at home until her nine-year-old daughter was four. But she went back to work part-time when Becky was only one month old. Becky, now three, goes to nursery school two days a week. From nursery school, a friend takes her to a sitter for the remainder of the day. On another day, she goes to yet a different sitter. "I don't feel good," Amanda says. "I don't feel she has adequate care in one of the daycare settings because they have too many children, and it's just custodial care. But I don't know what to do."

Because she believes she must make up for this deficiency, Amanda feels she is wasting valuable quality time if she cooks, does the laundry, or runs errands when Becky is with her. Instead, she tries to devote their time together to teaching her colors, numbers, and letters. But for Amanda, these activities add to her work load at home by eating into the only time available for household duties. When she complains of these problems to her husband, she says, she gets little support. An architect, he works so hard himself he is rarely home to help with household chores. "He tells me that I don't have to work. But that's no help, because I want to work."

Like Audrey Wilson, Amanda Emory could opt to provide her child with more early "being-together," rather than more early learning, but she seems to devalue more nurturing approaches to child rearing. "I'm disappointed in the nursery school. What's lacking is organized activities. They have this huge room, and they just let kids wander around and do whatever they want. I'd like her to have more activities I couldn't do at home with her. I haven't seen any reading readiness at all. They do things like take trips to the zoo. I don't need to send her to nursery school to have her go to the zoo and stand in line and go to see the zebra and giraffe. We've done that. As far as I can tell," she says derisively, "the nursery school is just socialization."

Unfortunately, parents like Amanda Emory fail to factor several important things into their judgments about less academically oriented preschools and nursery schools. First, they do not understand the philosophy of and level of educational, analytic, and organizational skills that go into planning sound, developmentally appropriate programs for their children. Jean Potter, an early-childhood educator and director of a nursery school in Arlington, Massachusetts, explains that the apparently random play that laymen and parents observe in many childcare centers and nursery schools is, in fact, carefully designed by experts in children's psychological development. "One of the key things we do is help a child develop a sense of self-esteem in the first four or five years. This is extremely important because if a person doesn't develop that in those years, it's very hard to recover. So we work to provide an environment that is developmentally appropriate for young children. This means that we don't require too much of them — thus making them feel frustrated and incompetent — yet we also don't put limits on what they can explore, learn, and develop."

This balance is attained through hard work. "We try to arrange everything so that children feel good about themselves and experience themselves as competent little people. We have to capitalize on their strengths and support their weaknesses," Potter elaborates. "That takes a lot of thought, a lot of observing, analyzing, and evaluating. And then a lot of work to create activities that do this."

The problem is that this work is invisible and some parents don't always understand the relationship between self-esteem, play, and cognitive development and between socialization and cognitive development. "Play allows children to master their impulses and ideas," Potter continues. "And when they're able to play in the company of other children their own age, they're able to expand this world of impulses and ideas to include others. They're able to learn to take other people into account. This is what we call socialization. It's not 'just socialization' — something unimportant or icing on the cake — it's one of the most important aspects of growth and development. If a child is not socialized, he or she will be very lonely indeed. Moreover, to master the world of ideas, children must learn to master their own ideas and impulses so they can test their ideas with others and share with others."

In an effort to give their children more than "just socialization," many advocates of high-powered parenting enroll them in academically oriented preschools and kindergartens. Because greater demand for their services has made entrance competition more intense, the fast-track three- or four- or five-year-old may have to take entrance exams — conducted by the Educational Records Bureau (ERB) — as well as go through interviews at the schools to which their parents have applied. To prepare them for these tests, parents often pay $1,000 or more for tutoring for those tests. To save money, they may themselves supervise pretest preparation.

In a 1988 article in *New York* magazine entitled "Making the Private-School Grade," which reached thousands of overanxious parents, Manhattan pediatrician Beatriz Rubinstein prescribed that such parental preparation cover a wide cognitive curriculum for the toddler facing the ERBs at four. The most mundane exchanges between parent and child, for instance, should be viewed as opportunities to enhance verbal skills. Rather than playing with pots and pans or building blocks, Rubinstein recommended investing in a set of expensive educational toys designed to enhance performance.

Without specifically mentioning race or class, she warned mothers that their affectionate Jamaican baby-sitter or white working-class family-daycare provider may actually be damaging their child. "If you work, or for some reason do not have the time to play with your child as much as you would like, consider the person who acts as your substitute. Your child will copy the way she speaks and does things. If your youngster is being cared for by a trusted foreign woman with extremely poor English, it makes sense to try to compensate for her weak points. You could do that by hiring a high school student to come in for a few hours once or twice a week and sit on the floor and read, talk or play games with your child."[14]

Rubinstein advised parents to select the outfit the child will wear for the test ahead of time and to dress the child in it on suitable occasions so that he or she will feel comfortable in it at the interview. She also suggests that parent and child visit the site where the test will be taken to familiarize the toddler with the scene of his or her upcoming competition.

Karen Honig, a veteran early-childhood educator, teacher, and former director of children's programs in one of Manhattan's most prestigious private schools, is very concerned because parental pushing of young children has become a national trend. "Fifteen years ago, parents had a lot more faith in their kids. If a child wasn't reading at five, it wasn't such a problem. Now it's looked at through a microscope. There's a big fear that children won't learn to read at an early age. Parents would come to me and say, 'My child has watched "Sesame Street" and knows his letters and numbers, what are you going to do? I don't want him to just play. I want him to learn something.'

"Or a parent brings in a four-year-old," Honig continues, "and describes all the things he did at three and then says, 'What are you going to teach him that's different?' " She laughs as she responds, "Just things like how to go to the bathroom by himself, not fight, little things like that."

But some parents, she says, scoff at such suggestions. Because these parents don't seem to understand that social skills are also learned, they don't value the time teachers spend socializing their

children. "We worked with parents of a five-year-old," Honig recounts, "who was reading fluently, having trouble writing, and
who had no ability to get along with other children. And of the
goals we set for the child with the parents, they didn't care about
social things. All they wanted us to do was work on writing. This
child was severely in need of help learning how to play with others.
Maybe these people were an extreme case, but a lot of people think
social skills are the last thing you need to worry about."

Honig attributes this dramatic shift in parental attitudes to the
spate of recent books that stress the importance of early learning
and to the testing services designed to determine whether a child
is "gifted" or just "average." "Parents get their kids tested either
through testing services or through the application process to private schools. Then they're told their kids are gifted and that they
should 'watch out' for their education. The parents come to us and
are floating on air. But they're also shouldering a tremendous burden. They feel that if they don't teach their children early, they're
losing out on some optimum opportunity." Honig groans when she
considers what has happened to early childhood. "Where are the
books that tell parents how important it is to let their children just
play?"

Ironically, when parents try to get their children to master cognitive skills at earlier and earlier ages, they compromise, rather
than enhance, their educational prospects. According to many specialists in childhood development, this kind of pushing serves no
real educational function. Trying to "teach" children to learn almost as soon as they are able to smile and say goo-goo is a misguided exercise in miseducation, contends David Elkind, professor
of child study at Tufts University. In his book *Miseducation: Preschoolers at Risk*, Elkind explains that, in so doing, we are putting
children at risk "for short-term stress and long-term personality
damage for no useful purpose. There is no evidence that such early
instruction has lasting benefits and considerable evidence that it
can do lasting harm."[15]

Elkind argues that academic preschools, accelerated kindergartens, and programs that teach parents how to have a brighter child
and other such formal and informal educational schemes push
children far ahead of their level of development, pay too little

attention to individual learning styles, focus on isolated skill development, and deprive children of more enjoyable natural learning experiences.

Specialists in emotional development and motivation like Virginia Demos, a child psychologist who teaches at the Harvard Graduate School of Education, believe that some parents disregard warnings like Elkind's because they simply don't understand how and why children learn. According to Demos, "Children will learn when they're interested in something because they're trying to solve a problem that's salient to their needs and interests." Such problem solving can be facilitated by an adult who can talk to them and lead them, Demos adds. But this interaction between child and adult has to be a collaboration in which the adult really follows the child's lead.

"Learning is determined by this collaboration," Demos continues. "It's also determined by neurological factors that differ in each child. No child is the same. Some children learn to read at four and some at a later age. What might make a difference is seeing that the parent values reading. Not because they flash cards at a child or buy expensive reading-readiness programs, but because they read to a child, or because the child sees his or her parents reading themselves."

What some parents do not realize is that many so-called skills training advocates base their claims and programs for accelerated learning on distorted interpretations of research findings. "We've learned a lot about young children's incredible capacity to master their environment," observes Demos. "But, while theorists like Jean Piaget have demonstrated a great deal about children's innate abilities, they've also cautioned about pushing children. In America, people have not heeded those cautionary warnings. Instead, they've turned these insights into curricula for very young children because they figure that if kids can perform some intellectual task at age seven, then maybe, with enough work, they'll be able to do it at age four."

Some child psychologists also believe that this new emphasis on the mass production of gifted children distorts research in another significant way. "While many thinkers and researchers in cognitive development zero in on one part of the child's whole being, most of them understand that this is only one part of the whole and that the part should not be developed at the expense of the whole," says Dr. Gerald Stechler, professor of psychiatry at Boston University's School of Medicine.

"But people who are pushing children to advance and achieve at young ages don't appreciate that fact. Their understanding of children is partial at best, and so they overemphasize one aspect of development at the expense of other equally important developmental functions."

Stechler stresses the importance of helping young children acquire a sense of self-esteem. "During the second year of life, and particularly during the third, parents have to cope with the tension between the child's omnipotent sense of himself and the omnipotence with which they invest their parents. During these two crucial developmental years, the parents have to let a child down gently — to make him see that neither he nor his parents is endowed with magical omnipotent qualities. Parents do this by enhancing a child's self-esteem."

Stechler believes that many contemporary parents misunderstand this crucial concept. "The sense of self-esteem that parents must give a child is created not because parents praise a child for what he *does*, but rather because they are thrilled just because the child *is*. If you only praise children for what they do, rather than because of who they are, you can, in fact, exacerbate the very problems and qualities you're trying to temper. Children become addicted to performing because they feel that's the only way to get a parent's love."

T. Berry Brazelton also believes this performance-oriented approach fails to develop self-esteem. "Nobody really knows what self-esteem is," he comments. "But it definitely comes from within a child. Adults wouldn't know this unless they watched their children very carefully. It's something you see in a baby's or child's behavior. In their face, if you watch and pay attention. You do not encourage self-esteem by pushing young children. That's the opposite of self-esteem."

The emphasis on teaching children to perform, compete, and achieve overshadows another important aspect of women's caring

agenda — the effort to help little boys become more sensitive, nurturing, and less competitive and aggressive. In the early days of
the women's movement, feminists were committed to the goal of
nonsexist child rearing. This meant more than teaching girls how
to project themselves into roles traditionally reserved for boys. It
meant helping little boys learn to be more emotionally expressive
and relationship centered — not simply by encouraging fathers to
share child rearing and thus provide boys with nurturing male role
models, but by altering child-rearing practices geared toward
raising boy children. But this objective seems to have been abandoned by many parents and child-rearing experts. Parents of
little girls may be very concerned about helping them master
competitive skills, and look forward to the moment when their
daughters will enter Little League and learn to be team players. But many of those who have little boys do not seem to be
concerned enough about helping them develop their "feminine
side."

This is admittedly very challenging work. Many psychologists
feel that little boys really are more aggressive and less relationally
oriented than little girls. This does not mean, they hasten to add,
that boys cannot be taught to be more caring and sensitive by
parents who encourage relational awareness. "When Joey is playing with a friend," says child psychiatrist Arnold M. Kerzner, "and
takes his baseball bat away from the other boy, you don't punish
him. You ask him to think about how the other little boy feels. All
too often, parents of small boys make things either-or." Kerzner
illustrates this approach with the example of an interaction between two young children. A little boy tries to take a toy away
from a little girl. His parents immediately tell him he's bad and
insist he return the toy, but they don't explain why, and — most
importantly — they don't illuminate the relational component of
the interaction by explaining how the boy's conduct makes the
little girl feel. When the little boy refuses to return the toy, they
take him into the house and tell him he can't play anymore. Thus,
the little boy learns that relationships jeopardize what he wants.
In order to have a relationship with either his parents or his playmate, he has to give up what he wants — the toy. Or he has to
give up both the toy and his playmate and gets nothing in return,

all of which reinforces the masculine notion that relationships are threatening rather than enriching.

Cognitive, competitively oriented instruction also undermines relational awareness. "When parents are overly concerned with cognitive development," Kerzner explains, "the interaction between the parents and children does not model the kind of relational content they want to encourage and loses the emotional tone they would want to create. Quality time these days tends to consist of educational discussions rather than relational sharing."

Similarly, when parents make mountains out of molehills — which Kerzner says they should do — they often choose the wrong molehill. Thus parents who are trying to encourage their children at a sporting event will push them to score goals, rather than point out the relational component of their interaction with others. "Imagine how powerful it could be, from the relational point of view, if a parent would say to a child, 'That was very nice the way you made that assist, how you helped that other child.' That would stress the assist, the pass, not the goal and would tell children that cooperation and collaboration, as well as competition and individual achievement, is valuable."

Discussions about making boys more relationship centered are relatively rare. Indeed, some studies confirm that even mothers continue to raise their sons in stereotypical ways. Many mothers and fathers allow their infant boys to cry much longer than their infant girls before picking them up. When they are older, some child educators and psychologists report, mothers still attend to their daughters' emotional needs much more quickly than to their sons'.

That we should continue to reproduce age-old behavior patterns is understandable. What is unfortunate is that there is so little societal discussion — such as there was in the sixties and early seventies — about transforming boys' behavior. There are no bestsellers countering the masculine, performance-oriented messages of *How to Raise a Brighter Child* with *How to Make Boys More Emotionally Expressive*. In fact, the opposite kind of behavior — competitive, aggressive conduct — is emphasized not only in children's educational toys and books but in cartoons and videos that are directly marketed to young children. Cartoons continue to be traditionally sex stereotyped, the better to sell toymakers' wares to an easily identified target audience. While cartoons aimed at an audience of boys remain warlike and violent and include few female characters in the male characters' almost exclusively masculine universes, many cartoons aimed at girls now teach them how to be competitive and materialistic. And movie and video makers now consider frighteningly aggressive and violent films — and toys based on them — like *Friday the Thirteenth* and *Nightmare on Elm Street* to be age-appropriate viewing even for four-year-olds.

It will take a renewed social discussion of how we rear young boys to raise parental consciousness about the importance of helping them be more sensitive and nurturing. Unfortunately, those parents who are overly concerned with individual performance, independence, and self-reliance are likely to be poor relational tutors. A mother who thinks a three-year-old boy should get down to business and learn to compete will probably not encourage him to prize his relationships, express his feelings, or see himself as connected to others. A father who thinks equality and enlightenment consists of teaching both sons and daughters to compete in sports and play rough at home may be helping little girls learn about competitive individualism but is doing very little to encourage an appreciation of nurturing and caring in either sex.

What is perhaps even worse is that some of the women who complain that men are unexpressive, unsupportive, and lacking in empathy do not realize their own child-rearing practices can have a positive impact on these oft-lamented male patterns of behavior. Indeed, by instituting competition-centered rather than relation- and care-centered child-rearing practices, many may actually be bequeathing to another generation of women the very behavior they complain about today.

As we have seen, performance-oriented parenting does little to foster the joy of learning, but it definitely takes the joy out of early childhood. Of course, no parent can guarantee her sons or daughters a pressure-free childhood. But instead of sacrificing a warm and supportive relationship with one's child in the pursuit of some vision of future success, parents can use this precious time — time they will never be able to recapture — to learn to value being rather than doing, and to reward their children and themselves for *who* they are rather than *what* they may become.

In so doing, we gain faith in ourselves and our own parenting abilities and absorb perhaps the most important lesson of all: if our children are not emotionally or physically handicapped, they do not need to learn to grow; they will grow at their own pace.

This is, after all, the remarkable thing about human beings. Evolution has furnished us with a built-in program that drives us to develop our talents and to master our world. Long before self-help experts published their tendentious tomes about infant intelligence and toy manufacturers glutted the market with their educational wares, children were learning to talk, read, write, do their sums, and turn into productive, sometimes even quite brilliant, adults. Given human history, going by the books, faithfully following the latest parenting fad isn't only a ridiculous exercise in futility; it can destroy our faith in ourselves and our children by injecting tension into the spontaneous play that is such an important part of childhood.

When I was researching Discovery Toys for this book, the company sent me several toys to sample with my child. Then about seventeen months old, my daughter decided we should play with a yellow pegboard that came with assorted colored pegs. I sat by her side as she randomly plucked the purples, blues, greens, and reds and plopped them into the lines of holes covering the square. At some point in her play, I decided to read the instructions that accompanied the toy and began to guide her play, suggesting she make rows of one particular color so she could, as the toymaker counseled, begin to identify colors.

As I tried to guide her tiny hand, her play became our mutual work. Not surprisingly, she balked at this directorial effort. She had been happy doing it her way. She didn't care about distinguishing red from green before she was two. She just wanted to have a good time. When I decided to turn play into a performance, our "being time" together was instantaneously transformed into "doing time" — an instrumental engagement that neither of us wanted or needed. I quickly abandoned the effort, and we were both palpably relieved.

Assuaging the anxieties and guilts so many of us feel by pushing

cognitive development over social relationships does little to address the causes of our many parenting dilemmas. Indeed, it may
only compound them. Promoting cognitive development and
teaching our children competitive skills is no substitute for longer
parenting leaves, saner working schedules, real family time rather
than the sham substitute of quality time, an adequate supply of
well-trained, well-paid daycare providers, a community of parents
that can bolster our confidence and with whom we can share our
problems and joys, and a society that places caring on an equal
par with profit.

Addressing the many social problems we have today with a misguided effort to place our children on the fast track in effect only
shifts the locus of our problems from the larger society to the frail
shoulders of our children. We burden their development with our
failure to challenge the new conditions our society imposes on parenting. But in so doing, we get no more time off when we have a
new baby, our work schedules are no more flexible, the supply of
daycare providers does not increase, and our children's future is
no more stable.

Rather than viewing women's liberation as the vehicle to infuse
caring into the marketplace, the marketplace now views women
as the vehicle to infuse marketplace values into that most intimate
and important personal relationship — the rearing of young children. But if we don't rebel against being so used, we defeat both
our children and ourselves. If we infuse our children's play with
purpose and turn it into work for us all, we quite literally create
a world in which work is without end and allow the market to
invade every corner of our lives. And we deprive ourselves and our
society of the opportunity to develop the values and behaviors that
might one day transform our culture into one more hospitable not
only to children but to the adults they will become.

Conclusion

TOWARD A NEW FEMININE FUTURE

WHERE HAS women's anger gone? What has happened to us, to me?" Helena Walzer asks, as she sits in my kitchen one summer afternoon, while her nine-month-old daughter plays cheerfully at her side. "All of a sudden, after being a woman wasn't an issue and I was doing just fine by myself, I'm not anymore. I keep thinking, I'm one of the lucky ones. Compared to so many other women, I have everything going for me. And yet I feel totally stuck. So I just can't imagine what other people are feeling."

It has been a year and a half since our initial meeting, and Helena Walzer recounts the events that have transformed her life and her thinking. Shortly after we met, Walzer discovered she was pregnant, married her longtime boyfriend, and quit her job. Before having her baby, she worked as a consultant. Now she's trying to adjust to motherhood and plans to get a part-time job in the near future.

Walzer explains that she feels both tremendously relieved and incredibly confused. "I hated my job. My boss used to come into my office each day to chat about how the market was doing, and I realized I didn't know and I didn't care. I didn't care enough about the ups and downs of the market to really follow it. The men were really into gambling against the market and competing with each other. And I wasn't interested in beating either the market or other portfolio managers. So I was glad to get out. But after spending my life preparing to give my all to work, how do I think about the future?" she asks.

As she thinks about the choices she has made, she realizes that she had viewed work as a kind of panacea. "When I was a teenager," she recalls wistfully, "feminism was a big part of my growing up. My mother went through a heavy divorce, and there was a great deal of consciousness raising going on and a feeling that women should talk to and relate to other women.

"But, somehow, in my twenties, all that ended," Walzer explains. "I had women friends, but our relationships were no longer centered on women's issues or the prospect of change. I think I saw the solution to all my problems as attaining economic independence. My mother was thrown out into the street because she wasn't economically independent, and I didn't want that to happen to me. So I went to business school. I thought that if I got an MBA and a good job, all doors would open. I became less politically active and more concerned with my own life. I felt that if I was all right, then things in the world were all right and we were all advancing together."

But Walzer could not muster the requisite reverence for the Dow when she was an investment adviser and did not like what she was becoming. "I got this great fast-track job and found out that while I could take care of myself economically, it was at great cost. I had no time for myself. I would have had to give up having a family. So now I'm home, married, with a child, and it's blown my mind."

In attempting to redefine her personal sense of self-worth, Walzer says, she is constantly fighting an inner battle. "I keep thinking, I can work part-time, have kids, and have a really nice life. But somehow, I keep worrying that that won't be enough. I should be doing more with my life."

When I ask Walzer what she wants to be, what kind of life she wants, she ponders quietly for a moment and then unhesitatingly responds. "I would like balance in my life. I would like to work three or four days a week in a job where I'm learning, respected, and earning decently. I don't want to earn a huge salary or become president of the company. I want to do well and have time for my family."

And what is so unrealistic about that goal, I ask?

Those aren't the ground rules, she observes. That's not what you're supposed to want. "You're supposed to want it all — money and getting to the very pinnacle of your corporation. I know now that I don't want that, yet I don't know how to go about changing the rules."

Like many other women, Walzer privately acknowledges that her insights and sense of balance are much needed in the contemporary workplace. She has been taught, however, not to publicly voice her real feelings and opinions at work because, even for many of the female mentors who advise junior colleagues, feminine perceptions and perspectives have become the problem for which masculine ideals are the solution. Rather than challenging the masculine world she has entered, she and many other women feel demoralized because they have failed to adapt to rules they do not respect. "We don't know how to be angry about things anymore. Like now, I feel so sensitized to women and family, and it shocks me that we're not all in rebellion. It's as though we've gone back in time to the early sixties except that now, it's the lucky ones who get to stay home with their children and the unlucky ones who have to cope with work and family."

Although she does not hold feminism responsible for her choices or the disillusionment she has experienced, she does believe that women have lost the simple ability to talk to one another about their problems in a way that leads to collective action to solve them. "I lie awake at night obsessing about how to get good childcare. There must be thousands of women thinking about the very same thing. But where do you go? Mothers' groups aren't designed to do more than provide moral support and companionship. Women's business networks are there to help women advance in their careers."

Walzer says she is not worried about getting a good part-time job when she returns to work. In fact, she's already had several offers. But work, she feels, is only a partial solution to her problems. Instead, she wants to participate in a more collective approach to changing women's realities. She would like to work with other women to create a culture in which women do not have to become clones of men in the workplace and which would provide a sense of community both at work and at home. But she is not at all certain how to proceed. "It's like all that consciousness has just left," she says. "I used to have a sense that we were moving toward something, and now we're not and I suddenly feel like I woke up and I'm all alone."

Helena Walzer is not the only one who feels bereft when confronting the complicated social problems affecting women. Although Mary Jane Gibson, an eleven-year veteran of the Massachusetts House of Representatives, has been trying to improve women's lives for decades, she says that progressive legislators like herself often find themselves fighting alone because so many women have abdicated their civic responsibilities. As assistant majority whip in the Massachusetts House of Representatives, Gibson has initiated legislation that would give working parents parental leave with some form of wage replacement and many other programs and policies that would help women and men with their caregiving needs.

But the normally optimistic fifty-six-year-old has become increasingly discouraged when facing the antigovernment sentiment so prevalent in the nation today. In this climate, people who would benefit most from reforms are the least active in the political process. "Young working women who are married and feel a sense of responsibility to their families don't feel they have the energy to organize collectively or even to contact their legislators individually," she says as we talk in her Beacon Hill office. "Or, if they could make the time, they're often unaware of the importance of doing so. They aren't making enough demands, either at their workplaces or on their political representatives."

The resuts of this inaction, Gibson says, are palpably evident. "As legislators, we simply aren't asked by either individuals or organizations to make family issues a first priority. We don't get letters and phone calls from young families. Young families are not our campaign workers or our financial contributors. And so the people who we hear from are the people who oppose the bills that would benefit the majority of citizens. We get letters and phone calls from the business community. And their first priority is definitely to kill these care-related bills. They're much more explicit about what they don't want than citizens are about what they do want."

Donna Lemhoff, director of the Women's Legal Defense Fund in Washington, D.C., expressed similar concerns. One of the major lobbyists for the Family and Medical Leave Act — which would give women unpaid leave at the birth or adoption of a baby — the fund has been going into battle with a well-organized opposition led by the U.S. Chamber of Commerce. "Even though the Family and Medical Leave Act will not significantly add to the cost of doing business," says Lemhoff, "business is violently opposed to it because it sees the act as a foot in the door for a whole series of mandated benefits that women are seeking."

In the past, forces for change have made legislative gains when they were able to mobilize millions of Americans whose social and economic being was at stake. This historical lesson is more relevant today than ever before. But women are not heeding it.

"We constantly hear from legislators that they're always getting calls from local Chambers of Commerce and business people who oppose the Family and Medical Leave Act," says Lemhoff, "but they say they're just not getting calls from the working women and men who support it."

Luz Allende, assistant commissioner of human resources in the New York State Department of Transportation, who has been an activist in Democratic politics for years, agrees wholeheartedly. Women's political inaction, she feels, has had a serious impact on the feminist movement and the ability of women to field candidates who represent the interests of the majority rather than the interests of their own careers and the business community. "What a lot of women politicians are feeling is that campaigns are won on TV. And so whoever gives you the money to pay for TV ads are the ones who help you win, and that's usually the business community. No matter how much NOW [the National Organization for Women] loves you, if you don't have the TV ads, you're not elected and that's a matter of fact."

But, Allende says, the women's movement doesn't do much fund-raising and it can no longer mobilize women at the grassroots level as either voters or volunteers. "In the sixties, a woman candidate could rely on the women's movement to come out with a cadre of volunteers who would run your campaign. With all due respect to the women's movement, my experience is that it cannot produce volunteers for you. That's almost out of the question."

With no ability to guarantee money, bodies, or votes, it's no wonder, Allende says, that female candidates have to go to the business community for support. "The whole issue of who's going to pay for my campaign is number one today. Women's issues are number two."

What Helena Walzer, Mary Jane Gibson, and Luz Allende describe is both a feminine and feminist impasse. Helena Walzer realizes the limits of individual survival strategies: she cannot accomplish her goals alone. The limitations of exit, of opting out, are more than apparent to her. But how, she asks, can she join with other women in the exercise of voice? As politicians, working for women like Walzer, Mary Jane Gibson and Luz Allende are also stuck. They have attained a measure of political power, but without a movement to back them, they are limited in exercising that power for programs that will serve the majority.

Because women have been drawn into a society that does not know how to care, our liberation has been redefined. We ourselves now reproduce the values of a society that denies the reality and importance of care.

Care is life. It is through caring, connection, and community — not in spite of it — that we achieve and create. Care is an integral part of our world, but in our society we have diminished and subverted it. In our lives and our work, we have radically over-valued competition, independence, self-reliance, and aggression, making of them the only organizing principles around which we construct our politics and policies, our morality, and, increasingly today, even our personal and social relationships.

But no society, no individual, can function without care. That is why, in so many respects, our lives no longer work: why so many of us find our lives so unfulfilled both at work and at home. And why we complain that the people upon whom we depend for gentleness and generosity, empathy and concern no longer seem to have the time or energy to care. The social devaluation of care threatens to corrupt and compromise all who need it and give it.

Our society has tried to entrap us all in the seductive masculine dream that we can deny care and simultaneously be cared for. We have been programmed to believe there is no higher human purpose than the relentless individual climb up the ladder of traditional American success. Thirty or forty years ago men who achieved the most power in our society were those who gave their lives to work. The rest of us, however, were allowed to make our eight-hour contributions to the market and then call it a day. Workaholics were the exception rather than the rule, and we viewed them with equal parts admiration and skepticism. Today, we believe that we must all emulate the work and lifestyles of the male — and now female — workaholics who sacrifice a personal, community, and civic life to the endless quest for more money, power, and status.

Remember that wonderful scene from the movie *Wall Street* in which Charlie Sheen — the poor boy who made good — and Daryl Hannah — the woman who's determined never to be a loser — engage in an orgy of acquisition to decorate his newly purchased Manhattan condo? They fill it with extravagantly expensive furnishings and the most up-to-date culinary gadgets. The only thing they lack is the time to enjoy anything they've worked so hard to acquire. They have goods and a lifestyle but no life.

Too many of us have been reduced to the same state of emotional deprivation in the midst of material plenty. We have children other people care for, friends we have no time to socialize with, spouses about whom we complain but with whom we have no time to struggle to create more fulfilling relationships. We have also — perhaps unwittingly and surely unwisely — abdicated our moral responsibilities as citizens. Too many of us don't even bother to vote these days, and those who do too often vote against — not for — care. Many citizens' main concern is to pay fewer taxes rather than to create a politics of care that will support and sustain the kind of caring culture that will nourish us all.

We can — we must — create that politics, culture, and community of care by striking out together for a new feminine and human future — a future in which working and caring are not opposites. As individuals and in groups we can begin to struggle in our communities, workplaces, and in the political arena for nothing less than a radical restructuring of our communal and corporate values. Working must be infused with caring, and caring is work. They are life's partners who have been forcibly divorced by a "masculine" marketplace concerned only with profit. They demand a second chance.

Women and our real liberation are that chance. Women for human liberation must take that chance.

The promise of feminism within our advanced technological world is not just the liberation of women but of the human capacity to care, create, and be responsible for ourselves, the world we produce, and the other human beings with whom we share it. Women together must help society breathe life into what writer Richard Margolis has called "the civic heart."[1] By showing us that caring makes life richer, energizes and mobilizes us, we can teach each other that the conflicts and work required to create a society that supports and sustains care are worthwhile.

Millions of Americans are already fighting for such goals. Feminists, for example, are working for what's become known as the family agenda — a set of demands that includes unpaid (and, in some versions, paid) parental and medical leave, increased public support for childcare, and more family-oriented workplace arrangements like job-sharing, part-time work, and flex-time.

But in the face of this country's massive crisis in caring, we need to be much braver and bolder. In the United States today we need far more than a family agenda; we need a National Care Agenda — a platform that weaves together our caring needs over a lifetime. We must not compromise in articulating this agenda but rather demand the recognition that we, as human beings, are entitled to the time to care for ourselves and others and to the social and financial supports that make caregiving possible.

Time is, perhaps, the central component of this National Care Agenda. Our nation must return to the forty-hour week as its basic standard. As we become a nation of work addicts and moonlighters, we are creating a culture in which work is viewed as the most important human activity, and we are depriving ourselves of the

nonwork time necessary for child rearing and other family or leisure activities — in other words, the time required to live a rich
and varied life.

Men and women who work between forty-eight and eighty hours
a week have no time to be more than survivors, careerists, and
consumers. In this context, alternative work arrangements like
part-time work, flex-time, and job-sharing do little more than
rearrange an unacceptable status quo. If we retain the fiction that
the eight-hour day, forty-hour week is still our standard, in today's
world women are, in fact, working more than the second shift.
When you add commuting time to a ten- to fourteen-hour day for
professionals, or consider the fact that many working-class and
lower-income women are, in fact, working two jobs, housework
and child rearing actually constitute a third — graveyard — shift
that's squeezed in at nights and on weekends. And men who work
nights and weekends are, in fact, working two shifts. How can we
persuade them to share more of the work of any shift when their
homes are little more than hotel rooms or boardinghouses? As for
children, the main victims of a society that believes it is far more
important to work than to care, we leave them undefended because
the adults upon whom they depend for affection and protection
are all too often imprisoned in a world of work without end.

The forty-hour week is not an option. It is a necessity. It is not
an end point but a new beginning. Once we have recovered the
forty-hour week, we can move toward even more significant re-
ductions in work time. Several European countries, like West Germany, have already begun to work toward a thirty-five-hour week.
And here in the United States, we can follow in their footsteps, as
well as those of American progressives who hoped that a six-hour
day would follow the eight-hour-a-day standard.

Minimum annual paid vacations of at least one month —
guaranteed by statute from the moment a worker enters the work
force — is another key component of a National Care Agenda. Although the norm in Western Europe for many years, longer vacations have rarely, if ever, been mentioned in the debate about
family and work in the United States. Yet, a first step toward
securing adequate family and leisure time would be the establishment of a national vacation period and a universal right to a fixed

month of paid vacation that would not be denied or traded away.

In this country we continue to believe that our individualized system of vacation benefits, negotiated company by company, worker by worker will give us freedom from work. But look at reality. Many of us can barely get away from work because there is no slack time in our frenetic schedules. To make such a vacation policy effective, we will have to consider establishing annual vacation periods — like those of our Western European trading partners — to reduce pressure on employees to relinquish their vacation entitlements.

Giving citizens time to care also means helping them take time off work when their families need care the most. Paid parental leave policies that allow either parent to take at least up to six months off work when they have or adopt a newborn and time off to care for sick children, parents, or spouses are necessary to our progress, as is a high-quality subsidized childcare system for both preschool and school-aged children. Under a National Care Agenda, childcare would not be limited to families in which both parents work outside the home: it would be available, on a part-time basis, to families in which parents work inside the home.

A well-financed public education system that allows all of us to educate ourselves and our children — again the norm in Western Europe — is sorely needed. One of the mandates of care is to train and educate the young so that they can help determine and design their own futures and contribute fully to society. A society that does not care about educating its children and does not value the teachers who are their moral and pedagogical guides does not care. And a society that makes education too expensive subtly discourages young people from entering professions that are concerned with care.

Universal access to high-quality, cost-effective health care that is both community and hospital based must be available to all Americans. No one should labor under the fear that the loss of a job will mean the loss of health care benefits. A national health care system must provide quality short- and long-term nursing and convalescent care to the elderly so that senior citizens do not have to bankrupt themselves and their families to pay for the privilege of dying. It must provide respite care for home caregivers who want to continue caring for sick children, relatives, or spouses in the home and need support, education, and help to do it. Moreover, such a health care system must give nurses and other non-physician providers far more respect and remuneration as well as a major voice in determining and evaluating how care is delivered. This is the only way to make our health care system not only cost, but *care*, effective.

Finally, a National Care Agenda must help provide quality affordable housing for the nation's homeless and those of us who now have to sell their souls and their dreams to pay for a roof over their heads. And it must establish a national pension system that assures the elderly that they will not be rewarded for years of hard work by poverty in old age, thus forcing them to take the highest-paying job possible when they are young.

In response to any such proposal for a cohesive and extensive National Care Agenda, political and business leaders will certainly raise the usual objections. Although they seem perfectly content to throw money at the Pentagon or the savings and loan industry, they will insist that throwing money at social problems solves nothing. Besides, they will insist, a National Care Agenda is too costly. There is no money to pay for care.

But we can indeed pay for such a National Care Agenda.

The United States is not India or Bangladesh. It is one of the richest countries on the face of the earth. The obstacle to such a care agenda is not lack of money; it is lack of vision and the will to realize it. We construct our spending policies either to support competition, acquisition, and consumption or to finance aggression and war.

But both the events in Eastern Europe and our crisis of care at home present us with an extraordinary — perhaps unprecedented — opportunity to move in a new direction. We now spend almost $300 billion on defense to protect ourselves from the "Communist threat." Since that threat seems to have evaporated almost overnight, credible economic and political experts now believe it is eminently realistic to cut our defense budget by at least 50 percent in the next five to seven years. This would give us more than $150 billion (in real dollars) with which to finance a National Care Agenda.

Political analyst Jack Beatty, to cite only one example, has suggested numerous ways this money could be redistributed.[2] For the cost of the Trident II submarine-based missile, says Beatty, we could return federal aid to education to its 1980 level in percentage terms. Thus, we could expand the Head Start program to cover all eligible children for at least one year; serve every child eligible for aid under Chapter I of the Elementary and Secondary Education Act of 1965; and make it possible for more poor and middle-income young people to go to college. With more money available for college loans, young people could afford to care. They could enter caregiving professions. Or even in traditional, male-dominated professions, they would feel liberated to "rock the boat" by fighting for realistic working hours and care-related policies.

We could continue to support the stationing of 31,000 army and 12,000 air force members in South Korea, to the annual tune of $2.6 billion, or we could bring home 10,000 of these soldiers and spend more money feeding women, infants, and children through the underfunded federal WIC program. We could continue the Strategic Defense Initiative, throw $150 billion annually at NATO, and build the Stealth bomber, at $600 million per plane. Or we could subsidize the training of preschool and elementary school teachers. This would allow us to pay such teachers comparable salaries, as the French government currently does, thus reducing preschool teacher turnover in this country, where over 40 percent of preschool teachers leave the field each year. And we could build affordable housing for the homeless and lower-income Americans and improve the pension system for the elderly.

Or how about equalizing the tax rate for those Americans who earn $50,000 or more a year? Today, those Americans who earn from $50,000 to $200,000 are taxed at the marginal rate of 33 percent, while those who earn $200,000 or more pay 28 percent. If these affluent Americans were taxed at the rate of 33 percent, we'd net another $10 billion annually for care.

President Bush asked us to read his lips. Armed with these arguments, we ask him to read our lives.

Grounding our social programs on the imperatives of care rather than on the marketplace also promises to release even more money with which to finance a care agenda. Consider, for example, the current waste in our national health care budget. Because the health care system has become almost entirely market driven, we spend more on health care than any other nation in the world and get less return on our investment. Thirty-seven million people in this country are uninsured, and twenty to thirty million are under-insured (a serious illness would therefore bankrupt them). Yet we spend 12 percent of our GNP on health care, and our medical costs are escalating faster than those of any other developed nation. In Canada, a country with a well-financed, effective national health insurance system, only 8.5 percent of GNP is spent on health care, and everyone in the country is insured.

In this country, we spend 23 percent of our health care budget on administrative costs. A typical Canadian hospital has only three people, who use a single personal computer, in its billing depart-ment. A typical American hospital must employ over fifty workers and a two million dollar computer in order to fathom and service the byzantine world of more than fifteen hundred different insur-ance plans. Some estimate that a large proportion of our surgical operations are unnecessary, and, in a costly experiment that adds neither to length or quality of life, we now spend great sums of money prolonging death. According to prominent health care ex-perts, there is now enough money in our health care system to pay for high-quality care for every American without increasing ex-penditures at all.

There has never been a more propitious moment to create a truly caring society. Not only is the money available to finance it, but a vast constituency can be mobilized to fight for a culture and politics of care in the community, workplace, and political arena. Over the past several decade the millions of citizens who so des-perately need a care agenda have been divided and disempowered. In the conventional political approach today, citizens tend to be seen as target audiences for a series of disconnected single-issue messages. But people who are viewed — and who view them-selves — as passive political consumers often get drawn, as con-testants, into futile struggles over resource allocation. In a system seemingly quite dedicated to the creation of artificial scarcity, this tends to fragment and divide actual and potential allies.

Rather than looking at society as a whole, and creating a rational, social structure that answers all our needs, our policy makers reluctantly move from one group desperately needing care to another, applying inadequate resources in each case. In the process we create a competitive victimization, in which those who represent groups needing care don't work together but argue about whose need is more pressing and who can afford to be passed by so the needs of the neediest can be — at least — partially met. Unfortunately, this game of "who'll be the loser this year" does not create many winners.

Similarly, the tendency to identify with one "special interest" to the exclusion of all others is intensified rather than ameliorated. Parents interested in childcare for young children fail to focus on their later educational needs until it is too late to save schools that are deteriorating now. Parents with children who are finally in school feel that they have left the struggle for parental leave or full-time daycare behind them because they no longer have infants or toddlers. Middle-aged men and women preoccupied with caring for ailing or dying parents hear about the "family agenda" and conclude that it applies only to working parents with young children. (People who are well and have health insurance erroneously believe they will never suffer from the nation's health care crisis. That's a problem only for the uninsured.) Minority women, women in lower-paying jobs, and those who are homemakers hear talk about "equal opportunities" for upscale working women and wonder what dressing for success has to do with their burdens and dilemmas. As a result, they may decide that the women's movement is for professional women with "careers," not jobs, and that it has little or nothing to offer them.

By linking the needs and interests of various constituencies in a general movement for care, such divisions can be overcome. Translating the family agenda into a care agenda, for example, allows us to fight critics who counterpose the needs of stay-at-home mothers against those of mothers who work outside the home. Those of us who appreciate and respect the demands of caregiving work — no matter what the setting — understand that mothers who work full-time in the home often need as much support and relief as women who work outside the home.

Stay-at-home mothers don't get negotiated coffee and lunch breaks. There is no closing time or weekends off the job. And today, when so many women commute to jobs elsewhere, it's harder than ever for stay-at-home mothers to enlist a neighbor, friend, or family member to look after their children so they can get some respite from their taxing responsibilities.

There is no reason stay-at-home mothers should not have access to expanded childcare as well. In France, for example, nursery schools are part of the public education system and many stay-at-home mothers utilize these *écoles maternelles.* In Scandinavia, mothers are allowed to use community childcare centers for a certain number of hours per week. Mothers who remain at home to care for children with handicaps or long-term illnesses would benefit from more respite care and visiting nurse services. Furthermore, their families — which must depend on the health care coverage of only one spouse — also face a far greater risk of being under-insured or of having no insurance in the event of the wage earner's job loss or layoff. They are a logical part of the constituency for national health insurance not tied to private medical plans or employment.

A National Care Agenda would help attract the many millions of men who are now taking care of young children and elderly parents or relatives, or who will be faced with such responsibilities in the future and will need adequate social and financial support. Despite major changes in the attitudes of men toward family life and their greater involvement in parenting, fathers have been ignored in debates about family policy. Needless to say, their relative invisibility does not contribute to successful lobbying efforts. More importantly, if men are not furloughed from the prison of work through shorter hours and extended vacation periods, they will never play a greater role in family life, and women's liberation will remain the stalled revolution about which so many now speak with such despair and sorrow.

If we have the political and social will, such a unified constituency for a caring society can begin to exercise its collective voice to urge candidates and political parties to support and vote for a cohesive care agenda. To do this, all of us must become active again and use our collective voice to promote care.

To make caring issues number one means devoting our most precious individual resource — time — to working for care in our neighborhoods, communities, and workplaces. For contemporary women time is one of the scarcest resources and most complicated issues. Many claim they simply have no time in their busy schedules for political activity. In some instances, this is certainly true. But in others the problem is not that we have no time, it's that we just don't understand how important it is to make it.

Some of us who work outside the home think our situation is unique. Our problems are different, we believe, from those of women who stay at home to raise children today, or who did so in the past. But are they really? It is, of course, true that thirty or forty years ago, far fewer women left home to go to work. Nonetheless, they still worked all day in their own homes. Most had more than our two point eight children and worked from seven in the morning till nine or ten at night on domestic duties and child rearing, without any assistance from baby-sitters, au pairs, or husbands (in those days, men contributed far less to housework than they do today). Yet these busy women found time to be active in their communities.

Today, minority political leaders like Luz Allende also point out that poor and lower-income women, who are often single heads of households and have no help at home, work for political change because they have to. The excuse of lack of time by elite, white professionals appears to Allende and others to be simply a cop-out.

The fact is that many of us — particularly upper-income professionals — believe that we can purchase an exit visa from the erosion of the public sphere. Some think they don't need to fight for childcare subsidies because they can afford quality care. They don't need to vote for increased taxes to support public education because they can send their children to private school. Most importantly, they can exit from the problems of increased poverty and remain insulated from the devastating conditions in which so many live today.

Moreover, just as so many have been convinced that political exit is possible, they've also been assured that moral exit is preferable. Many educated, affluent female professionals — precisely the group that we expect to be informed, active citizens — have been tutored in a definition of citizenship and moral obligation that precludes action on behalf of — or even reflection about the needs of — a wider community. In today's political marketplace, some may be consumers of single-issue political offerings. But on the whole, many of us have become part of an educated, depoliticized elite who have bought what mass culture has been selling for the past two decades: the idea that our only moral obligation is to look out for oneself, and our immediate family, and our only social obligation is to succeed and get ahead.

What women are discovering, of course, is that there is no such thing as total exit from the larger social whole. Which is why we have to redefine the obligations of citizenship and make time to fulfill them. Perhaps the simplest and least time-consuming thing all of us can do is register to vote — not only in national but also in state and local elections — and vote for candidates who support care. We can vote generously, not defensively, for each other and in the long-term interests of the human community, rather than in the short-term interests of our single-issue selves.

We can also avoid the single-issue trap when we consider which candidates to vote for, having the courage to vote for men and women not only because of gender or their position on any single issue but because they are willing to support a broad care agenda. This is a difficult problem today, when so few candidates do, in fact, represent that agenda — which is why we must do more than vote. The only way to encourage candidates to support caring programs is to penalize them if they don't. If we want to influence the direction of our public policy, we must express our opinions in the public debate about this country's direction as well as the purpose of government.

One very effective vehicle would be a coalition of women and men who work in the caregiving professions. In the current battle over the 1.5 and 2.5 percent of our GNP devoted to state and federal programs for human services, we often see nurses pitted against teachers, teachers against social workers, social workers against childcare workers. Each group is forced to petition local, state, and national government for a piece of a shrinking pie to save their particular profession and the portion of the public it serves. In this scramble for society's crumbs, they are often depicted as an isolated "single" interest acting against, rather than in, the larger public interest.

Imagine, then, how important it would be if 2.1 million registered nurses, 3.4 million teachers, 527,000 social workers, and 1,219,000 childcare workers coalesced around the National Care Agenda to fight for both a positive image of caring and the resources to make caring possible. Organized into a National Care Coalition, they would educate the public about the importance of care, respond to attacks on care and the caregiving professions, and lobby political and business leaders to implement a National Care Agenda. If a National Care Coalition became more than a letterhead organization made up of leaders of various professional associations, its moral and political force would be considerable. By organizing members of the caregiving professions from the bottom up, caregivers could not only support or oppose candidates but field their own candidates and proposals whenever necessary. Their influence would increase exponentially if they were also able to mobilize those who benefit from their services — parents of schoolchildren, patients in hospitals and clinics, home caregivers, the elderly, families of the physically and emotionally handicapped, as well as lower-income Americans — to join their campaign.

The fact is that all Americans concerned with care can be part of this coalition. The most minimal donation of time will make a big difference. It takes only a few moments to write a letter to a political representative at the local, state, or national level asking him or her to vote for or initiate care-related legislation. No one is too busy to invest five or ten minutes in writing a letter or making a telephone call. Some will say each letter or call is only a drop in the bucket. But it is drop by drop that the bucket is filled.

It is hour by hour that a caring culture is built. Are we willing to take an hour a week away from the marketplace to devote to relationships and community? Are we willing to accumulate fewer possessions? Can we not fill the relational void in our lives by getting to know our neighbors, rebuilding community institutions that have suffered so much in recent decades?

We can each give an hour a week or even every two weeks and join a neighborhood block watch, form or work in a parent-teacher association, attend school committee meetings, run for town government, volunteer to be part of a recycling or conservation committee, or — among many other possibilities — work in a women's health collective. Within these organizations we can help initiate discussions about our common social purpose, thus expanding their agenda of caring concerns.

For example, a group of preschool parents organize to support a campaign to increase town revenues available to local schools. In the process, they urge new parents to focus on more than the struggle to obtain high-quality childcare for their infants or toddlers, but to inform themselves about the fiscal problems the town faces. After the campaign, these parents decide to organize a preschool P.T.A. to draw a continuous stream of preschool parents into community affairs. And they go one step further. Rather than urging parents to attend local school committee meetings, the group asks them to take part in the state and national debate about educational spending — thus connecting their local problems to national policy.

It is through such promotion of human and societal interdependence that a caring culture is constructed.

Such a caring culture, moreover, can be built not only in our communities but also in our workplaces. If, that is, women are willing to come out of the caring closet in which they have been told to take refuge.

We will never be able to change corporate culture if we do not reveal our caring commitments to others and proudly advertise our desire to fulfill them. How can we prevail on our employers to create policies that help us meet our caring responsibilities if we are too timid to talk to one another about our care-related joys or dilemmas? Just as women's conversations and consciousness-raising groups created, nourished, and expanded the feminist movement in the late sixties and early seventies, so, too, raising our common consciousness about care can rekindle that movement in the nineties.

No matter how or where we begin — be it a lunch-hour con-

versation or at a meeting of a women's network — we must bring
our concerns out into the open. We must bring our baby pictures
to work when we return to the office after parental leave, and talk
about our children at work. We must not disclaim our femininity
when men accuse of us acting "just like a woman." We must voice
our legitimate concerns about the excessive time demands of the
workplace or our employers' belief that a good worker gives 100
percent of him or herself to his or her job.

Creating care networks in the workplace may mean transforming women's business and professional networks so that they are
as concerned with career enhancement as they are with career
advancement. It will mean asking more labor unions to consider
our caregiving needs as well as our need for better wages and
working conditions. Or it may mean forming new networks,
unions, or collective organizations grounded in care.

Yes, it will take time to create such networks — time that would
normally be devoted to personal, career, or other concerns. But
this time will be more than well spent. Not only will our investment
in *each other* change workplace culture and practices that are
pushing women out of corporate institutions, it will create a much
needed sense of collaboration and community within the workplace. Rather than feeling that other women are, at worst, ruthless
competitors or, at best, sympathetic listeners to whom we confide
our private woes, we will recognize that at least some of us are
true allies.

With these allies, we can work toward the next step — expanding the workplace constituency for care to include all who are
concerned with caregiving issues. This means bringing men into
discussions about care-related issues. As we have said before,
many men now care about caring. They want to help more at
home. Many are now grappling with the same issues that preoc-
cupy so many women. They are taking personal and sick days off
to take care of children. They are pretending they have to leave
work early to "go to a meeting" in order to fulfill family responsibilities. It may not be easy, but with work, they can be enlisted
in the struggle to create a caring culture. Similarly, we must include women and men who do not have young children but are

taking care of elderly relatives or are concerned about health care issues, pensions, or other care-related concerns. Every effort should be made to include employees at every level of the corporate ladder.

Slowly, employees who have built trust with one another can begin to challenge company policies and attitudes. One logical starting point is the excessive work demands so many are saddled with today. We must talk to each other about putting work back into perspective — considering it to be a part, but not all, of life. This does not have to lead to a flight from the work world, nor to the creation of discriminatory "mommy tracks" in the workplace. What we do need is a *normal track* — a set of work-related schedules and goals, as well as a model of career development that conforms to the needs of the majority of human beings.

Today, as we have seen, the fast track is the only valued track. If you are not driven in the workplace, you are considered to have no drive. If you do not aim for the very top, you do not deserve to stay in the middle. With everybody going for the gold, nobody's going home.

This leaves many people who want to have a life outside of work — whether or not it includes family — out of luck. Yet, most of us want that kind of life. We are not, will never be, and may not even care about, being number one. It is our job to insist that this is not failure but success, and to defend the legitimacy of the idea that people can work to live as well as live to work.

To do this will require slow and patient discussion and action. In our caring networks, we can begin to raise the issue of overwork and build a consensus for resisting the demands that are imposed on us. We can slowly cut back, even if it's only by an hour on Friday night, and resist the idea that a committed worker is the one who never leaves the office.

We can, for example, explain that it is not our job to stay at the office to present the appearance of commitment. It is our job to get our work done. We can reinforce rather than criticize women and men who leave the office after an eight-hour day. We can applaud rather than penalize people who take their proper allotment of vacation time, or maternity or paternity leave, and encourage each other to be honest rather than duplicitous when we must take time off to care for a sick child or relative or fulfill a family-related obligation.

When we feel more confident in our own beliefs, we can take our arguments to the leaders of our corporations, who must become aware that obsession with work to the exclusion of a personal life is not the path to excellence. Although I do not believe this should be our main argument, it will serve their personal and business interests if employees are allowed to have a life outside of work. Employees who are forced to be frantic workaholics have no time to reflect about the work they do. Men and women who are overly preoccupied with their efforts to juggle their personal and professional responsibilities cannot, in fact, work effectively and efficiently. Moreover, the job stress they experience has been linked to a variety of physical and emotional problems that compromise productivity and reduce corporate profits.

When women move to more open proposals for changing discriminatory practices in the workplace, they can also expand their agenda beyond traditional demands for better pay and a more equitable promotional ladder to include challenges that will hopefully transform corporate culture. Women editors at the *Boston Globe*, for example, did just this when they formed a group called Women on the Verge. Top editors organized over a period of a year to document and then protest inequalities in promotional ladders in the newsroom. They also addressed the more subtle problems created by a competitive corporate culture. Women on the Verge is gradually trying to deal with the kind of excessive time demands that make for twelve-hour workdays. The group argues that women who care about a relational life outside of work will never be able to advance if this corporate culture doesn't change.

And corporate culture will not change if there is not more collaboration and less competition in the workplace. To a degree, the group explains, editors are now judged by who can get the most stories on page one. They don't feel free to leave work at a reasonable hour, because they believe that they personally need to shepherd their stories through the evening's editorial process. Because so many of the top editors at the *Globe* are men, female

editors explain, discussions about how big stories are covered or
played in the paper take on an aggressive tone that discourages
participation by those women who are uncomfortable with such
"masculine" styles. Rather than following the traditional route of
asking women to adopt the male model, Women on the Verge
wants the *Globe*'s culture to be broadened to include a wider di-
versity of managerial styles.

To integrate women's way of knowing, being, and acting into
the workplace, women must also be willing to work to extend
individually negotiated benefits to the entire work force. In the
contemporary work setting many women, like senior banking executive Meredith Jameson, all too often negotiate individual family, care-related benefits. They do not work together with their
peers to institutionalize these benefits for higher-level employees
and they often refuse or fear to act on behalf of those below them.
But if women are not to be pitted against one another, we have to
begin to work together to create corporation-wide benefits for all
who need them. This is not a risk-free strategy. But as most
women, when pressed, will admit, they have far more power than
they think. Corporate America has already begun to respond haltingly to these needs, and it can do far more if pushed.

Arnold Hiatt, chairman of the board of the Stride Rite Corporation — a company that has responded positively to its employees' care-related needs — agrees. Corporate America, Hiatt
insists, will respond to pressure, if, that is, pressure is applied. "If
employees do not put pressure on their companies, then CEO's
will respond to other kinds of pressures when formulating policies.
And if women conceal their care-related needs, companies will
never implement policies that respond to them."

In order to act effectively for care, employees must also initiate
their own care-related programs and proposals rather than wait
for their companies to act on their behalf. And they must measure
any company-initiated proposals against a standard of care rather
than against that of work performance and competitiveness. Consider, for example, the issue of corporate-sponsored daycare programs. Today a number of companies have received good reviews
from the press and the public for creating backup or emergency

daycare programs in their firms, or for setting up childcare referral services for their employees. These Band-Aid programs are a response to employee interest in on-site or near-site childcare and societal concern with providing parents with mandated sick leave so they can take care of an ailing child.

Instead of supporting broader social programs, law firms like Washington's Wilmer, Cutler and Pickering, Arnold and Porter, and Boston's Goodwin, Proctor and Hoar have set up backup daycare centers available to a limited number of children when normal daycare arrangements fall through or parents have to work on snow days, holidays, and weekends. A group of seven major employers in New York have pooled their resources to send a home health care worker to the home of an employee whose daycare provider is out sick or who has a mildly sick child so the former can come to work. And IBM and AT&T, among many others, have established childcare referral services for their employees.

In fact, backup daycare centers that are open on weekends, snow days, and holidays help companies get more work out of already overworked employees. More important, children who may have spent the entire week in daycare must now spend part of their weekend in yet another institutional setting. Emergency services that send strangers to the home when a child is ill keep parents at work when their children need them the most. And childcare referral services do nothing to help relieve the critical shortage of childcare workers. They do not create the kind of much needed new jobs, with decent salaries and benefits, that will attract people to the childcare field. Instead, they simply refer more employees to an already overburdened and underfunded system, thereby adding to the demand.

Although many of these emergency programs have been initiated by well-intentioned women, working parents must insist that they don't need programs that help them work longer and harder. They need more time off, not less; more corporate-subsidized on-site or near-site daycare centers, and more corporate commitment, rather than opposition, to nationally mandated care-related programs.

We need to remember, moreover, that voluntary initiatives can be wolves in sheep's clothing and may ultimately be used to legitimize business opposition to even the most minimal legislative mandates. Pointing to the small number of employer-sponsored childcare or parental leave programs that currently exist (and ignoring the fact that, in many cases, employees had to fight long and hard for them), the private sector argues that all employers will eventually follow the lead of the more enlightened, thus making legislative solutions unnecessary.

Arnold Hiatt, for one, argues that individual corporate policies are no replacement for a national daycare policy. "We have a national policy for five-year-olds, that's kindergarten. We have a national policy for eight-year-olds, who go to school. Why shouldn't we have a national policy for children from birth to age five?" he asks. National policies are the only protection children have against the vicissitudes of the market. Some firms that provide daycare for their employees when they're doing well, Hiatt points out, may sacrifice those programs when earnings are down. That's what happened when Stride Rite encouraged a nearby high-tech company to open two daycare centers. As soon as it began to lose money, the company closed those centers.

Because of shortages of qualified workers, Hiatt adds, many corporations have begun to consider providing some childcare relief. But what will happen to such voluntary programs when firms no longer have problems recruiting workers? "We keep talking about children being our most important resource, but no one is doing much to help them," he says.

In organizing for care in our society, another important agent of much needed change is young women — and men — on college and university campuses. As network television producer Claire Riso says so eloquently, young women must worry not only about getting to the top but about what happens to them while they're climbing and what kind of lives they will have when they achieve the goals the American success ethic has set for them. Just as women have to come out of the caring closet when they're at work, women should resist being pushed into that closet when they're preparing to enter the marketplace.

Young women must begin to voice in public what they currently worry about in private. They must hold and participate in open discussions about the costs of success in a world that does not accommodate the imperatives of care. Many of their professors and advisers are already trying to initiate such public conversations. But many more could join in. They could supplement their lessons in how to master masculine marketplace skills, fight discrimination in the workplace, or struggle for reproductive rights with open discussions about how men and women can value and share in a world of care. This would encourage students to risk now, rather than sacrifice their caring selves later. If such discussions do not become the norm, rather than the exception, young women and men will continue to pursue a narrow definition of self-interest that eventually pits them against those who are trying to fulfill caregiving responsibilities in the workplace. In the process of concealing their care-related concerns, they will become their own jailers, locking themselves into the prison of men's dreams, and foreclosing the possibility of alliances that will help us all escape.

In discussions about care among young and old, women and men, in workplaces, on college campuses, in the media and the political arena, we can approach the ultimate solution to the business world's denial of care: a challenge to the ideology that drives corporate culture and thus much of our society. Too often, we've allowed our way of life to serve perceived corporate needs rather than asking our corporations to serve our human needs. In the contemporary world we all, in fact, contribute to corporate culture's consummate lack of care. By legitimating the idea that the bottom line of short-term profit and greed is the only one that counts, we allow business and individuals in it to operate according to a different moral standard than that which we wish for the wider society. If it's "good for the economy," we argue, even against our own individual and communal self-interest, it's good for us all. But we never ask what an economy is for, to whom it belongs, what human purpose it should serve. Those who embrace a care agenda must begin to ask these questions and to provide answers that will require corporate culture to meet our individual and social needs.

There are many paths we can follow as we move away from the masculine dream toward a new feminine and human future. Some we have already mapped. Others we will invent along the way.

One thing is, however, certain: we must change our world if we want to make our own lives easier. We cannot afford not to work for change if we want to protect the gains we've already made and provide care and community for ourselves, our children, and generations to come. There is, moreover, no risk-free road to social and personal transformation. But today, perhaps the greatest risk for women and our world is inaction and adaptation.

In spite of the fact that our agenda for change is eminently realistic, we will certainly be accused of wild-eyed radicalism, or worse, starry-eyed idealism if we move together toward a world of care. Our most compelling task will be demystifying the myth of "realism" and legitimizing the kind of idealism without which women could not have begun the transformation of our world.

As we contemplate such an "idealistic" agenda, our very discontents and frustrations should empower us. Our disaffection and disillusionment are powerful tools for change. Obviously, they have not yet produced a cohesive opposition to the status quo, but anger and disenchantment are essential prerequisites.

To understand the potential of this kind of dissent, we have only to look at the example of recent events in Eastern Europe to see how quickly and dramatically popular frustration and personal despair can give way first to glimmers of hope and then to a surge of activity aimed at remaking entire societies. Contrary to conventional Western wisdom, these momentous events were not the result of activity on the part of cold-warriors in the West, but of years of slow, patient, and courageous labor by a few lonely individuals and small groups in country after country in the Eastern Bloc. Working quietly for reform, under circumstances far more daunting than exist here, they have succeeded in mobilizing the mass opposition necessary to effect change. Suddenly, citizens of these countries who were reluctant to act, speak out, or even dream of change have joined them to create transformations few thought possible.

In East Germany, ministers, intellectuals, students, and workers used the East German church to build first an environmental, then an antinuclear and antimilitary, and, finally, a feminist movement. In Hungary, students, priests, and churchgoers formed small community groups working against militarism in that country. In

Czechoslovakia, students, political activists from the "Prague Spring," and young people in the cultural underground protested against human rights abuses. And in Poland, millions of workers formed the core of a new society.

In each case, what these ordinary citizens did was rebuild community in societies where the very concept had been undermined by years of distrust and oppression. When they had no access to the mass media, they created their own media. When the state banned or corrupted their churches, they created new forms of spirituality. When party-controlled unions failed to represent them, they created their own. In each case a major thrust of the politics of reform is the creation of what Eastern Europeans call "civil society" — constructing a new set of interdependent social relationships based on individuals caring for and aiding each other. In each instance, what these activists did was expand the boundaries of what they called "free space," determining where they could safely act together to express their collective voices and broaden their limited freedoms. And perhaps most importantly, these activists rejected exit in favor of voice. In the face of police harassment and arrest, they stayed, even when, as in East Germany, it would have been easy for them to escape to the West.

What began as a drop in the bucket became the bucket, a virtual sea of dissent that has resulted in transformations no one could have ever predicted.

The example of Eastern Europe is not as remote as we in the United States like to think. We are certainly not surrounded by an Iron Curtain of political oppression, but we have been sequestered in the marketplace's obsession with self. How can we be number one? we ask. Are we loving too much? What's in it for me? What has feminism done for me? But while those questions may be relevant to some parts of our lives, they are not relevant to all of our lives. Sociologist Diane Margolis asks us to think of life as an artist's palette of varied hues. Marketplace models have made the palette of life appear to be monochromatic — a world in which personal success is determined only by marketplace success.

Those of us who try to conform to that muted vision of the human tapestry have become unidimensional. Because without care we belong only to ourselves and to be true only to the self is to belong to nothing. It is through care that we become, quite simply, better, fuller, happier human beings. Care is central to our liberation. We all have a moral duty that we can, indeed must, fulfill: to reclaim the central precept of transformative feminism, making the human capacity for individual and social caring the core value of our society.

NOTES

INTRODUCTION. *Women at Risk*

1. Betty Friedan, *The Feminine Mystique* (New York: Dell Publishing Company, 1963), 360.
2. Lisa Belkin, "Bars to Equality of Sexes Seen as Eroding, Slowly," *New York Times*, August 20, 1989.
3. Betty Friedan, *The Second Stage* (New York: Summit Books, 1986), 70, 80.
4. Beverly Kempton, "Great Transformations," *Working Woman*, January 1989.

CHAPTER ONE. *The Masculine Mystique*

1. Sara M. Evans, "Women in Twentieth Century America: An Overview," in *The American Woman 1987–88*, edited by Sara E. Rix (New York: W. W. Norton and Company, 1987), 32.
2. Interview with Susan Shank, U.S. Department of Labor, Bureau of Labor Statistics.
3. Nancy Barrett, "Women and the Economy," in Rix, ed., 120.
4. Interview, U.S. Department of Labor, Bureau of Labor Statistics.
5. Ibid.
6. Adam Smith, *The Wealth of Nations* (Chicago: University of Chicago Press, 1976), 18.
7. See Jean Baker Miller, *Toward a New Psychology of Women* (Boston: Beacon Press, 1986); Jessica Benjamin, *The Bonds of Love* (New York: Pantheon, 1988); Carol Gilligan, *In a Different Voice* (Cambridge: Harvard University Press, 1982) for a full elaboration of these ideas.
8. Richard Hofstadter, *The American Political Tradition* (New York: Vintage Books, 1973), xxxvii.

9. Ibid., 160.

10. Roslyn S. Willett, "Working in 'A Man's World': The Woman Executive," in *Woman in Sexist Society*, edited by Vivian Gornick and Barbara K. Moran (New York: New American Library, 1971), 532.

11. Gornick and Moran, eds., xxx.

12. Robin Morgan, *Sisterhood Is Powerful* (New York: Vintage Books, 1970), xxxv.

13. Kate Millett, *Sexual Politics* (New York: Ballantine Books, 1970), 507.

14. Richard M. Huber, *The American Idea of Success* (New York: McGraw-Hill Book Company, 1971), 1.

15. Quoted in Huber, 8.

16. Margaret Fenn, *In the Spotlight: Women Executives in a Changing Environment* (Englewood Cliffs, N.J.: Prentice Hall, 1980), 3.

17. Margaret V. Higginson and Thomas L. Quick, *The Ambitious Woman's Guide to a Successful Career* (New York: AMACOM, 1980), 15.

18. Ibid., 8.

19. Ibid., 26.

20. Fenn, 3.

21. Higginson and Quick, 236.

22. Judith Daniels, *Savvy*, January 1980, 4.

23. Friedan, *The Feminine Mystique*, 361.

24. Colette Dowling, *The Cinderella Complex: Women's Hidden Fear of Independence* (New York: Summit Books, 1981), 31.

25. Fenn, 44, 45.

26. Ibid., 51.

27. Betty Lehan Harragan, *Games Mother Never Taught You: Corporate Gamesmanship for Women* (New York: Warner Books, 1977), 21, 22, 35.

28. Courtenay Beinhorn, "In Search of Stamina," *Savvy*, September 1986, 31, 32.

29. Higginson and Quick, 165, 166.

30. Fenn, 12.

31. Suzanne Gordon, "The New Corporate Feminism," *The Nation*, February 5, 1983, 146.

32. Harragan, 293.

33. *Savvy*, 146.

34. Jane Wilson, "The New Girl Network: A Power System for the Future," *Savvy*, January 1980, 18–23.

35. Ibid., 22.

36. Harragan, 384.

37. Tom Richman, "Assets and Liabilities," *Inc.*, May 1985, 91.

38. Asta Lubin, *Managing Success: High-Echelon Careers and Motherhood* (New York: Columbia University Press, 1987), 49.

39. Ibid., 29.

40. Harragan, 75.

41. Huber, 7.

42. Anne Taylor Flemming, "Women and the Spoils of Success," *New York Times Magazine*, August 6, 1981, 30.

43. Mary Anne Dolan, "When Feminism Failed," *New York Times Magazine*, June 26, 1988, 21.

44. Ibid.

45. Ibid., 66.

46. Huber, 5.

CHAPTER TWO. *The New Jerusalem*

1. U.S. Department of Labor, Bureau of Labor Statistics.

2. Ronald E. Kutscher, "Projections 2000," *Monthly Labor Review*, September 1987.

3. As quoted in William Appleman Williams, *The Contours of American History* (Chicago: Quadrangle Paperbacks, 1966), 390.

4. As quoted in Dana Jack and Rand Jack, "Women Lawyers: Archetype and Alternatives," in *Mapping the Moral Domain*, edited by Carol Gilligan et al. (Cambridge: Harvard University Press, 1988), 267.

5. Lorraine Dusky, "The Awful Truth about Office Politics," *Mademoiselle*, February 1989, 142.

6. Sally Jacobs, "New York Jogger Ran on Fast Track to Tragedy," *Boston Globe*, April 30, 1989, 1.

7. Americans and the Arts, conducted by the National Research Center of the Arts, an affiliate of Louis Harris Associates, Inc., January 1988, 22.

8. Ibid., 21.

9. Employee Benefits in Medium and Large Firms, 1986, U.S. Department of Labor, Bureau of Labor Statistics, June 1987, Bulletin 2281; Employee Benefits in State and Local Governments, 1987, U.S. Department of Labor, Bureau of Labor Statistics, May 1988, Bulletin 2309.

10. Hidesuke Nagashima, "No End in Sight for Overwork Problem," *Japan Times*, June 17, 1989, 3, and Randolph Winn, "Squeezing in a Holiday," *PHP Intersect*, November 1988.

11. Benjamin Kline Hunnicutt, *Work without End: Abandoning Shorter Hours for the Right to Work* (Philadelphia: Temple University Press, 1988), 2.

12. Ibid., 3.

13. Peter T. Kilborn, "For Many Women, One Job Just Isn't Enough," *New York Times*, February 15, 1990.

14. U.S. Department of Commerce, Bureau of the Census. Current Population Reports, Consumer Income Series P-60, No. 166, October 1989.

15. Stephen J. Rose, *The American Economy Poster and Fact Book* (New York: Pantheon, 1987), 50.

16. Ibid.

17. Alan Wolfe, *Whose Keeper: Social Science and Moral Obligation* (Berkeley: University of California Press, 1989), 63.

18. James B. Treece, "Gloom in the Showroom," *Business Week*, October 16, 1989, 31.

19. Rose, 52.

20. Hunnicutt, 50.

21. Rosabeth Moss Kanter, *Men and Women of the Corporation* (New York: Basic Books, 1977), 63.

22. "Futures That 'Look, Act, and Feel Like a Dollar,' " *Business Week*, November 18, 1985.

23. Christine Hogan, "Elaine Garzarelli: The Wizard of Wall Street," *Ms.*, February 1988, 72, 73.

24. Tom Peters, "The Power of Information," *Marriott's Portfolio*, May/June 1989, 19.

25. As quoted in Suzanne Gordon, "Roe V. Wade: Sixteen Years and Counting," *Washington Post*, April 4, 1989, 17, Health Section.

26. Richard L. Berke, "Late Childbirth Is Found on Rise," *New York Times*, June 22, 1989.

27. Interview with Howard Hagey, U.S. Department of Labor, Bureau of Labor Statistics.

28. Interview with Susan Shank.

29. Interview with Howard Hagey.

30. U.S. Census Bureau.

31. Interview with Mathy Mezey, professor of gerontological nursing, University of Pennsylvania School of Nursing.

32. Bulletin, Family and Medical Leave, International Comparisons, source, Women at Work, International Labor Office Global Survey.

33. The Staff of Catalyst, "Workplace Policies: New Options for Fathers," in *Fatherhood Today*, edited by Phyllis Bronstein and Carolyn Pape Cowan (New York: John Wiley and Sons, 1988), 328.

34. Interview with Sally Styfco, Yale Bush Center for Child Development.

35. Ibid.

36. Ibid.

37. Juliette Brudney, "New England Medical Center Program to Raise Day-Care Horizons," *Boston Globe*, August 8, 1989, 31.

CHAPTER THREE. *Targeting the Top — Gain and Pain*

1. Barbara Ehrenreich, *Fear of Falling: The Inner Life of the Middle Class* (New York: Pantheon, 1989), 78–82.

2. Jack and Jack, in Gilligan et al., 266.

3. N. Strachan, "A Map for Women on the Road to Success," as quoted in Gilligan et al., 266–67.

4. Kathleen A. Hughes, "Businesswomen's Broader Latitude in Dress Codes Goes Just So Far," *Wall Street Journal.* September 1, 1987.

5. Tamar Lewin, "Women Say They Face Obstacles as Lawyers," *New York Times*, December 4, 1989.

6. Rosanna Hertz, *More Equal Than Others: Women and Men in Dual-Career Marriages* (Berkeley: University of California Press, 1986), 158.

7. Laurie Baum, "Corporate Women: They're About to Break Through to the Top," *Business Week*, June 22, 1987, 73.

8. Betty M. Vetter, in Rix, ed., 208.

9. An excellent book on this subject is Evelyn Fox Keller's *Reflections on Gender and Science* (New Haven: Yale University Press, 1985).

10. Vetter, 209.

11. Ibid., 212.

12. Ibid.

13. Ehrenreich, 136.

14. Belkin.

CHAPTER FOUR. *Targeting the Top — Fight and Flight*

1. Albert O. Hirschman, *Exit, Voice and Loyalty: Responses to Decline in Firms, Organizations and States* (Cambridge: Harvard University Press, 1970), 4.

2. Ibid., 43.

3. Carol Gilligan, *In a Different Voice: Psychological Theory and Women's Development* (Cambridge: Harvard University Press, 1982), 21.

4. Ibid., 79.

5. Felice Schwartz, "Management, Women and the New Facts of Life," *Harvard Business Review*, January–February 1989.

6. "Are You a Victim of Vacation Anxiety?" *Working Woman*, January 1988, 15.

7. Lynn S. Baker, "Superwomen Don't Get Sick," *Working Woman*, January 1988, 78.

8. "Fear of Tears: Crying at the Office," *Working Woman*, March 1988, 111.

9. Leah Rosch, "Managing Your Way Out of the Work Swamp," *Working Woman*, April 1988, 91.

10. Judith Briles, *Woman to Woman: From Sabotage to Support* (Far Hills, N.J.: New Horizon Press, 1987), 253.

11. Robert Jelinek, "How to Be a Corporate Kremlinologist," *Working Woman*, March 1988, 118.

12. Briles, 264, 265.

13. Marguerite Michaels and James Willwerth, "How America Has Run Out of Time," *Time* magazine, April 24, 1989, 67.

14. Baum, 76, 77.

15. Ethel Klein, *Gender Politics: From Consciousness to Mass Politics* (Cambridge: Harvard University Press, 1984), 127.

CHAPTER FIVE. *The Crisis of Women's Work*

1. Patricia Benner and Judith Wrubel, *The Primacy of Caring* (Menlo Park, Calif.: Addison-Wesley, 1989), 16.

2. Nel Noddings, *Caring: A Feminine Approach to Ethics and Moral Education* (Berkeley: University of California Press, 1984), 16.

3. Heinz Kohut, as quoted in Judith Jordan et al., *Women and Empathy: Implications for Psychological Development and Psychotherapy.* Stone Center for Developmental Services and Studies, No. 82–02, 1983, 5.

4. U.S. Department of Labor, Bureau of Labor Statistics.

5. Burton Gummer, "Competing Perspectives on the Concept of 'Effectiveness' in the Analysis of Social Services," in *Managing for Service Effectiveness*

in Social Welfare Organizations, edited by Rino Patti et al. (New York: Haworth Press, 1988), 257.

6. As quoted in Robert L. Turner, "Personal Values: A Lesson to Learn," *Boston Globe,* October 5, 1989.

7. Ehrenreich, 38–41.

8. Friedan, *The Feminine Mystique,* 153.

9. Doris B. Gold, "Women and Voluntarism," in Gornick and Moran, eds., 50.

10. Anita Shreve, *Remaking Motherhood: How Working Mothers Are Shaping Our Children's Future* (New York: Viking, 1987), 43.

11. Robin Norwood, *Women Who Love Too Much* (New York: Pocket Books, 1985), 17.

12. *Working Woman,* July 1988, 65–66.

13. Kempton, 87–92.

14. Letty Cottin Pogrebin, "It Still Takes a Bride and Groom," *New York Times Magazine,* July 2, 1989, 32–33.

15. For a full discussion of this subject see John Ehrenreich, *The Altruistic Imagination: A History of Social Work and Social Policy in the United States* (Ithaca: Cornell University Press, 1985).

16. Interview with Marilyn Rogers, National Education Association.

17. Linda H. Aiken and Connie Flynt Mullinix, *Recurring Hospital Nurse Shortages: Explanations and Solutions,* The Robert Wood Johnson Foundation, Princeton, N.J., 1986.

18. Jordan, 2.

CHAPTER SIX. *Is Sisterhood Powerful?*

1. Jessica Benjamin, *The Bonds of Love* (New York: Pantheon Books, 1988), 220.

2. Ibid., 9.

3. For an excellent discussion of the problems of women's work in this context see Arlie Russell Hochschild, *The Managed Heart: Commercialization of Human Feeling* (Berkeley: University of California Press, 1983).

4. See Richard Parker, *The Myth of the Middle Class: Notes on Affluence and Equality* (New York: Liveright, 1972).

5. Employment and Earnings, Bureau of Labor Statistics, U.S. Department of Labor, January 1990, Table 22.

6. Kanter, 79. This book contains an extensive discussion of the secretarial role. Although it deals with women working for men, much that it describes is as applicable, unfortunately, to many women who work for women in status hierarchies.

7. Ibid., 98, 99.

8. Harragan, 316.

9. Fenn, 12.

10. Higginson and Quick, 166.

11. Nancy F. Cott, *The Grounding of Modern Feminism* (New Haven: Yale University Press, 1987), 237. Cott's analysis of professionalization at the turn of the century and of the class divisions within the women's and woman movement is invaluable.

CHAPTER SEVEN. *Domestic Disturbances*

1. See Benjamin, Miller, and Gilligan for excellent analyses of this male developmental trajectory.

2. See Ray Oldenburg, *The Great Good Place* (New York: Paragon House, 1989). Oldenburg's description of the value of what he calls "neutral third places" and the loss of community in the United States is as apt as it is bleak.

3. See Suzanne Gordon, *Lonely in America* (New York: Simon and Schuster, 1976). Chapters on marriage and community present a fuller elaboration of this argument.

4. Arlie Hochschild's recent book *The Second Shift: Working Parents and the Revolution at Home* (New York: Viking, 1989) presents the best articulation and analysis of this phenomenon to date.

5. Kyle D. Pruett, *The Nurturing Father: Journey toward the Complete Man* (New York: Warner Books, 1987).

6. Bradley Googins and Dianne S. Burden, *Managing Work and Family Stress in Corporations* (Boston: Boston University School of Social Work, 1987), 25.

7. Joseph Pleck, *Family-Supportive Employer Policies and Men's Participation*, Wheaton College, Norton, Mass., 1989, 5–8.

CHAPTER EIGHT. *The Enemies of Childhood*

1. See David Elkind, *The Hurried Child: Growing Up Too Fast Too Soon* (Reading, Mass.: Addison-Wesley, 1981).

2. See Burton L. White, *The First Three Years of Life* (New York: Prentice Hall, 1985).

3. Sara Ruddick, *Maternal Thinking* (Boston: Beacon Press, 1989), 23.

4. David Michaelis, "The Baby Formula," *Manhattan, inc.*, July 1985, 82, 83.

5. Ibid., 82.

6. Ibid., 83.

7. Stuart Ewen, *Captains of Consciousness* (New York: McGraw-Hill, 1976), 39.

8. *American Baby*, "The First Year of Life," 1986.

9. Ibid., 22.

10. Elizabeth Tener, "Your Success, Your Child's Success," *Working Woman*, January 1988, 96.

11. "The Managerial Mother," *Working Woman*, December 1987, 126.

12. Bruce Lansky, *Baby Talk* (Deephaven, Minn.: Meadowbrook Inc., 1986).

13. Dorothy Einon, *Play with a Purpose: Learning Games for Children Six Weeks to Ten Years* (New York: Pantheon, 1985).

14. Beatriz Rubinstein, "Making the Private-School Grade," *New York*, October 20, 1986, 54–57.

15. David Elkind, *Miseducation: Preschoolers at Risk* (New York: Alfred A. Knopf, 1987), 3, 4.

CONCLUSION. *Toward a New Feminine Future*

1. Richard J. Margolis, *Risking Old Age in America* (Boulder, Colo.: Westview Press, 1990).
2. Jack Beatty, "A Post–Cold War Budget," *Atlantic Monthly*, February 1990, 74–82.

SELECTED
BIBLIOGRAPHY

Aisenberg, Nadya, and Mona Harrington. 1988. *Women of Academe: Outsiders in the Sacred Grove.* Amherst: University of Massachusetts Press.

Alvino, James. 1985. *Parents' Guide to Raising a Gifted Child: Recognizing and Developing Your Child's Potential.* Boston: Little, Brown and Company.

Arendt, Hannah. 1965. *On Revolution.* New York: Viking Penguin.

Ariès, Philippe. 1962. *Centuries of Childhood: A Social History of Family Life.* New York: Vintage Books.

Beatty, Jack. "A Post–Cold War Budget." *Atlantic,* February 1990.

Beck, Jean. 1986. *How to Raise a Brighter Child.* New York: Pocket Books.

Beinhorn, Courtenay. "In Search of Stamina." *Savvy,* September 1986.

Belensky, Mary Field, Blythe McVicker Clinchy, Nancy Rule Goldberger, and Jill Mattuck Tarule. 1986. *Women's Ways of Knowing: The Development of Self, Voice, and Mind.* New York: Basic Books.

Benhabib, Seyla. 1987. *Feminism as Critique.* Minneapolis: University of Minnesota Press.

Benjamin, Jessica. 1988. *The Bonds of Love: Psychoanalysis, Feminism, and the Problem of Domination.* New York: Pantheon Books.

Benner, Patricia. 1984. *From Novice to Expert: Excellence and Power in Clinical Nursing Practice.* Menlo Park, Calif.: Addison-Wesley.

Benner, Patricia, and Judith Wrubel. 1989. *The Primacy of Caring: Stress and Coping in Health and Illness.* Menlo Park, Calif.: Addison-Wesley.

Berg, Barbara. 1986. *The Crisis of the Working Mother: Resolving the Conflict Between Family and Work.* New York: Summit Books.

Bettelheim, Bruno. 1987. *A Good Enough Parent.* New York: Alfred A. Knopf.

Brazelton, T. Berry. 1985. *Working and Caring.* Reading, Mass.: Addison-Wesley.

Briles, Judith. 1987. *Woman to Woman: From Sabotage to Support.* Far Hills, N.J.: New Horizon Press.

Bronstein, Phyllis, and Carolyn Pape Cowan. 1988. *Fatherhood Today: Men's Changing Role in the Family.* New York: John Wiley and Sons.

Brownmiller, Susan. 1984. *Femininity.* New York: Simon and Schuster, Linden Press.

Brumberg, Joan Jacobs. 1988. *Fasting Girls: The Emergence of Anorexia Nervosa as a Modern Disease.* Cambridge: Harvard University Press.

Burch, Frances Wells. 1986. *Mothers Talking: Sharing Secrets.* New York: St. Martin's Press.

Callahan, Daniel. 1990. *What Kind of Life: The Limits of Medical Progress.* New York: Simon and Schuster.

Carroll, Jackson W. 1981. *Women of the Cloth: A New Opportunity for the Churches.* San Francisco: Harper and Row.

Caster, Steven. 1987. *Men Who Can't Love: When a Man's Fear Makes Him Run from Commitment.* New York: Berkley Books.

Chodorow, Nancy. 1978. *The Reproduction of Mothering: Psychoanalysis and the Sociology of Gender.* Berkeley: University of California Press.

Clayre, Alasdair. 1974. *Work and Play: Ideas and Experience of Work and Leisure.* New York: Harper and Row.

Cott, Nancy F. 1987. *The Grounding of Modern Feminism.* New Haven: Yale University Press.

Dinnerstein, Dorothy. 1963. *The Mermaid and the Minotaur: Sexual Arrangements and Human Malaise.* New York: Harper and Row.

Douglas, Ann. 1977. *The Feminization of American Culture.* New York: Avon.

Dowling, Colette. 1981. *The Cinderella Complex: Women's Hidden Fear of Independence.* New York: Summit Books.

Dowling, Colette. 1988. *Perfect Women: Hidden Fears of Inadequacy and the Drive to Perform.* New York: Summit Books.

Ehrenreich, Barbara. 1983. *The Hearts of Men: American Dreams and the Flight from Commitment.* Garden City, N.Y.: Doubleday, Anchor Books.

Ehrenreich, Barbara. 1986. *Re-making Love: The Feminization of Sex.* Garden City, N.Y.: Doubleday, Anchor Books.

Ehrenreich, Barbara. 1989. *Fear of Falling: The Inner Life of the Middle Class.* New York: Pantheon Books.

Ehrenreich, John. 1985. *The Altruistic Imagination: A History of Social Work and Social Policy in the United States.* Ithaca: Cornell University Press.

Eichenbaum, Luise, and Susan Auerbach. 1987. *Between Women: Love, Envy, and Competition in Women's Friendships.* New York: Viking Books.

Einon, Dorothy. 1985. *Play with a Purpose: Learning Games for Children Six Weeks to Ten Years.* New York: Pantheon Books.

Eisenstein, Hester. 1980. *The Future of Difference.* New Brunswick, N.J.: Rutgers University Press.

Eisler, Riane. 1987. *The Chalice and the Blade: Our History, Our Future.* San Francisco: Harper and Row.

Elkind, David. 1981. *The Hurried Child: Growing Up Too Fast Too Soon.* Reading, Mass.: Addison-Wesley.

Elkind, David. 1987. *Miseducation: Preschoolers at Risk.* New York: Alfred A. Knopf.

Ewen, Stuart. 1976. *Captains of Consciousness: Advertising and the Social Roots of Consumer Culture.* New York: McGraw-Hill Book Company.

Ewen, Stuart. 1988. *All Consuming Images: The Politics of Style in Contemporary Culture.* New York: Basic Books.

Fein, Rashi. 1986. *Medical Care, Medical Costs: The Search for a Health Insurance Policy.* Cambridge: Harvard University Press.

Fenn, Margaret. 1980. *In the Spotlight: Women Executives in a Changing Environment.* Englewood Cliffs, N.J.: Prentice Hall.

Figes, Eva. 1970. *Patriarchal Attitudes.* Greenwich: Fawcett Publications.

Finch, Janet. 1983. *A Labour of Love: Women, Work and Caring.* London: Routledge and Kegan Paul.

Forward, Susan. 1986. *Men Who Hate Women and the Women Who Love Them.* New York: Bantam Books.

Friday, Nancy. 1987. *My Mother/My Self,* tenth anniversary edition. New York: Delacorte Press.

Friedan, Betty. 1963. *The Feminine Mystique.* New York: Dell Publishing Company.

Friedan, Betty. 1986. *The Second Stage.* New York: Summit Books.

Friedman, Meyer, and Ray H. Rosenman. 1974. *Type A Behavior and Your Heart.* New York: Alfred A. Knopf.

Gilligan, Carol. 1982. *In a Different Voice: Psychological Theory and Women's Development.* Cambridge: Harvard University Press.

Gilligan, Carol et al., editors. 1988. *Mapping the Moral Domain.* Cambridge: Harvard University Press.

Goodale, Thomas L. 1985. *Recreation and Leisure: Issues in an Era of Change.* State College, Pa.: Venture Publishing.

Googins, Bradley, and Dianne S. Burden. 1987. *Managing Work and Family Stress in Corporations.* Boston: Boston University School of Social Work.

Gordon, Linda. 1988. *Heroes of Their Own Lives: The Politics and History of Family Violence.* New York: Viking.

Gornick, Vivian, and Barbara K. Moran. 1971. *Woman in Sexist Society: Studies in Power and Powerlessness.* New York: New American Library.

Harragan, Betty Lehan. 1977. *Games Mother Never Taught You: Corporate Gamesmanship for Women.* New York: Warner Books.

Henning, Margaret, and Anne Jardim. 1976. *The Managerial Woman.* New York: Pocket Books.

Henry, Fran Worden. 1983. *Toughing It Out at Harvard: The Making of a Woman MBA.* New York: G. P. Putnam and Sons.

Hertz, Rosanna. 1986. *More Equal Than Others: Women and Men in Dual-Career Marriages.* Berkeley: University of California Press.

Hewlett, Sylvia Ann. 1986. *A Lesser Life: The Myth of Women's Liberation in America.* New York: William Morrow and Company.

Higginson, Margaret V., and Thomas L. Quick. 1980. *The Ambitious Woman's Guide to a Successful Career.* Rev. ed. New York: AMACOM.

Hirschman, Albert O. 1970. *Exit, Voice and Loyalty: Responses to Decline in Firms, Organizations, and States.* Cambridge: Harvard University Press.

Hirschman, Albert O. 1982. *Shifting Involvements: Private Interest and Public Action.* Princeton: Princeton University Press.

Hochschild, Arlie Russell. 1983. *The Managed Heart: Commercialization of Human Feeling.* Berkeley: University of California Press.

Hochschild, Arlie Russell. 1989. *The Second Shift: Working Parents and the Revolution at Home.* New York: Viking.

Hofstadter, Richard. 1973. *The American Political Tradition and the Men Who Made It.* New York: Vintage.

Huber, Richard M. 1971. *The American Idea of Success.* New York: McGraw-Hill Book Company.

Hunnicutt, Benjamin Kline. 1988. *Work without End: Abandoning Shorter Hours for the Right to Work.* Philadelphia: Temple University Press.

Hyatt, Carole. 1979. *The Woman's Selling Game: How to Sell Yourself and Anything Else.* New York: Warner Books.

Jardine, Alice, editor. 1987. *Men in Feminism.* New York: Routledge, Chapman, and Hall, Methuen.

Jones, Anne Hudson. 1988. *Images of Nurses: Perspectives from History, Art, and Literature.* Philadelphia: University of Pennsylvania Press.

Jordan, Judith V., Janet L. Surrey, and Alexandra G. Kaplan. 1983. *Women and Empathy: Implications for Psychological Development and Psychotherapy.* Stone Center for Developmental Services and Studies. No. 82–02.

Kagan, Jerome. 1984. *The Nature of the Child.* New York: Basic Books.

Kalisch, Philip A., and Beatrice J. Kalisch. 1987. *The Changing Image of the Nurse.* Menlo Park, Calif.: Addison-Wesley.

Kanter, Rosabeth Moss. 1977. *Men and Women of the Corporation.* New York: Basic Books.

Kasasek, Robert, and Tores Theorell. 1990. *Healthy Work: Stress, Productivity, and the Reconstruction of Working Life.* New York: Basic Books.

Keller, Evelyn Fox. 1985. *Reflections on Gender and Science.* New Haven: Yale University Press.

Klein, Ethel. 1984. *Gender Politics: From Consciousness to Mass Politics.* Cambridge: Harvard University Press.

Kohn, Alfie. 1986. *No Contest: The Case Against Competition.* Boston: Houghton Mifflin Company.

Lamb, Michael E. 1986. *The Father's Role: Applied Perspectives.* New York: John Wiley and Sons.

Lasch, Christopher. 1978. *The Culture of Narcissism: American Life in an Age of Diminishing Expectations.* New York: W. W. Norton and Company.

Lasch, Christopher. 1984. *The Minimal Self: Psychic Survival in Troubled Times.* New York: W. W. Norton and Company.

Lee, Nancy. 1980. *Targeting the Top: Everything a Woman Needs to Know to Develop a Successful Career in Business, Year after Year.* Garden City, N.Y.: Doubleday and Company.

Lerner, Gerda. 1986. *The Creation of Patriarchy.* New York: Oxford University Press.

Levinson, Daniel J. 1978. *The Seasons of a Man's Life.* New York: Ballantine Books.

Lightfoot, Sara Lawrence. 1988. *Balm in Gilead: Journey of a Healer.* Reading, Mass.: Addison-Wesley.

Lowenberg, June S. 1989. *Caring and Responsibility: The Crossroads Between*

Holistic Practice and Traditional Medicine. Philadelphia: University of Pennsylvania Press.

Lubin, Asta S. 1987. *Managing Success: High-Echelon Careers and Motherhood.* New York: Columbia University Press.

Margolis, Diane Rothbard. 1979. *The Managers: Corporate Life in America.* New York: William Morrow and Company.

Margolis, Richard J. 1990. *Risking Old Age in America.* Boulder, Colo.: Westview Press.

Marzollo, Jean. 1989. *Your Maternity Leave: How to Leave Work, Have a Baby, and Go Back to Work without Getting Lost, Trapped or Sandbagged Along the Way.* New York: Poseidon Press.

Meakin, David. 1976. *Man and Work: Literature and Culture in Industrial Society.* London: Routledge, Chapman, and Hall, Methuen.

Miller, Jean Baker. 1986. *Toward a New Psychology of Women.* Boston: Beacon Press.

Millett, Kate. 1970. *Sexual Politics.* New York: Ballantine Books.

Miner, Valerie. 1987. *Competition: A Feminist Taboo.* New York: The Feminist Press at the City University of New York.

Mitchell, Juliet. 1984. *Women: The Longest Revolution.* New York: Pantheon Books.

Morgan, Robin. 1970. *Sisterhood Is Powerful: An Anthology of Writings from the Woman's Liberation Movement.* New York: Vintage.

Morrison, Ann M. 1987. *Breaking the Glass Ceiling: Can Women Reach the Top of America's Largest Corporations?* Reading, Mass.: Addison-Wesley.

Mulroy, Elizabeth A. 1988. *Women as Single Parents: Confronting Institutional Barriers in the Courts, the Workplace, and the Housing Market.* Dover, Mass.: Auburn House Publishing Company.

Noddings, Nel. 1984. *Caring: A Feminine Approach to Ethics and Moral Education.* Berkeley: University of California Press.

Norwood, Robin. 1985. *Women Who Love Too Much: When You Keep Wishing and Hoping He'll Change.* New York: Pocket Books.

Odent, Michel. 1984. *Birth Reborn.* New York: Pantheon Books.

Oldenburg, Ray. 1989. *The Great Good Place.* New York: Paragon House.

Parker, Richard. 1972. *The Myth of the Middle Class: Notes on Affluence and Equality.* New York: Liveright.

Patti, Rino et al. 1988. *Managing for Service Effectiveness in Social Welfare Organizations.* New York: Haworth Press.

Payer, Lynn. 1988. *Medicine and Culture.* New York: Penguin Books.

Petrie, Pat. 1987. *Baby Play: Activities for Discovery and Development During the First Year of Life.* New York: Pantheon Books.

Phillips, Adam. 1988. *Winnicott.* Cambridge: Cambridge University Press.

Porterfield, Kay. 1989. *Violent Voices: 12 Steps to Freedom from Verbal and Emotional Abuse.* Deerfield Beach, Fla.: Health Communications.

Pruett, Kyle D. 1987. *The Nurturing Father: Journey toward the Complete Man.* New York: Warner Books.

Randall, Vicky. 1987. *Women and Politics: An Internal Perspective.* Chicago: University of Chicago Press.

Rendall, Jane. 1985. *The Origins of Modern Feminism: Women in Britain, France, and the United States 1780–1860.* London: Macmillan.

Reverby, Susan M. 1987. *Ordered to Care: The Dilemma of American Nursing.* Cambridge: Cambridge University Press.

Rose, Stephen J. 1987. *The American Economy Poster and Fact Book.* New York: Pantheon Books.

Rosenberg, Charles E. 1987. *The Care of Strangers: The Rise of America's Hospital System.* New York: Basic Books.

Rubin, Lillian B., 1983. *Intimate Strangers: Men and Women Together.* New York: Harper and Row.

Ruddick, Sara. 1989. *Maternal Thinking: Toward a Politics of Peace.* Boston: Beacon Press.

Sandel, Michael, editor. 1984. *Liberalism and Its Critics.* New York: New York University Press.

Sanger, Singay. 1987. *The Woman Who Works, the Parent Who Cares: A Revolutionary Program for Raising Your Child.* Boston: Little, Brown and Company.

Schwartz, Felice. "Management, Women and the New Facts of Life." *Harvard Business Review.* January–February 1989.

The Secretary of Health, Education and Welfare. 1973. *Work in America: Report of a Special Task Force to the Secretary of Health, Education and Welfare.* Cambridge: MIT Press.

Shreve, Anita. 1987. *Remaking Motherhood: How Working Mothers Are Shaping Our Children's Future.* New York: Viking.

Smith, Adam. 1976. *An Inquiry into the Nature and Causes of the Wealth of Nations.* Chicago: University of Chicago Press.

Stanton, Jeanne Deschamps. 1988. *Being All Things: How to Be a Wife, Lover, Boss, and Mother and Still Be Yourself.* New York: Doubleday and Company.

Stein, Harry. 1988. *One of the Guys: The Wising Up of an American Man.* New York: Simon and Schuster.

Steinem, Gloria. 1983. *Outrageous Acts and Everyday Rebellions.* New York: Signet Books.

Stern, Daniel M. 1985. *The Interpersonal World of the Infant: A View from Psychoanalysis and Developmental Psychology.* New York: Basic Books.

Stewart, Abigail, and M. Brinton Lykes. 1985. *Gender and Personality: Current Perspectives on Theory and Research.* Durham, N.C.: Duke University Press.

Swackhamer, Annette, and Ralph W. Moss. 1986. *Caring.* Garden City, N.Y.: Doubleday and Company.

Taylor, Charles. 1989. *Sources of the Self: The Making of the Modern Identity.* Cambridge: Harvard University Press.

Terkel, Studs. 1985. *Working.* New York: Ballantine Books.

Tocqueville, Alexis de. 1945. *Democracy in America.* 2 vols. New York: Vintage.

Todd, Emmanuel. 1985. *The Explanation of Ideology: Family Structures and Social Systems.* New York: Basil Blackwell.

Tonnies, Ferdinand. 1957. *Community and Society.* New York: Harper and Row.

Turow, Joseph. 1989. *Playing Doctor: Television, Story Telling, and Medical Power.* New York: Oxford University Press.

Walsh, Mary Roth. 1987. *The Psychology of Women: Ongoing Debates.* New Haven: Yale University Press.

Watson, Jean. 1988. *Nursing: Human Sciences and Human Care, a Theory of Nursing.* New York: National League for Nursing.

White, Burton L. 1985. *The First Three Years of Life.* New York: Prentice Hall Press.

Winnicott, Clare, et al., editors. 1989. *Psychoanalytic Explorations: D. W. Winnicott.* Cambridge: Harvard University Press.

Winnicott, D. W. 1987. *The Child, the Family, and the Outside World.* Reading, Mass.: Addison-Wesley.

Wolfe, Alan. 1989. *Whose Keeper: Social Science and Moral Obligation.* Berkeley: University of California Press.

Yoder, Barbara. 1990. *The Recovery Resource Book.* New York: Simon and Schuster.

Zuboff, Shoshana. 1989. *In the Age of the Smart Machine.* New York: Basic Books.

INDEX